Ida Maria Lipsius, Bettina Walker

My Musical Experiences

Ida Maria Lipsius, Bettina Walker

My Musical Experiences

ISBN/EAN: 9783337084967

Printed in Europe, USA, Canada, Australia, Japan

Cover: Foto ©Thomas Meinert / pixelio.de

More available books at **www.hansebooks.com**

MY
MUSICAL EXPERIENCES

BY

BETTINA WALKER

'What I aspired to be,
And was not, comforts me'

A NEW EDITION

LONDON

RICHARD BENTLEY & SON | NOVELLO, EWER & CO.
Publishers in Ordinary to Her Majesty | And at New York

1892

TO MY SISTERS

PREFACE

When the first edition of the book called 'My Musical Experiences' had gone into the press and was about to be published, I could but little have anticipated that it would have met with so favourable a reception. Not only from various parts of Great Britain and the Continent, but even from the shores of the far Pacific, I have received letters expressive of hearty sympathy and grateful thanks from both amateur and professional musicians. These letters have been to me at once a source of mingled pleasure and perplexity. In their pathetic confessions of failure, their allusions to foiled aspirations and chilled enthusiasm, they have helped me to realize, as I had, perhaps, never done before to the same degree, that in the difficulties which so often impede our upward progress, the cross currents in struggling against which so many of us lose much of our primal native power and elasticity, there is not a single individual who stands so entirely by himself as he is so often apt to imagine.

The perplexity which these letters have occasioned

me has been caused by the many appeals made to me for counsel and guidance—appeals that have laid on me the burthen of a responsibility which I never could have foreseen and still less desired, since they contained such questions as could never be adequately dealt with by any amount of correspondence.

Among the questions which have been put to me, there is, however, one which I have no difficulty in answering, and the appearance of this second edition seems to offer a very suitable opportunity for doing so. That question is, 'What is the Henselt method?'

To this I reply that it is a method of pianoforte study which may be divided into two heads—considered under two aspects.

I. The purely technical or physical—a preparatory drill which, according as it may be more or less completely carried out, is intended to fit the hand for approaching and mastering every imaginable difficulty presented to us in the works of pianoforte composers.

II. The mental, or that method of studying pianoforte pieces which has for its aim an intelligent appreciation of the composer's intentions, and a thorough carrying out of the same.

Now, as regards the first or technical aspect of the school, I am of opinion that, apart from personally conveyed teaching, no amount either of talking or writing on the subject could enable the student to get a definite hold of it.

The mental aspect of the method is, however, admirably outlined in a little work called 'Advice to Teachers,' by Adolf Henselt, which will, I hope, shortly appear in print.

I likewise take this opportunity of thanking the friends whose sympathy encouraged me both to begin and to go on relating my musical experiences. My warmest and best thanks are, however, due to Mrs. Alfred Marks, known in literary circles as the authoress of 'The Masters of the World,' 'A Great Treason,' and many other interesting and admirably written novels. This lady, while my book was in progress, gave me the benefit of her wide literary experience in the form of many valuable hints and suggestions, and when, owing to a severe attack of ophthalmia, which during several weeks rendered it impossible for me either to read or write, I would have had to give up the idea of finishing it at least for months to come, this kind friend, although then deeply absorbed in a new work of her own, gave up entire days not only to writing from my dictation, but to the ungrateful drudgery of copying large portions of my somewhat illegible writing, and seeing that the whole MS. was in a fit condition for being sent to the publisher.

The fresh matter contained in this edition consists—

I. Of two traits relating to Sterndale Bennett, pages 24-32.

II. A short paragraph at page 83, and another at page 212.

III. The following letters:

A letter from Wagner to the head of the Schott firm at Mayence. Signor Sgambati gave me a reproduction of this letter, and it is with his sanction that I translate and give a considerable portion of it to the public.

Two letters from the Fräulein Hummel, who, at my request, were kind enough not only to give me their written assurance that the lock of Beethoven's hair and the pen which he last used are in the possession of their (the Hummel) family, but still further verified my reference to the same by giving the dates of the visits to the dying musician during which her grandparents (Hummel and his wife) came into possession of these 'precious relics.'

IV. An interesting sketch of Henselt's life and career from the German of La Mara, an author whose 'Musical Portraits,' and other works referring to music, are highly valued in musical circles abroad.

This sketch contains a long letter by Henselt written in early youth, two letters by Schumann, written before his marriage, and several by Henselt, which are highly characteristic of him.

It is with the author's permission that the above sketch is here given.

V. Copies of letters from Rubinstein, Liszt, and Von Bülow, handed to me for translation and publication by Frau Mila, of Berlin (Henselt's niece by marriage).

CONTENTS

		PAGE
I.	SIR STERNDALE BENNETT	1
II.	TAUSIG	37
III.	SGAMBATI	44
IV.	LISZT	85
V.	DEPPE AND SCHARWENCKA	115
VI.	HENSELT	153
	ARTICLE ON HENSELT BY LA MARA, FROM THE 'LEIPZIGER ZEITUNG'	279
	LETTERS TO HENSELT FROM LISZT, VON BÜLOW, AND RUBINSTEIN	319

MY MUSICAL EXPERIENCES

I.

SIR STERNDALE BENNETT.

A FULL and faithful account of the efforts and studies of an individual (especially if these efforts and studies be self-chosen) is, in fact, the history of that individual's life.

But I do not mean to write my life; and the following pages do not, therefore, contain every single fact in my musical experience, but only such selections from it as I believe may possibly interest those who are working in the same field as myself.

How many *whys* there are in this world of ours, to which scarce one of the answers given ever seems to do more than circle and wheel round the central point, never once hitting it right to the core! How many hundreds of persons have, like myself, asked themselves over and over again, *why* they go on from year to year, giving some of the best hours in their lives to pianoforte-playing! Their aim is—or ought to be—to reproduce, in all the glow and life and pulsation of the moment when they were first breathed into being, those exquisite tone-poems, in which the master-spirits of the divine art have embodied some of the subtlest thoughts, the most weird and wonderful fancies—some of the most impassioned yearnings of the human soul.

But leaving this *why* for everyone to answer for himself, the fascination remains as an undeniable fact—a source at once of joy and pain to the individual who has once come under its spell. Joy, because in all effort, in all quest, there is joy; and pain, because we can never attain to our ideal. We advance, indeed, but only to realize that there are fresh vistas opening in every direction round us; and when the shadows fall, we only seem to have reached the true starting-point.

But the spell does not lose its power, and I could tell of an artist, still with us when I began to write these experiences, but now departed—a giant in his art—who, at the age of seventy-six, was still wrestling and fighting with 'the flesh' (his name for *technique*), in order to render it ever a fitter medium for embodying his ideal aspirations. I allude to Adolf von Henselt, composer, artist, and teacher. Of him I shall speak more later.

The musical natures to whom these pages are addressed will like to have some little clue to the whole—something to explain, at least partly, the experiences which I am about to narrate. I shall try to do this in the simplest manner possible, colouring nothing, and putting in no fancy-spun incident to make it more interesting.

The first nine years of my life were passed in a remote country village, to which no news from the outward world ever seemed to come. My first conscious sensations of delight were the joy I felt in sunshine, in the scent and colour of certain flowers, in the sound of running water, which always sent me off into a sort of waking dream, and in the wind, every varied tone of which never failed to arrest my attention. If it were sighing among the leaves, I felt pleased and happy; if it were wild and stormy, I loved to run before it in an exuberant flow of animal spirits; if it whistled round the corners of the house, and moaned at night up in the chimney-top, I shuddered and shivered, and seemed to see an endless sweep of desolate moorland, beneath as endless a sweep of cloud, which grew ever grayer and grayer. I seemed to myself to be out there, seeking for shelter, for companionship, knowing all the while that the search would ever, ever be in vain.

But every other sensation I had in those early days grew pale and shadowy before what I felt when my small fingers first drew sounds from the old grand-square Broadwood pianoforte, on which I got my first lesson, before I was five years old. I ran to it as often as I could, and was soon able to play little pieces by heart; but I was taught almost entirely by ear, and could not, even years afterwards, have spelt out the simplest thing for myself. There seemed to be (as I look back to those days) a great natural facility in the small fingers, and an instinctive yearning towards the tender and pathetic in the child-heart, and withal an ambition of one day doing something which was to surprise and charm numbers of people.

In my ninth year I heard for the first time many voices singing together in church (probably in parts); and what I felt *then* I have never again experienced with the same degree of intensity. It seemed to me that the heavens opened, and there was a floating to and fro of the angel-choirs between earth and heaven. I was quite overcome, and I began to cry as if my heart were breaking; and yet I would have died rather than confess that I was crying because I was happy—oh, *so* happy! I believe they took me home, thinking that I had a pain somewhere, and did not know how to tell it, or that I was frightened by the noise.

It is difficult to believe that, although my family belonged to the better middle-class, and had much education, and some culture (my father's library contained most of the standard works in literature and history), I yet passed through childhood without having so much as heard the names of Handel, or

Bach, or Beethoven. My governesses taught me Czerny's Exercises in the most slovenly and incorrect manner, also some of Herz, Plachy, Rosellen, and even Thalberg; and the more facility I got—and I rattled through these—the more I began to dislike the pianoforte, and often wished that I were grown up, and not forced to sit at it for two long hours every day.

All my love for music at this time went into singing; for I had a voice which seemed to grow with my growth, and was so clear and sweet and strong, that I had to try and hold it back in church, lest people should turn round to look where the voice came from. Not only had I never been in a theatre or a concert-room, but I had never even heard of such places. I had read, however, of troubadours and wandering singers; and it came over me sometimes that my voice would bring me out into the world, and I longed to sing to a great crowd. But then I grew frightened at my thoughts (which, having been reared in a Puritan school, I regarded as sinful), and I believed that I ought to pray that they might not come to me; and this I did, poor child! often with many tears; still, singing became more and more to me, and whatever troubled, whatever pleased me, was all confessed in song. I used to start away out into the fields, or get up into the attics of the house, where no one could see that I often wept as I sang; and there was a strange charm in those solitary tears!

Miss Davis's simple song of *Ruth*, and Russell's *Woodman, spare that Tree*, brought, each in the most vivid manner, a scene of the deepest pathos before me. I saw Naomi, old and childless, called by God to return to the land of her birth, leaving behind her all that she had been left to love; and it seemed to me that I could see how she looked when the young warm-hearted Ruth clung to her. And then the 'old tree,' under whose shadow so much had happened! To be cut down—just perhaps to make room for one of a later growth! I took part with the singer. I sang to the woodman as if he could actually hear me. I was making him understand that a tree which had seen so much had a right to live out all its time, even if it had grown bare and gnarled.

Leaving these childish reminiscences behind me, I pass on to the evening when I was for the first time in a concert-room, and for the first time heard not only an orchestra and a great pianist, but the orchestra playing a Beethoven symphony, and the pianist (Sir Charles Hallé) playing a Beethoven concerto. The effect on me was such that I made up my mind then and there to devote my life to music.

By a singular coincidence, this happened to me just at the time when I lost my voice, owing to the ignorant attempt of a professor (who ought to have known better) to make me produce chest-notes far above my natural register. It was a bitter grief to me, and for some time I would not give up the hope held out to me by another eminent professor of singing, that a long spell of complete silence would undo the mischief which had been done; but this was not the case, and having meanwhile begun to feel the charm of the pianoforte, I grew by degrees to accept it as a substitute for the voice which I had lost for ever.

I came home after nine months' lessons in London from an excellent master (but having only been able to practise an hour and a half daily during that time) with my whole heart set on becoming a musician. Easier said than done! There was but one piano in our house, and there were two other people to practise on it besides myself. It was, moreover, in the drawing-room; and there were naturally times when, even in a quiet family like ours, practising would have been inconvenient. Moreover, I was supposed to play as well, or indeed better, than was at all necessary for an amateur; and an hour a day (when convenient) was surely enough for keeping up all I had learned! Many a time was I laughed at for my strange fancies; but what I had heard, and the nine months of teaching, had set something agoing within me that would out, and I fumed and worried because I was checked in my endeavours. Whenever it was possible to stay at home when the others went out, I did so; and rushing at once to the pianoforte, I sat there until the knock at the hall-door told that they had come home again. But these occasional 'incursions' into the clover naturally did not satisfy me; on the contrary, I fumed and worried all the more. But I said nothing, until finally I lost both sleep and appetite, and the doctor was called in; he, not finding any ailment which he could define, ordered me 'change of air and scene.' Now, this was rather a puzzle in our family, for my mother was too delicate to leave home, and there was no unmarried aunt to come to the rescue. When I saw they all were really anxious about me, I suddenly took courage and said, 'There is something that will cure me without sending me away, but I am afraid you will not care to do it.' And when they pressed me to say what this something might be, I said, 'Give me a piano all to myself, and let me play on it as much as I like!'

They were much amused at this novel remedy, but it seemed worth trying. A piano was put into the dining-room, and I was allowed to play on it to my heart's content; and after one month, to my mother's delight and surprise, I was as full of life and brightness as I had before been of languor and depression. How I did rush through the classics in every direction! Mozart, Beethoven, Weber—wherever I tried them there seemed to be mines of wonderful jewels. Months over which an enchanted light still gleams as I look back on them! I believed that everything was possible; and by natural facility I got a mass of beautiful things under my fingers without ever perceiving the gaps, the gulfs rather, that lay between what I wished to do and what I actually accomplished. But the consciousness dawned on me at last; and though I had as yet not the faintest idea of the toil that must be undergone before one reaches even the most moderate degree of excellence, still it became clear to me that I wanted guidance for my head and my fingers. Lady Eastlake's charming musical novel, *Charles Anchester*, chanced into our house just about this time: and we all were charmed with Starwood Burney, the little boy who called the key-board of the piano 'the beautiful cold keys.' We were told that 'Sterndale Bennett' was meant by 'Starwood Burney'; and, curiously enough, much about the same date, a friend gave me some copies of the *Musical World*, which were written when Sterndale Bennett was a boy. In this' paper, his beautiful playing of his own compositions at twelve years old was graphically described; and how, later on, he went to Leipzig, and how Mendelssohn had loved and valued him. It is a singular fact that it is to these two apparently chance influences from without that I owe the good fortune of having studied under Sterndale Bennett—for no one whom we knew believed that an Englishman *could* be a musician; and in the school where I had spent nine months, the feeling was distinctly in favour of everything foreign, and against everything English. I began at once to beset my mother to send me to London and let me study under him, of whom we all that time, and ever afterwards, always spoke as 'Starwood'; but I had to beg and pray for some time before my wish was granted. My mother did, however, at last write to Sterndale Bennett, and ask him whether he would give lessons to a young lady who would be sent for that purpose to London, for a few weeks. He replied that his time was so fully taken up just then that he could not spare a single hour; that he could not even promise to give lessons in three months hence.

This letter naturally impressed us all (my mother especially) with an idea of Sterndale Bennett's position, and the value which was attached to his lessons. He had in his reply kindly offered to recommend another professor, but this I would not hear of; and at my entreaty another letter was written to him, saying that we would wait, but that my mother hoped he would be able to receive me at Easter. (I believe she put in a little word suggestive of my being very much absorbed in music.) At Easter, to my joy, a letter came, which named 'a possible date' in about a fortnight's time; and in a few days after the receipt of this letter I started for London, under the charge of a middle-aged family friend.

On arriving there, we took rooms in Gower Street, and hired a very nice Broadwood; and the same evening a letter, announcing our arrival, was sent to Sterndale Bennett. He, however, to my extreme disappointment, could not give me my first lesson for five days. How well I remember every circumstance of that time—even the fact that, trusting to a warm and lovely spring, I had brought nothing to London but summer dresses ; and though it was on the 17th of May that I had my first lesson, the weather had suddenly become so cold and rainy, that both my friend and I were extremely glad to find a good fire burning in the drawing-room into which we were ushered. After a minute or two Sterndale Bennett came in, and in an extremely easy and natural manner addressed us both, and turning to me, said something to the effect, ' This is, then, the young lady who has been waiting so long to have lessons from me.' He then opened the piano, and asked me to play to him, and after I had only got through about four or five bars, exclaimed, ' Why, we have an enthusiast here !' But I was painfully shy and timid ; all we three sisters were hero-worshippers, and I especially so, and I don't believe that I even ventured a glance in reply. I certainly made no audible answer.

A letter written home, which I found a little while ago, describes my first impressions of Sir Sterndale Bennett. ' He is very pale, and to my thinking quite unlike anything you see every day ; very quaint—in fact, like a face you see in an old picture.' Indeed, I described him as resembling Ary Schaeffer's *Dante*, which I had seen at an exhibition.

The presence of my kind-hearted but very prosaic

friend, who I knew well looked on the motive of this visit to London as utterly absurd, made me still more timid than I would naturally have been; and Sterndale Bennett, finding that I uttered scarcely a word, did not know, I should say, what to make of me. I played several times to him, and each time was disturbed by the wish to ask him whether he thought favourably of me, and the fear lest his reply would dash my hopes for ever. What with this, and my natural shyness, I played each time rather worse instead of better. I thought of writing to him, but could not bring myself to do this, and I owe it again to a seeming chance that I did not return home, believing all my hopes to be a delusion. My friend luckily took cold just then, and I had to fare off alone to take my lesson from Sterndale Bennett; and strangely enough, after playing one movement of Dussek's *Invocation*—and as badly as possible, to my way of thinking—I forgot myself, and suddenly exclaimed, 'It is no use; I know I shall never be able to play!' and then I was so ashamed of having said so much that I would have gone on with the piece, but for his kind words, and the still kinder tone in which they were uttered. I cannot recall them exactly, but they were in the form of a question— 'what it was in my playing that I felt was not as I wished it.' And then I told him how I loved music, and wondered why I should be able to do so little, when so many, to whom it was nothing, were yet able

to do so much. He said little, but that little was all
I wanted to hear, and, indeed, far more than I had
dared to hope. I knew I had got just the help and
direction for which I had been so long craving.

I returned home then for the summer, and coming
back to London in October, was received as parlour-
boarder in a ladies' school for three months, during
which time it was arranged that I should have two
lessons a week from Sterndale Bennett. He now took
me thoroughly in hand. I had expected to be given
no end of scales and studies; but, to my surprise, he
gave me Bach's *Clavier bien tempéré*, as a study for
bringing strong, firm tone from the fingers. He also
gave me much of Dussek, Clementi, Moscheles, and
Hummel for scale-passages and rapid playing; and
anticipating the unuttered question, which no doubt
he read in my surprised glance, he said, ' I must not
give you much scale-playing or exercises, or you will
become stupid,' and then, enlarging on his words, he
added, ' There are people who must be always on the
strain, and if you demand anything from them but
the highest—what, in fact, they can't do—they
become languid and relaxed. You cannot actually do
what I am giving you at present, but in the effort to
do it you are kept on the strain, you are roused and
stimulated, and this is what you need.' I pondered
long over his words without fully realizing their
meaning; nor did I take in their entire import until
long after he had passed away for ever. Need I say

that my respect for him was profound, and that I never dreamed of calling any dictum of his into question? He was indeed a strict, but a most kind and sympathetic, teacher. In using the preludes and fugues of Bach's *Clavier bien tempéré* as finger-exercises, he made me bring out every single tone as clearly and distinctly as if each note were a separate step of a stair—lifting the fingers well, and taking great care that the action or exertion should come right from the knuckle-joints. He often said that when the *fingers* are tired, it is a sign that one has practised well; and he constantly warned me from letting any other part of my body become engaged in the work—it took, he said, from 'the strength that ought to be in the fingers.' He had a power peculiarly his own of at once stimulating and tranquillizing. He never stopped one suddenly to comment on a fault or an oversight; but at the end of a page, or of a movement, he would say with a gentleness which did not exclude authority, but, on the contrary, rather suggested it, 'You did so and so—did you perceive it?' and he would then indicate what he wished, and make me repeat the page or movement in question, often more than once. He never allowed me to pause in a passage or page where I was either uncertain, or had done badly, but insisted on my going on as if nothing was wrong. He held that the next best thing to having played a passage well is to go on and betray no immediate consciousness of having done it badly. I remember once in the middle of a fugue, when I slipped in a passage, I heard his gentle but decisive voice telling me not to stop, but to keep it up; and the ring of that voice was so bracing, that I *did* keep it up, and played on, though I never got right until I had reached almost the last line in the fugue, and he said, 'You have won a victory,' and praised me as if I had really performed a feat.

He demanded much, and this demand forced the pupil to strenuous exertion; but, on the other hand, he had such a fine instinct for divining all one had wished to do, even when the intention was but very faintly carried out, that one felt sure of being given credit for all earnest work. This gave me a sense of rest, and a freedom from morbid anxiety—so much so, that after one of his lessons, even though I might have played badly, I was never either out of humour or discouraged. Indeed, far from this, I invariably felt cheered, and wound up for fresh efforts. In fact, while studying with him I acquired such self-possession, and had such an implicit belief in his knowing better than I knew myself what I was able to do, that had he desired me to sit down and to play in a concert-room for the first time, I am assured that I should have done so without the slightest danger of falling much below my best.

His phrasing was absolutely perfect—not insistent nor angular, but wave-like and persuasive. He communicated his feeling of a movement by a gesture—a word, a light touch on the pupil's arm, or by playing with one hand along with the pupil. His glance was full of power, and he moved with so much dignity that he did not suggest at the first glance that he was 'a little man' (though he was much below the average height); and every line of his face told of thought, feeling, and sensibility held in lifelong restraint by a will that never let go the reins. His voice was (excepting two others, one of whom was a little-known poet who has ' *also gone to his rest*') the sweetest, the most refined in *timbre*, that I have ever heard. Its tone seemed to come right from the heart. His words were few, and ever well chosen and to the point; and there was a ring of truth in all he uttered, that carried conviction to the hearer that here was one who could not and would not lie—no, nor dilute the truth by telling it by halves. His laugh was gleeful and childlike; I remember it well, as one of his most characteristic outward traits. Another was a habit he had of rubbing his hands energetically together when something had especially pleased him. When a lesson had been exceptionally satisfactory, he would go off rubbing his hands, and once or twice he has even laughed to himself as he left the room. He had thrown himself so heart and soul into the lesson, with all his attention concentrated in helping, encouraging, and fully understanding the pupil, that he in fact identified himself with the result; and he said himself more than once that it was not a mere lesson he gave, but an hour of his life, in the fullest sense of the word. Although he gave from ten to twelve hour-lessons a day when the season was at its height, I have never caught him looking either jaded or absent, and he has given me more than once the last hour of his long day's work. I add, for the benefit of those who may perhaps say, 'He may not have been so with all,' that in a school where for many years he gave from ten to twelve consecutive hours, it was impossible to gather from his manner which was the *most* or the *least clever* pupil, so thoroughly did he interest himself in each individual. From the zest with which he went into every special beauty of the composition which was being studied, it would have been difficult to realize that he was not just entering a new and enchanting region, instead of (as was the case) walking over well-trodden, old, familiar ground. And his sense of enjoyment communicated itself to the pupil, and gave life and charm to all one learned from him. There must be many of his pupils whose experience would confirm mine on this point.

His instruction as to how the time of a piece should be started was the best I have ever heard. I will try to give it, though I cannot remember the telling and concise words in which he expressed it. 'People begin to play, and don't get into swing until they have played one or two bars. The *moto*, the beat of the piece, ought to have begun in the mind, in the feeling of the performer, before he put a finger on the key-board.'

He told me that, when practising, one should listen to what one was doing; but in *playing*, once having set off, one should play the thing through—go on without listening or looking back. I have myself benefited by this exhortation, and with complete success, more than once, when about to face a large audience. He was not, like Von Bülow, inclined to believe that general studies in other directions give greater breadth, or variety, or charm to one's playing; and once, when I told him that I was about to begin a course of English literature, his expressive silence showed that he did not approve of the plan; and he made me give up the concertina, which I had played very well when I came to him. He had far too many pupils to form any personal acquaintance with them outside the lesson-hour, and yet he found a way to favour those who were enthusiastic and hard-working. For instance, he invited me to go to his house during his absence, and look through his library. His own words were, 'You may rummage about in it to your heart's content.' I made, one may be sure, full use of this kind permission, and saw some very interesting manuscripts —amongst others the first sketch of the lovely *barcarolle* in his F Minor Concerto, and a few words which suggested the mood in which the melody came to him.

A book with a black morocco binding contained the correspondence between him and Mendelssohn, and I read the whole so many times over that, even at this distance of time, I could write much of it down word for word, but to quote from it would be a breach of faith. Once, when he had been pleased with my work, he said, 'I will lend you the album which I have had since I was a boy, and your sister can perhaps copy for you a picture which Mendelssohn painted in it for me before I left Leipzig.' This view was taken from Sterndale Bennett's window, and showed the roof of the Conservatoire, on which the wintry snow was lying. The copy which my sister made of it was so exact that the next time Sterndale Bennett came to give me a lesson, he exclaimed as he came into the room, 'Is that my picture out of the album?' This water-colour drawing is to me a sacred relic—*his* clear, very characteristic handwriting on the margin tells that the picture is a copy of the one in *his* album, who it was painted by, for whom, and what it represented. But the picture has an even still deeper interest for me, inasmuch as it recalls to me 'the touch of a vanished hand' (the copyist of the picture).

One other way he took of showing kindness, which, now that I look back, and realize, as I could not in those days of youth, what an amount of kindly interest it implied, surprises me and fills me with tender gratitude. Knowing that I could read a little from the orchestral score, he never once forgot either to bring or send the score of whatever symphony was about to be performed at the Philharmonic, of which he was then the conductor.

Speaking of public playing as a profession, he said, and with much emphasis, 'Nowadays it is not worth anyone's while to take up public performance as a profession; things are so different to what they were when I was a boy. *Then* no one ever thought of giving themselves entirely to it, unless they had a natural and most unmistakable gift for the "pianoforte." In the present day the advance in the mechanical (the means which bring one to a certain point) is so great, that numbers of clever people, who have but little natural talent for music, become players through a system of admirable training.'

For the benefit of those who are pleased to think and assert that schools and methods are quite superfluous things, I quote an observation which was made to us by Sterndale Bennett in the course of the second winter that I was studying with him.

My mother and I had been one day telling him about a very gifted friend of ours, who without having had a single lesson from any master, either at home or abroad, had yet, in our opinion, become a good musician and a very fine performer on the pianoforte. Sterndale Bennett listened to all we said about our friend, with the grave smile so peculiarly his own.

He then, without giving either in tone or glance

the slightest impression that he in any way doubted the possibility of our friend being all we had described him to be, observed, with that gentleness which carries with it far more conviction to the mind of the hearer than any strongly and dogmatically expressed opinion of dissent: 'I can quite believe that persons of talent may be able to find out a great deal for themselves without the help of a teacher. There can be no doubt that such do often succeed in doing many things admirably without having had any instruction. Yet, for all that, I think' (and here Sterndale Bennett made a slight pause before continuing) 'that sooner or later you are sure to discover great gaps in the acquirements — the knowledge of anyone who has had no regular schooling.'

Speaking again of the difference between amateurs and professionals, he observed, 'We are the servants of the public, and the public wishes to be *surprised* as well as pleased, and for this reason the artist is often tempted to play a piece much faster than the composer ever intended. With an amateur it is different: he can, if *he will*, adhere rigidly to the composer's intentions, whereas the artist cannot invariably do so.'

This was in reply to a question of mine regarding a piece which I had the evening before heard played by an artist of eminence. One movement had been taken at nearly double the time which Sterndale Bennett had in a previous lesson indicated to me.

He added, 'There is, indeed, one training which the amateur does not get—that of public opinion—and yet to this the artist is at times compelled to sacrifice his convictions.' He also said that an amateur who has high attainments will be an object of hostility to second-class professionals; such will always sit on a musicianly amateur when they can.

In all that concerned art, and his position as guide and teacher, Sterndale Bennett always stood on a pedestal, and would tolerate no trifling. He had promised me at the start that he would give me the same training as if I were to play in public, that he would be as exacting in his demands as if I were an Academy student; and he kept his word to the letter. He always marked what he wished to be prepared, and once—only once—when I told him I had not got as far as he had marked, he just said, in a tone from which there was no appeal, 'If you have not prepared it, you shall read it through.' It was not a pleasant lesson, for he kept saying, quietly but firmly, 'Go on.' I believe I played as many wrong notes as right ones, and the lesson was so effectual that I never again came to him with an excuse of the kind.

Another time I wanted, in a mood of girlish frolic, to see how he would take it if I brought him a piece of modern music instead of the Weber Sonata which he had chosen for me. I laid the piece on the desk and looked at him, and wondered what he would say; with a grave glance, he lifted it from the desk, and said in a decided tone, 'This is not what I told you to play; please let us have it.' The piece he had given me was luckily at hand; I had studied it, and it went rather well. But the characteristic point of the whole was, that he *then* said, in a tone and manner that was commanding, ' Now play the other.' I understood as clearly as if he had said it in so many words that he meant, ' Since you placed it there to play to *me*, I expect it will have been studied as thoroughly and carefully as everything you bring to me always is;' and I was conscious that he would have looked on the fact of its being otherwise as an act of disrespect—a departure from the attitude which a pupil owed to one who felt himself to be in a very special sense ' a master.'

But my veneration for him was profound, and I had never dreamed of playing a trick in a vulgar sense. I played the piece from beginning to end quite correctly; and I can just recall, as if it were yesterday, how stiff he looked when I began, and how, as the piece went on, he relaxed; and though he said nothing when I had finished, except to show me where to improve some passages, yet there was a look of amusement in his face.

Speaking once to me of the amount of practice an artist must give to a piece before he plays it in public, he related of himself that once he had practised a piece of his own composition, which he was to play at a concert in Leipzig, with such steady persistence up into the night, that at last an exasperated next-door neighbour not only hammered to hinder his practice at night, but in the daytime, whenever he began, would beat counter-time against the wall, and Mendelssohn had to get a magistrate to interfere.

The question of facing the public was, he said, a problem which all could not solve. 'The difficulty is,' he said, 'to play even before one person just as you may feel. Some can never do this; and some can do it before the few, but cannot face a crowd. It is a question how much of one's attainments one can *faire valoir*.'

Speaking to my mother of progress in pianoforte-playing, and trying to convey a clear idea on the subject to one who, though highly intelligent in many directions, had yet no *artistic* perceptions, he said, 'Making progress on the pianoforte is not like walking along a road, where you can see what you have just left behind, and what you are just about to walk over. Here, you advance by leaps and pauses. You seem to have a barrier before you, and you can't climb over it, and you keep struggling and striving either to get over it or push it aside, and some happy day you find yourself over it, and for a short space you feel you have made a stride; but there before you lies another barrier, and you are restless again, and the struggle and the effort must begin afresh.'

Sterndale Bennett did not give me his own music

to study, unless I asked him to do so. The lovely *Rondo Piacerole*, his *Studies*, *Preludes*, and *Lessons*, the fine F Minor *Concerto*, with the *barcarolle* — all recall to me happy hours when I believed that I should attain all I aspired to! Sterndale Bennett told us that, from the beginning of his own career as a professor, he had set his face against teaching any but classical music; and he was so severely classical that he could not bring himself to accept many modern composers, without whom we should feel ourselves at the present moment in a sense orphaned. Schumann had been his personal friend, but with Schumann's compositions he had no sympathy; and though he did not say 'no,' when I asked him to give me a piece of Chopin's to study, yet I felt that he had no such love for Chopin as he had for Handel, Bach, Beethoven, Mozart, Hummel, Weber, and even Moscheles. The result was, that when with him I gradually lost all wish either to play Chopin myself or to hear him played by others.

It may easily be imagined that he could not admire Rubinstein either as an artist or composer; and, curiously enough, I, who was at that time a disciple even to fanaticism of the classical school, was always carried away and transported with delight whenever I heard Rubinstein. Never did I miss any possible chance of going to a concert at which he was to appear; and all the while I believed that I was wrong, for when I told Sterndale Bennett how I was enchanted with Rubinstein's exuberant flights and warm glow, I seem still to see his grave look, and to hear the words, 'I am sorry for you.' And I can see how he folded his hands when he said this.

It was not my good fortune ever to hear Sterndale Bennett play, except a few bars as a prelude, just as I was taking off my hat before the lesson began. (The lessons were sometimes at his own house, but he most frequently came to us.) When I had lessons from him he had not only ceased to play in public, but he gave so many lessons that he could have had but odd scraps of time to play for himself, not to speak of study or practice. He told us from the first that he never played to his pupils, and though the snatches one got now and then filled one with longing to hear more, such was our respect for him that we never ventured to suggest anything of the kind. I used to hope that some time or other he would indulge me with a little of what I knew must be something most sweet and rare and exquisite. His deep rich tone, the phrasing that charmed without being insistent, all suggested something remote from the dusty highway of life, something fragrant and sweet as the meadows in June. At last, however, we took courage, and told him how much we longed for *even ever so little* of that which we knew he had to give; and I can still recall the mood of deep sadness which came over me when he said what amounted to, 'You never shall hear me.' They were words which none but a master of his art would have or could have ventured to utter. 'When I *could* study,' he said, 'then my playing was a pleasure to myself, and I knew it must be so to others; it has long since ceased to be so, and I do not mean to offer to others what does not satisfy myself.'

I have said before that he would have resented anything which looked like playing with art, or failing in deference to him as a guide and teacher; but he could enjoy a harmless joke, as the following will prove:

I longed for a little fun in the midst of my serious studies, and I induced my mother to help and abet me. She asked him a question, just as I had come to a pause for a moment in my playing, and as he turned away from the piano to speak to her in reply, I laid a chocolate beetle which I had prepared for the occasion on the keyboard, and then suddenly pushed back my chair with an exclamation. He at once— for he was one of the most perfect gentlemen I have ever known—took out his pocket-handkerchief, and was about to apply it as a means of getting rid of the ugly intruder, when he saw what it was—and our faces. And how he laughed! and how we all laughed, for nearly five minutes! And then the lesson went on, and I remember that I played none the worse for our laughing trio.

I here add another trait which speaks for itself of an exquisite refinement and gentle dignity in which, as far as my knowledge of men and manners go, I have up to the present time seldom if ever found anyone to whom I could compare him. When the hour's lesson was over—and never by any chance did he curtail this even by a few seconds—no one could have realized, from the quiet way he stood up from the piano and wished us good-bye as he turned to leave the room, that every one of his minutes was precious, and every single hour of the day filled with pressing engagements. He always seemed to find time for a few words of encouragement to me, and a few more of kindly courtesy to my mother.

When the lesson was at his own house, although his carriage was waiting at the door, he would look as unpreoccupied, and chat with us as pleasantly while I was putting on my outdoor wraps, as if he had hours of leisure before him. He then accompanied us to the top of the stairs, where I still seem to see him stand, and make us a parting bow as we walked down to the hall, and the servant opened the door to show us out. My mother and I took such note of the fact that Sterndale Bennett never seemed to be in a hurry, that I often wondered if it would be possible to stir him out of this repose and restfulness of manner. One day, accordingly, when the lesson was over and I was preparing to go, I took at least double as much time as usual in putting on both hat and mantle, and wound up by fastening to the last button a pair of new and very closely-fitting gloves. The experiment was, however, an utter failure. Sterndale Bennett did not seem to observe the slowness of my movements, and the conclusion to which both of us came after that day was that, however numerous and pressing his business engagements might be, it was either a need—a deep-seated instinct of Sterndale Bennett's nature—or a rule which he had laid down for himself, not to let these encroach on the gentle courtesies of life.

It is with a sense of wonder at what his memory must have been that I look back and remember that he never seemed to have forgotten any piece I had ever studied with him. It was one of his habits to ask for some piece which I had perhaps not played for weeks; and if I tried to avoid playing it by the excuse, 'But I have not played it lately,' 'No matter,' he would say, in his gentle, but for all that singularly authoritative way; 'you shall play it now.'

In speaking of learning pieces quickly, sight-reading, etc., I have heard him say more than once, 'No one can form a true idea of what a pianist's attainments are who has not heard him in music with which he has been familiar for years.'

And again, reverting to the question of time in music, and especially in the old classical composers, he often repeated that there was more gain than loss in taking a movement somewhat slowly. On one occasion I remember I was playing Beethoven's Sonata,

Op. 7, No. 4, and in the second part of the first movement, where a motive in A minor modulates into D minor, and, beginning *pp*, gradually works up to a climax marked *ff*, I increased the rapidity of the beat in proportion as I got up to the *crescendo*. He did not stop me at the moment, as almost any other musician would have done, but when a suitable place for a pause occurred, pointing to the bars where I had hurried the time, he asked me what reason I had for doing so. I replied, 'It is very intense, it is very insistent; I feel as if it *must* get on.' 'I am glad,' he replied, 'that you have the keen feeling for beauty there which makes you try to hurry on; but, remember, it is not by merely quickening the time that the feeling of intensity shows itself. It is by means much less obvious, much deeper-lying than this, that such an impression is conveyed. It must be done by the tone, the turn of the phrase. Think well over this,' he added.

On another occasion, in adverting to the fact that love for and enjoyment in music deepens rather than lessens as we advance in life, he observed, 'Association comes in then to strengthen and reinforce the feeling, and every beautiful thing which we have loved in our early years brings back with it a whole host of memories.' I cannot recall the exact words he used, but I remember that as he uttered them a sensation came over me as if I had been wafted into a vast cathedral, where, amid solemn records of the past, the sweet voices of many young choristers were chanting some quaint mediæval hymn.

He had a special love for Mozart's music, and he told me that on the day when he came by chance on Mozart's F Major Sonata in the library of a country house, he felt as if he had 'found a diamond.'

It may be imagined all the while that, as there is no absolute perfection in this world of ours, there would be from time to time some dissonance in the relation even between a young and most profoundly respectful pupil, and one who felt that in teaching he was giving some of the very best he had to give, and who demanded with reason implicit confidence in all his dicta. Well I remember how stern a tone his voice took, and how his face clouded over, when, after being more than usually in earnest about conquering some difficulty, and, as I thought, doing but little towards it, his kind words of encouragement brought from me the hasty words, 'Oh, don't say that! I get angrier with myself than ever when you speak so!' 'Do you think for a moment,' he replied, 'that *I* would give you undeserved approval? You don't *appreciate* what I give, and I must say you are most ungrateful.' I was dumfounded—in fact, horrified—at what his words suggested, and lost not a moment in apologizing, and assuring him that at the time I had only thought of myself, without any reference to him. He was satisfied, I believe, even more by what I looked than what I said, and, telling me to continue my playing, dropped by degrees into his usual tone and manner. Need I say that I never again gave him cause for displeasure on these grounds? There came, indeed, times when I was taken aback by getting praise where I looked for blame; but I grew in time to understand that the praise was given to what I had intended to do, and when I once realized this, and felt that he really did study every pupil's case, and had 'mastered mine,' a great calm came over me. All that trepidation and flutter of nervous excitement, which so often spoils an interview or a lesson, entirely vanished. If I had played a page, or even a whole movement, badly to him, instead of chiding myself for the failure, and thus marring what was coming next, I learnt from him, as one among the many other conditions for becoming a performer, to go on cheerfully, and not think of what had just happened before. The result was that, from a growing sense of self-possession, I began to think of doing far more than I had ever dreamed of when I first went to him. The possibility of one day being a concert-player dawned upon me with fresh clearness every month. But my mother could not bring herself to think of such a possibility. She had indulged my desire to study to play, and to seclude myself for the purpose. But public life—no! Even if I reached the height of a Clara Schumann, it would make no difference in her feeling about it; and she would say this often to Sterndale Bennett, and he would reply,

'Well, it is a problem; it will work itself out some day.' And then, turning to me, he would observe that in a concert-room there are perhaps not more than five or six among the listeners who are really giving themselves up to take in what the player is offering to them. 'You are choosing,' he used to say, 'a path which is beset with thorns.' The natural result of all this was, that without actually saying that I would give up the idea of playing in public, I did what amounted to quite the same thing. My mother's wishes and Sterndale Bennett's sombre view of public life damped my ardour for such a career. I paused, without realizing that not to advance is to retreat; and indulging the hope that circumstances might come in to help me, I consented to stay quietly at home, and content myself with occasional visits to London for the purpose of showing Sir Sterndale Bennett how I continued to work. The next step may be foreseen; for if art was to be only my pleasure, and not my life's vocation, what right had I just for this pleasure to turn all family arrangements upside down?

I found myself, moreover, looked on in our circle as a star, a wonder, a sort of oracle; and though I knew well that there was no honour in being admired by people who had no art-perceptions, yet I let myself drift into a sort of stagnation, and slowly, but none the less surely, did I cease 'to be on the strain.' Waves of circumstance, beginning with a disappointment in friendship, in which music and musical associations were strongly entwined, and ending with a family sorrow, which for a long, long space of time so utterly benumbed me that I neither wished to play myself nor even to hear music, submerged, if I may so express myself, all my musical past.

I was for two whole years quite unable to find any charm in music, though able to pursue other studies with plenty of energy. And then at last—it was on a day in spring—I laid my hand on the keys, and perceived that music had once more awakened up within me, and I was glad, and I set myself in a manner to 'get into step' again.

Many changes had in the meanwhile passed over our home, and it was no longer possible for me to go off alone, and give myself up to practice as I had once done, though only during a few years, and not for a sufficient period to bring anything to maturity. But I now began again to work a little, and that little very thoroughly; and as we passed through London the following year, Sir Sterndale Bennett kindly received us for a long visit, and at his request I played to him several pieces by heart: *Scherzo to the Midsummer Night's Dream*, Beethoven's Sonata in D Minor, Scarlatti's Sonata in A Major; and as I still retained the ease and freedom from undue anxiety which I had ever felt in his presence, these pieces went well, and he was much pleased, telling me, however, as truly and faithfully as he had ever done, where the weak points lay, and saying to my mother, 'It is a pity she is not in the profession, for the wish is still there.' As we stood at his door, and he shook hands with us, his parting words to me (the last I ever heard him utter) were, 'Though you are not a public player, yet remember that I tell you you have not for all that missed your vocation.'

Time went on, and, with many an ebb and flow, I alternately grasped and let go the piano. At last some hindrances passed out of the way, and it seemed possible to recommence my studies with Sir Sterndale Bennett. I took to working regularly every day in January, 187—, and in the first week of February, in the postscript of a letter from a London friend, I was scared by the words, 'The papers this morning say, "Sir Sterndale Bennett is in a state of great exhaustion."' But I would not believe that it was anything but an idle report, and I think it must have been the same day that I went to the house of a friend, and began to play Mozart's Sonata in F Major (one of Sterndale Bennett's favourite pieces, and one of those which I had been intending to play to him, perhaps in a month or two later on). But this was never to be, for at the close of the first movement a gentleman who had just come in, and who, only knowing that I had once been a pupil of Sir Sterndale Bennett, had no idea that the news would affect me particularly, observed, 'You know, of course, that your old master is dead.' And as I repeated the last word in a sort of daze, he continued, in the same tone as we use in mentioning odd scraps of news in society, 'Yes, the papers say he died last night.' Will it be thought an incredible thing, a heartless trait in me, that I just turned round, and played the piece to the very last note? No one there had the slightest idea what that death meant to me, and I was not going to let them know it then. But as soon as I could I left the room and went home, with the feeling that, as regarded pianoforte-playing, I was stranded.

II.

TAUSIG.

During the time when I was still a pupil of Sterndale Bennett, I came accidentally into contact with Tausig. I brought away from the one occasion on which I heard him an impression which no lapse of time has been able to efface. It was in the month of February, and my mother and I were staying in Berlin, where we had been detained by my having had scarlet fever in a very severe form. We were both anxious to return home, and the day of our departure had been nearly settled on, when some friends of the lady in whose house we were staying mentioned a concert to be given in the following week by an artist whose name, though unknown to us, was, it appeared, of Continental celebrity. The manner in which this lady spoke of Tausig excited in me a great desire to hear him. He was to play nothing but Chopin that evening, and the tickets, though expensive for Germany, were only to be had through a private source, as the performance was to take place in the house of people belonging to the aristocracy, and the audience was to be very exclusive and select. But to defer a journey just in order to hear even a great artist play was the very last thing which would have suggested itself to my mother. She observed that it was a pity the concert had not taken place sooner; that if he were so wonderful, she would like me to have heard him if it had been possible. My musical instincts protested against missing such a chance; but common-sense said that I had no right to make all plans give way to an infatuation which my family did not share. We spoke no further on the subject, and were really going to leave Berlin on the next day but one. But a quite exceptionally heavy fall of snow supervened. The papers spoke of trains being stopped midway on their route, and in places where there was no possibility of getting anything to eat or drink. Our kind friends entreated us not to risk a journey under such circumstances, and it was arranged that we should wait in Berlin until the weather should have become less severe.

Need it be said that, since our journey had been definitely put off, I at once thought of the Tausig concert? My mother, accordingly, asked our friend if it would still be possible to get us tickets for it. We heard, however, to our extreme vexation, that all the tickets had been sold, and that there was not the slightest chance of procuring even one—in fact, that it was useless to think any more about the matter. On hearing this I was in great dismay, when my mother suddenly proposed that we should visit the artist; that she should introduce me to him as a pupil of Sterndale Bennett, and ask if he could not instruct someone to sell us a ticket for his performance. We were told that Tausig was haughty and inaccessible, that if we went to his rooms he would not receive us; and, even supposing that we got an interview, that he would say, 'selling tickets was no business of his.' Fortune, however, favoured us in a way of which our German friends had little thought. Tausig was not at home when we reached his rooms, but we succeeded in persuading the woman who opened when we rung to allow us to come in and await her master's return in his rooms. We sat there for an hour or more, and I well remember the impression produced on me by this first glimpse into an artist's sanctum. A confusion prevailed here such as I had never before seen. Unbound volumes of French philosophy— Cousin, for instance—were scattered about on the broad window-sills. Music of Bach, in more than one edition, was lying on chairs near the piano. There was no look of comfort in the room, no suggestion of the refinement given by a woman's ordering hand. The atmosphere, nevertheless, wafted in on me in a subtle and mysterious way the sensation of a life centred in art—a life whose poetry, comfort, refinement, were all comprehended in art.

Finally, we heard a voice at the door, and then Tausig, having been told that there were visitors in his room, walked quickly in, and with a slight bow approached us. My mother at once apologized for being 'in possession of his sanctum,' and presenting me to him as a pupil of Sterndale Bennett, asked him, as an artist, not to send away such a devoted lover of music without giving her the chance of hearing him play once. She, in fact, told him in a few words how we had in the first instance declined tickets because we were leaving Berlin, and how afterwards we had been told it was hopeless to think of getting any. Tausig was both polite and kind, for he at once said, 'I cannot sell tickets for my concert, but I will with pleasure write an order which will admit you and your daughter.' And as he bowed us out at the door, he added with a smile: 'There are no reserved seats, and it is, therefore, not in my power to offer you and your daughter a place near the piano.'

I refrain from passing any criticism on a performance of which my then entire inexperience of modern pianoforte-playing rendered me a very incompetent judge. Suffice it, I was charmed, excited, carried away by the electric emanation which is always present in great artists. All sorts of wishes welled up within me as I listened. 'If it were but possible to stay in Germany, and have lessons from such an artist!' was the thought which kept returning to me again and again. But there were ever so many hindrances in the way—too many, at least, for anyone to surmount who was not strong-willed enough to carry all before her.

My mother and I called on Tausig, to thank him for his great courtesy to us. We found him at home, and were at once asked to walk in. He looked quite pleased to see us, and spoke of wishing to visit London. He told us that Mr. Ella had invited him to come and play at the Musical Union; 'but one engagement would not afford me sufficient inducement to undertake the journey,' he said. 'Nor would it suit my position as an artist to visit London and play only at the Union. If the Philharmonic invite me over, then it will be worth my while, otherwise London will never see me.' Tausig then asked how I liked his playing, and looked so genial when I told him what had pleased me most, that I actually had the audacity to say that I wished I could hear him play Bach. 'The greatest player of Bach's music is Hans von Bülow, pianist to the Austrian court,' was his rejoinder: 'but you shall hear me play Bach, mademoiselle, if you and your mother care to come here on next Sunday afternoon.' 'We English do not visit or go to concerts on Sunday,' said my mother; and then there was a pause. Tausig looked at me, and seeing probably that I was disappointed, seemed to be considering for a moment or two, and then named the afternoon of the following Friday. My mother knew quite well that I was longing to study with Tausig, but she did not suppose he took pupils, nor had she any idea of either staying with me in Germany herself, or leaving me in that country without her. She, however, observed to him in the course of conversation that she presumed he did not give lessons. 'I do not care to take private pupils,' was the reply. 'My terms, besides, are so high that few care to give them. But, madame, when you and your daughter visit me next week, I will hear her play; and if the young lady is as musical as her appearance suggests to me, it is not impossible that I might consent to take her as a pupil.' My mother had not intended her question to be answered so directly, and was not only a little embarrassed how to respond to Tausig's courteous speech, but a little disturbed by my half-confessed wish being thus met by him half-way. We returned home, and for the next two or three days I indulged in many a delightful dream as to what Tausig would do for me. And then I thought of Sterndale Bennett. I wanted to be loyal to him, but the charm of the fiery and glowing playing I had heard that evening thrilled and dominated me.

It was on a Friday we had seen Tausig, and when we had told him that we could not accept his invitation for Sunday, he had named the following Friday (that day week) as being the earliest day at his disposal. Saturday, Sunday passed, and Monday's post brought letters from our own country, which

urged my mother's immediate return there. On the
same evening a thaw set in, and our journey was thus
rendered possible. My air-built castles melted with
the snow, for there was important business to be
attended to. It was impossible for my mother to
remain. My artistic nature made only one struggle,
and then succumbed to the inevitable. I just asked
my mother the question whether she would be
satisfied to leave me in Berlin until summer, and
when I recognised that she could not reconcile herself
to the idea, I saw there was no use in thinking any
more on the subject. Before we left Berlin she
enclosed her visiting-card to Tausig, and in a few
courteous lines thanked him for his kindness, and
begged him to come and see us if he ever found his
way to England.

We were, however, never to meet him, never to
hear him again; for in the following year he was
carried off by a fever. He had been the favourite,
and, according to some, the most gifted pupil Liszt
had ever had. In referring to him a few years back,
the Meister is said to have pronounced the dictum
that since his death there had been but one who
could be compared to him. That one was Eugène
d'Albert, to whom even then, and before his great
powers were quite matured, Liszt alluded as 'the
young,' or rather, '*our young lion*.'

III.

SGAMBATI.

I now come to speak of one of the greatest living exponents of the Liszt school at its point of highest perfection. Giovanni Sgambati (known among his friends as *Nino*) holds at the present moment a brilliant position in Rome, where he is the pianist *par excellence*, the favourite and much sought for professor, an honoured guest in the most aristocratic circles; a composer whose works for the pianoforte, concerted chamber music, and the orchestra are known both in France and Germany—to both of which countries he has been more than once invited to conduct his own symphonies, and to play his compositions both for the pianoforte solo, and for this instrument in concert with others.

In the high social circles where Sgambati is so often a guest, he is invariably accompanied by his wife; and as I saw them then they were indeed a singularly interesting and distinguished-looking pair.

She—beautiful and sympathetic, far above the middle height, with a form of faultless symmetry; he—not devoid of beauty, and with power shown in every line of his face. On these occasions he nearly always gave some specimen of his masterly art, and even played duets, if he happened to meet pupils of his who did not like playing solos.

The brother of an intimate friend of ours had often spoken to us of Sgambati, whom he knew personally, and had eulogized his playing in the warmest manner. When circumstances brought us to Italy, and we were joined there by one of the family who had been away from us for years, there seemed to be once more an opening for me to devote myself to music without neglecting any nearer duties. My mother now regretted that I had not followed my bent; and she urged me in the strongest manner to go to Germany, and there try to regain what I had lost during the years when music had been but one— and not the most important—element in my daily life.

All was nearly arranged for carrying out this plan, when I suddenly bethought me of Sgambati, and resolved to try and hear him play before I turned my back on Italy. I went to his house to find out if it were possible to get an interview with him; and, to my surprise, the servant who opened the door told me that if I could call at his dinner-hour, or a little after it, the Maestro would see me at once. (He had not, like the English professors, entrenched himself behind barriers of inaccessibility.) I called, therefore, the very next day, and was shown into a pretty little salon, where all was neat and elegant and refined.

The friend of his above alluded to had shown me an early likeness of Sgambati—a thin, determined-looking young man, with a remarkable nose, and eyes which sent out from under drooping eyelids a veiled and mysterious glance whose meaning one could not quite define. The door opened, and let in one who, in the full summer of his manhood, had little of that early likeness but the eyes. Slightly *embonpoint*, and looking as if he had grown up into leaf and flower in the full sunshine of happy hours, and the benign smile of the gods, Sgambati presented the appearance of one in complete harmony with all around him. He struck one as being both physically and mentally in perfect balance. His manners were most easy and engaging; and on the strength of having 'a mutual friend' whom we both admired, we got into a very pleasant talk; but, though much pleased with my visit to him, I had never got the chance of hinting my wish to hear him play, for he had received me in a room where there was neither music nor a pianoforte. On reaching the hotel, however, it all at once occurred to me that, even if I were going to Germany, here was an opportunity for learning something of Liszt's pianoforte music (I knew from report that Sgambati played Liszt to perfection), and at the same time by taking a few lessons from him, attaining my desire of hearing Sgambati play.

Strange fatality! if anyone had told me that I was going to step out of the mould into which I had been cast—to leave quite aside all my traditional notions as to how Bach and Beethoven should be interpreted, and become a persistent imitator of the Liszt school—I should have raised an indignant protest to the contrary. But 'it was to be'; and I wrote a few lines to Sgambati, saying that, although I did not expect to be more than three weeks in Rome, he would do me a great favour by allowing me to study one or two of Liszt's compositions with him. He was kind enough to name an hour the next day but one, and I betook myself to his house at the time fixed, without any presentiment of what was to come out of that one lesson.

Not being nervous, but merely timid, I played a good deal by heart to him, and he at once seemed much pleased and interested. He then sat down, and played three or four pieces of Liszt's, winding up the whole with a splendid reading of Bach's *Fantaisie Chromatique*. In everything that he played, Sgambati far exceeded all that I could have anticipated. His lovely elastic touch, the weight and yet the softness of his wrist-staccato, the swing and go of his rhythmic beat, the colouring rich and warm, and yet most exquisitely delicate, and over all the atmosphere of grace, the charm and the repose which perfect mastery alone can give.

What wonder, then, if I was at once captivated by the Liszt school in Sgambati, and all unconsciously at first, but most consciously in a very few lessons, gave myself up to the task of becoming a 'Lisztianerin,' with a zeal and devotion which Sgambati, in a letter introducing me to Liszt some months later, described as 'the enthusiasm of a neophyte who has just embraced a new faith'? There was no more thought then of going to Germany, for not only did I hear Sgambati play when he gave me a lesson, but I often met him in society, where he always played; and besides this, he never failed to let me know when there were practices going on at his house, or rehearsals at the Sala Dante, and he used to let me stand beside him and turn over the leaves for him on these occasions. The more I heard of his playing, the more I strove with all my might to follow in his steps, though 'afar off'; and perhaps I might have done so, though in a very limited sense, if Sgambati had not unluckily suggested my taking out the diploma of the St. Cecilia Academy. I say unluckily, for a great part of the work which the candidate for the diploma had to prepare was of a kind which I could not afterwards utilize, and it kept me, moreover, for a year and a half on a sort of strain that was not stimulating, but quite the contrary. To prepare up to metronomic time, and keep in practice the twenty-four preludes and fugues which are contained in the first book of Bach's *Clavier bien tempéré*, twenty-four studies from the *Gradus ad Parnassum*, to play a modern piece by heart, to read a short manuscript at sight, and to answer, *vivâ voce*, questions on the general principles of harmony—such are the requirements with which all who wish for the St. Cecilia diploma must comply. The Bach preludes and fugues were pretty familiar to me, and I did not object to study them again; but the Clementi I had never played, and Sgambati, who really took a cordial interest in me, thinking that Clementi would be especially useful to me, and perceiving the lack of interest I took in the studies as 'music,' thought to do me a kindness by letting me believe that I had *forty* instead of twenty-four studies from the *Gradus* to prepare for the examination.

How I can pity myself when I look back at the hours I sat grinding away at all these, at a season of the year when the thermometer remained steadily at eighty-three degrees by night and day, for long weeks, and in rooms where everything was done to keep out the heat! It must not, however, be supposed that the entire twenty-four preludes and fugues, or the entire twenty-four studies from the *Gradus*, had to be gone through at the examination; but they had to be so far ready that when I should go down to the academy on a given evening and draw a single number of each out of a box into which they had been thrown

4

for the purpose, I could be sure of playing the number I might draw reasonably well on the next day but one.

I became meanwhile acquainted with many of the young students in Rome—Signor Rosati, a musical nature, but unable *se faire valoir*, owing to 'the modern *pianistic* nervousness;' Alfredo di Lucca, now teaching in Florence; Ernesto Consolo, 'a child prodigy,' who has developed into a very fine player; Signorina Ballio, who gave a concert in the Sala Dante at the age of sixteen—a little creature, with a tremendous force of will. One instance of this I shall recall here. This young lady had just begun to study Liszt's enormously difficult *Tarantelle*, from the *Muette de Portici*, when Sophie Menter arrived in Rome, and played the piece at a concert given by her in the *sala* of the British Embassy. Signorina Ballio was at the concert, and I likewise: and though we did not get near enough to speak to each other that night, I wondered what the young student would think of Sophie's terrible, almost demoniac, mastery of the keyboard. Meeting her the next day in the street, she rushed up to me, and with that delicious *naïveté* which makes Italians so charming, she said:

'I am in despair, signorina—in despair! I thought I was beginning to play the Tarantelle quite nicely, and oh! I don't believe I shall ever get it up to the *tempo* that Madame Menter takes it; and if I don't, I shan't care to play it;' and saying this, her dark eyes filled with tears, and she added, 'I cried so much, so much, when I went home last night, signorina; but'—brightening up with a sudden flash—'I *will* do it!'

Another young lady student of the Conservatoire became intimate with us much about the same time, in the following somewhat unusual manner. The mother of Signor Sgambati asked me one Sunday afternoon if I would like to accompany her to a pupils' concert, which was to take place on that day in the academy. One or two of her son's best pupils were to play, and among those she mentioned a young lady of whom I had heard Sgambati himself speak more than once very favourably. It was, therefore, with pleasure that I accepted the invitation. What music we had at the beginning of the *séance* I do not now remember; but when Signora Sgambati called my attention to a young lady who had just seated herself at the pianoforte, saying as she did so, 'That is Signorina G——,' I at once looked at her with much interest and attention.

She was young and attractive-looking, with a graceful and harmonious form, and she began to play her piece so beautifully that I was quite charmed with her performance. All at once, however, I felt that she was threatened with a nervous panic, that there was a danger of her tottering—in fact, breaking down. Not venturing to glance at Signora Sgambati, I turned towards a young lady who was my neighbour at the other side, and, our eyes happening to meet, we instinctively interchanged a glance of inquiry, of alarm and anxiety. And our mutely expressed fears were, indeed, but too well founded; for in a few more seconds there was an abrupt pause in the playing, and the young lady got up from the piano, and, facing round on the audience as if she knew not what to do next, she wrung her hands, saying in a most plaintive and appealing tone, 'Dio mio, non so che fare!' or some words to the like effect. One of the professors stepped, however, quickly forward, led her back to the piano, and laying the music of the piece which she had been playing on the desk, with gentle but authoritative gestures bade her resume the performance. With the exception of one or two slight breaks, she on the whole played the piece very well, and when it was over the professor shook hands with her, and the girl, seeming to have quite recovered her balance, moved away quietly and joined her mother, who was sitting in the body of the *sala*. My young lady neighbour had meanwhile raised her handkerchief to her eyes, and was weeping bitterly. A boy of about ten who was sitting near us was sobbing, poor little fellow! as if his heart would break (I heard afterwards that he was a brother of the young pianist). Signor Alfredo di Lucca, whose name was next but one in the programme for a sonata of Weber, had been so overcome by the scene that a friend and fellow-student brought him out of the concert-room, and insisted on his having a glass of Vermuth, after which he recovered his usual swing and *élan*, and played his piece admirably.

On the following day, a young student of St. Cecilia, who came twice a week to read music arranged for four hands with me, told us much about Signorina G—— which was calculated to excite our interest in her. On my observing that I had wondered at the self-control she had shown in playing so well after such a break-down, and still more wondered at her power of keeping countenance and looking so calm as she sat by her mother for more than an hour afterwards—

'Ah,' signorina,' observed Signor R——, 'had you but seen her in the class this morning—how she wept as she begged Sgambati's pardon, and deplored having given way to such an unreasonable panic! And the professore was so kind to her. He told her she must not cry any more, but think of retrieving herself. He would give her the chance of doing so, by having her asked to play at the next pupils' concert, which would be in four weeks. She should play Mendelssohn's First *Concerto*, and he would accompany her on a second piano.'

My sister and I both felt great sympathy with Signorina G——, and we felt very anxious on her behalf as the time approached for her performance of the Mendelssohn concerto. We feared that she would brood over what had happened at her last appearance, and so mar her future prospects. We thought of going to see her, and telling her that some of the finest players had had similar experiences, but finally decided that the very best way to help her a little would be to give her some agreeable surprise during the hours of suspense, and thus to divert her thoughts into another channel at that critical time. But how to do this was the question; and, after many half-formed plans, we settled on the following. Not very English, my readers will say. We wrote a letter to the young lady, in which we praised her talent, expressed ourselves her sincere well-wishers, and begged her not to let her thoughts revert to what was after all, though a misfortune, yet one that could reflect no real discredit on her; the piece (a concert study by Liszt) being, moreover, of enormous difficulty—from beginning to end one maze of intricate passages. We did not sign our names to the letter, but concluded by telling her we should be at the concert, and fully expected that she would play admirably. I took the letter, accompanied by a book, called *Volere è potere,* to the floor on which the young lady lived; and being very anxious to avoid recognition, not only put on a very thick gauze veil, but when the door was opened by Signorina G——'s mother, handed her the parcel without saying a word, and hurried away. Had I spoken, my foreign accent would have betrayed my nationality, and given them a clue as to who I was. I hurried away, therefore, in silence, and reached home, congratulating myself that neither on the staircase nor at the street door had I met anyone who could have recognised me. But Rome is a small place, and our secret oozed out in a way for which I was not at all prepared. The young student who came to play duets with me knew my handwriting, and happening to pay a visit to the G—— family about an hour after I had left the book, he told them whose the writing was; and even before the concert had begun, Sgambati knew the whole thing. His mother was not present at this concert, but I met the young lady who had been my neighbour on the first occasion. We sat together, and both rejoiced as Signorina G—— came forward, looking happy and full of spirits, and played with fire, energy, and *élan*. Signor Sgambati looked all pleasure and satisfaction as he shook hands with his pupil at the conclusion of the piece. He then descended the platform, and I wondered whom he wanted, as he hurried down the room, glancing to the right and to the left as he moved along. He came nearer, and I perceived that his face wore a smile, his eyes were beaming with irrepressible amusement, and even before he addressed me, or indeed saw me, I feared that all was known, and felt that I was reddening in a very tell-tale manner. His first words to me seemed innocent of any special meaning—in fact, would have suggested nothing to an outsider; it was the smile that accompanied them, the tone in which they were uttered, that gave them any meaning at all. 'The family want, of course, to know you.' 'What family?' was my rejoinder. 'Ah, signorina, it is no use. If I did not know as much as I do, your colour would be quite enough to excite suspicion! Come, come, there's no use in fencing. The book and the letter! I have not only heard of them, but I have seen them! Don't blame me, if I convey to you the thanks of the whole family, and their wish to be at once presented to you.' It was rather an embarrassing position, for all who were near us must have pretty well guessed the import of what we were saying. Sgambati wanted me then and there to come up the room with him and be introduced to the G——s, a proceeding which would, I feared, have attracted general attention. I therefore begged him to tell them that I would wait where I was, and when the concert was over, and they were coming out, I would be very pleased to make their acquaintance. Father and mother were lavish in their expressions of gratitude to me for the sympathy, the interest, I had shown in their child. Signora G—— asked if she might pay me a visit on the following day; and when she came, brought with her the young lady who had sat beside me at both the pupils' concerts, and on the first occasion had shown such bitter grief at the break-down of Signorina G——, and the second time had been so full of genuine delight in her success. The young lady was Signorina Ballio, then the special and most intimate friend of Signorina G——. The result of this incident was that I came to know a good many of the St. Cecilian students. Not only did the two above-named young ladies come very often to our house, but one or two of the gentlemen-students would drop in of an evening. And we sometimes had 'a sham examination'; *i.e.*, we drew lots who was to play, and then again which of Bach's preludes and fugues, or which study from the *Gradus*, was to be performed by the player.

In the following year Signorina G——, being about to play before the examiners who award the St. Cecilian diploma, gratified me much by asking Sgambati if it would be possible for her to get permission to bring me into the examination room, for she felt that my presence would be a help and a stimulus to her. Sgambati kindly got her the required permission, and we went together to the academy. When the signorina was about to play, by her special wish I seated myself where my glance could meet hers all the time she was playing. She passed an admirable examination, and was given a high number of marks in taking out the diploma.

Several other students were going in for their examination on the same day. One of these was a gentleman I knew, and he asked both Signorina G—— and me to come into the room where he was awaiting his turn to appear before the examiners. He was rehearsing the different pieces he was about to play. Poor fellow! he was in such a highly wrought state, that although he was playing in a cool room, the beads of perspiration stood on his forehead, and he was all in a tremor. It was not the mere question of passing—getting through—that made all these young students so anxious, but they were teachers, and if they only passed with a minimum number of marks, though they might indeed get the diploma which carries with it the title of professor, yet they would take but a low place in the profession—a great disadvantage at the beginning of their career. This gentleman's turn came just after that of Signorina G——. We met him in the corridor, and he made us both promise that we would not either listen at the door while he was being examined, nor remain anywhere near enough to hear his performance. Giving him the required promise, we both went down the stairs into a distant part of the building with some other students, and there we anxiously awaited the event, for the gentleman was a favourite with his fellow-students. Far away as we had gone, however, we could hear, though not very distinctly, both the study from the *Gradus ad Parnassum*, and the prelude and fugue from Bach's 'well-tempered Clavier.' They both seemed to go very well, for there was no break in the performance. But then came a long pause. Ten minutes passed, and, becoming very uneasy, we stole softly up the staircase. At the top of the corridor leading to the examination-room, we met an attendant, who told us that he had just been in there, bringing water to recover a gentleman who had all but

fainted away. 'He is coming to, however,' added the
man; 'he is getting up his courage; he has already
spoken, and asked if he might be allowed to finish
his examination. Ah! there he is playing again;'
and, mindful of our promise, we once more retired to
a distant room, and in about twenty minutes were
joined by our friend and fellow-student. He looked
very happy, and so, indeed, he well might be; for he
had played his longest and most difficult trial-piece
quite exceptionally well, and he got a much higher
number of marks than he had ever dared to hope.

But to return to the relation of my studies with
Sgambati. He gave me the scales to practise in
thirds, and *arpeggios* in the diminished seventh, for
raising the fingers from the key-board—recommending these as the best possible daily drills for the
fingers. He also gave me some guidance in the first
book of Kullak's octave studies, and he tried to
initiate me into the elastic swing and movement of
the wrist, so important in the octave-playing of
modern compositions. Sgambati's playing of Liszt
was, now that I compare him with many others
whom I have since heard, more poetical than any.
In the sudden *fortissimi* so characteristic of the school
his tone was always rich and full, never wooden or
shrill; while his *pianissimi* were so subtle and
delicate, and the *nuances*, the touches of beauty,
were fraught with a sighing, lingering, quite inimit-
able sweetness, which one could compare to nothing

more material than the many hues where sky and ocean seem to melt and blend, in a dream of tender ecstasy, along the coast-line between Baia and Naples. His playing of Schumann was also 'a speciality'; and I remember vividly his delicious wrist-played staccato, from the first to the last bar in the left hand of the last variation but two of the *Etudes Symphoniques*. And yet I only heard him play it *en robe de chambre*, as it were—just to show me how it went; for he had little time for practice, and had not played it in public for years before I knew him. I also recall his playing of (Schumann's *Carneval*,) as one of the pieces which gave him great scope for showing his masterly range in many directions. Besides hearing him play it at a concert at the Sala Dante, I had the good luck to hear him rehearsing it in the concert *sala* a day or two previous to the concert. His wife, whom I had gone to visit that afternoon, told me that she was just then going to fetch him home, and asked me if I would accompany her. It was early in April, and there was a breath of coming summer in the air, and as the door opened to let us in, the rich tide of complex harmonies, fraught with all the mystery, the passionate questioning, which the magician Schumann has poured out there, floated through the *sala*—all the more weird and all the more mysterious because he who evoked the phantoms was brimful of life and strength, and a conscious delight in achievement.

Sgambati's playing of Beethoven's E Flat Concerto was (I should rather say *is*) one of the finest I have ever heard; such beautiful tone, such perfect taste, such broad simple phrasing, such reserve of force; never have I heard any artist sink so poetically from *forte* to *piano* in the two octave passages of the first movement. I had, moreover, the advantage of hearing him play it several times, both in the Sala Dante with the orchestra, and in his own house with the accompaniment of a second pianoforte. Like all great artists, Sgambati really shines most when *en robe de chambre*, and seeming scarcely to be trying to play at all. I have heard him, for instance, accompany some very promising young pianist in such pieces as the Mendelssohn Concertos, the *Concert Stück*, and others, when the pupil has had the good instrument and Sgambati a very inferior one; and yet, with Sgambati evidently out of practice, and taking no trouble, as he sat there with a cigar between his lips, looking all *nonchalance* and easy *insouciance*, one felt what he was, just as one feels that the sun is there behind the clouds. The pupil was brilliant, and was playing without apparent difficulty, and yet all the while one had a consciousness that under this apparent ease there *was* effort and strain, the anxious throb of endeavour not yet quite sure of itself. I have heard those who were not his friends call Sgambati 'a cold player'; but this is not true. The utmost I would say is that he is at times reserved, and cannot 'let go'—cannot always solve the problem which makes the playing of the greatest artists a tantalizing *forse*, the problem how to be at once self-contained and impassioned, at once firmly balanced and yet floating midway between earth and heaven. No artist, however great, ever invariably solves that problem; but either, like Rubinstein, lets impulsiveness lead him with headlong impetuosity into a wild storm of incoherent passion; or, if the artist's will holds the emotional element so much in check that the intellectual element predominates, then the artist stands before us dwarfed, a pianist indeed, and it may be one of no common order, but without the magic power, the soul-subduing thrill, for lack of which art is not living and vital, but a petrifaction, a crystal.

How Sgambati must have worked before he attained this mastery, the following anecdote will very clearly instance. The lady who told it to me was a near relation of Sgambati. I had been telling her that several of his pupils in the academy had complained to me that, after having done their best, the only praise he ever gave them—and that very rarely—was ' *Non c'è male* ' (' It is not amiss '). 'If he would but praise us a little more,' they said, ' we should get on ever so much better.'

'But, my dear signorina,' said the lady, ' only think what Sgambati's natural endowments are (when I tell you that at fifteen he was already a charming player, and yet all the while never flagged in his industry; and that at twenty, when he had obtained recognition, and was giving concerts, and was known to be a special favourite and highly valued pupil of Liszt, how he used to work at that time! Yes,' she continued, 'I have known him to begin practising some passage which he thought wanted improvement in a Mendelssohn concerto, and there he would sit on, from the closing in of a winter afternoon until near midnight, patient, absorbed, and untiring; nor would he leave off even then, had I not begged him to bethink himself that the other lodgers in the Palazzo might complain if he went on any longer! He who has done so much, and has shrunk from no effort, no fatigue, in the maturing of his great powers, how can he praise these young people, who, without a tithe of his natural talent, think to accomplish great things with comparatively little labour?'

Sgambati has formed some very fine players— Ernesto Consolo; Alfredo di Lucca; Emma Metler, a young Swiss girl, known in Germany as a concert-player; and several others, whom I do not name here.

Sgambati does not usually talk much, but is dreamy and contemplative, and often quite lost in musical reverie; but when he does speak, it is much to the purpose, and, in his own beautiful language, he is 'a virtuoso,' with a perfect accent, and a command of choice and elegant expressions. He speaks of his art like one who has thought much and deeply on the subject. I wish I could recall even the outline of what he said to me one day about Listz's *Venezia e Napoli*, and Beethoven's *Sonata Appassionata*; as it is, I only give a general impression.

'Nothing is so immaterial as music,' he said, referring to the vexed question of how much strict form is essential to the manifestation of a high form of an art idea. 'Great flashes of wonderful colour, in which we cannot exactly perceive a definite, clear outline or form, may call up in us streams of fascinating suggestion; and when this suggestiveness is present in a composition, who shall say that there is less of true art than when the form is clear and definite? I make no comparison,' he continued, 'between these two (the *Venezia e Napoli* and the *Appassionata*), for they are so essentially different as to exclude all possibility of comparison; I hold that there is as much beauty, though of a different kind, in the one as in the other.' ('There is a theory,' he said to me more than once, 'that music is the faint reminiscence of a language which we used, either in a previous and immaterial existence, or in some earlier stage of our development, but the meaning of which we have lost.) I am not saying,' he added, 'that I believe this, but there is much in it that would lead one to fancy such a conclusion may not be very far from the truth.'

For two summers I saw much of Sgambati, whose wife was my friend, and who asked me to join them in their daily evening walks and drives at the Bagni di Lucca, where they spent the *villeggiatura*. Learning thus to know Sgambati in his family relations, I was inspired with a personal respect and sympathy for him, which naturally enhanced my appreciation of him as an artist and musician. The life which he and his charming wife led was the precise opposite of what we English are but too apt to think that of foreigners in general and of artists in particular must be. Sgambati spent the whole of the long sultry summer days in composition, while his wife sat in the adjoining room with the door open between; and, with just the interruption of the one o'clock dinner and a short siesta afterwards, she either painted or did a little needlework, while he was deep in writing. They were supposed to go out for the evening ramble about five o'clock; but when Sgambati had not brought his work up to a given point, he lingered over it, and the wife would look in at him, and then sit down again, and recommence her work. More than once, when I have gone in by appointment, she has motioned me to a seat, and we have either carried on a conversation in subdued tones, or each taken a book to beguile the time, and an hour or more has slipped by, and the shadows of evening have approached, and I have thought to myself, 'What a pity to lose the most perfect hour of the day!' and just then the musician would come out of his sanctum, looking ready for rest and enjoyment, their beautiful child would join us, and we would set off for a walk, or, still oftener, for a drive. Sometimes we took donkeys, and all four ascended some of the heights, from which we got lovely views.

In the first year of my stay in Italy, our family sustained the darkest and dreariest and most abiding sorrow of my life—no less than the removal of 'the head of the household'; as after a previous loss, I shut the pianoforte, and but for the earnest entreaties of my sister, and the kindly sympathy of the Sgambatis, would probably not have opened it for long enough. I resumed, however.

A few months after this great loss it was necessary that I should go to Great Britain, and put our family affairs in order. Liszt happened to be in Italy just then, and Sgambati, who knew that it had long been a cherished wish of mine to see the great man—perhaps to hear him play, and even, it might be, have an opportunity of playing to him—kindly gave me a letter of introduction. Liszt was not in Rome, but at Tivoli, where he occupied a beautiful suite of rooms in the Villa d'Este.

The evening before our intended excursion to Tivoli, Sgambati sent me this letter of introduction, and my sister took a copy of it for me, which I still preserve. About an hour or so after we had got the letter, my sister had undressed her little girl, and put her into a bath, and I had gone for a moment into the next room, to run over the piece which I hoped to play to Liszt the next day, when all at once I perceived that Sgambati had come in, and was talking to my sister; and when I joined them, there he was, smiling at the little creature, whom my sister had, on his entrance, swathed up hastily in a couple of large towels. He said over and over again, as he looked at her, 'Quanto è carina! quanto è carina!'. ('What a darling!' etc.). Those who feel an interest in Sgambati as a composer and as an artist, will be still further interested in him when they hear that the dreamy, nonchalant, and often supremely disdainful-looking musician has an inborn capacity for letting himself down to the level of quite small children, and making them love him and feel at home with him.

How often has he not improvised a doll with a knotted pocket-handkerchief, and not only charmed my little niece, but also highly amused both her aunt and mother, by making his doll perform all sorts of ridiculous jumps and somersaults! So fond was our little one of him, and so firm a faith had she in his sympathy with her in all her childish troubles—scratches, bruises, bumps, and such-like—that when her mother and I applied the panacea usual in such cases, 'a kiss on the place to make it well,' the small creature has more than once said to us, 'But I want Sgambati to kiss it too.'

But to resume the thread of my narrative. Sgambati had come in order to tell me how I was to approach the great man, on whom he evidently wished me to make a favourable impression. 'With regard to his compositions, should you get an opportunity of alluding to them, don't refer to those which he has written for the pianoforte, for (though we don't quite agree with him there) Liszt believes that it is through his orchestral works that his fame will be handed down to posterity.' 'But how can I do this, for I have never heard any of Liszt's compositions for the orchestra?' was my reply to Sgambati. 'Yes, but you have played arrangements of the above, you know — Fest-Klänge, les Préludes, also Tasso and the Dante Symphony—and you can, at all events, tell Liszt that you look forward some day to the pleasure of hearing a complete orchestral performance of these, perhaps in Germany; and then,' continued Sgambati, 'when he asks you to play to him, don't rush over to the piano the minute he first broaches the subject, but stand up, to show your willingness to comply with his wishes, and then pause a little, and get into chat, to show that, though *willing*, you are not *anxious* to play to him.'

My sister and her little girl—a fragile creature then just three years old—came out with me to Tivoli, and leaving them both, in the first instance, at a little inn in the village, I went (as advised by Sgambati) to the Villa d'Este; and, giving my letter of introduction to Liszt's valet, I asked him what time I had best call and pay my respects to the Master. He replied, 'About half-past three; for after his early dinner the Master takes a nap, and is then ready to receive.' I returned then to the inn, where I had left my sister and her child, and as it had begun to pour with rain, we had to occupy ourselves with the little one, who found the place very dull, as her toys and dolls were all at home. We ordered an early dinner, and 'baby,' as we called her, dropped off asleep the moment she had done eating, and when it was time to go up to the Villa d'Este we could not rouse her; and even if we had done so, she would not have been quite *en train* for going into a strange room and seeing strange people, and I had therefore to go by myself to the Villa d'Este, and was amused by Liszt's valet asking me 'where were my friends.'

He was an inquisitive body, and had asked me in the morning whether I had come out from Rome 'all by myself,' and I had replied that my sister and her little girl had accompanied me; so now, seeing me without them, he asked me where they were. I satisfied his curiosity, and then was shown into a room in which there was a grand pianoforte and handsome antique furniture; but if I noticed anything here it was the glorious view of the campagna on which one looked out through the quaint windows.

After about five minutes, Liszt came in. He impressed me both then and since as one of the largest and most widely sympathetic natures I have ever come across. I had heard some things against him 'as a man,' and I heard more later on, and all I heard was what would prejudice one who never could quite lose the strong impressions of her early Puritan training. But Liszt's individuality was a thing apart; and in spite of the awe I had for his great genius, and the discomposing sensation of being in the presence of one who has 'a demon '—in Goethe's sense of the word—I was at home at once with him. He seated me on the sofa beside him, asked me about Sterndale Bennett, and then about Sgambati, and whether I liked Von Bülow's or Sgambati's playing best. I replied that, though I did greatly admire Von Bülow, yet I found more charm in Sgambati; and I even ventured to say to Liszt, 'Has not Sgambati *un poigs doux?*' (my way of describing Sgambati's wrist-playing). Liszt replied, 'Vous avez parfaitement raison, mademoiselle.' He then said he would like to hear me play; on which I rose, but, mindful of Sgambati's admonitory hint, chatted on with Liszt and made no motion to go to the piano. After two or three minutes, however, Liszt broke in with, 'But you are to play to me—yes, and now at once;' and so saying, he gave me a little push towards the instrument, at which I at once seated myself, and played the *Spinnerlied;* and though I confess that when I was leaving my sister, and while I was coming up to the Villa d'Este, I had felt much as if I were about to 'undergo an operation,' yet I kept my word to Sgambati, and played the piece from beginning to end very respectably, and with much go and swing. Liszt was kind enough to suggest that I should play another piece to him; but by not doing so, but simply saying, 'You are too good; you have heard enough of my attempt' (for I had a keen perception of whose presence I was in), I got something which Sgambati told me afterwards did not always fall to the lot of those who were admitted to Liszt on a letter of introduction. He sat down himself to the pianoforte, and played a long piece—a concert-study of his own. He thrilled even more than he astonished me by his sweet penetrative tone, and the tender pathetic ring which pervaded the whole. The winter afternoon sunlight streamed in, and lighted up the silvery hair that reached down to his shoulders, and I felt as I listened and looked, and realized that he was *aged*, and therefore could not be with us very long, that I would gladly give up my life just to add it to *his* precious existence. When he got up from the piano he ordered tea and toast, and he made me sit down beside him and talk, and told me in whatever city I found him I should be welcome, whenever I came. It was not he, but I, who brought the visit to a close; and having heard from me that my sister was waiting for me at a hotel in the village, he put on his mantle, and escorted me to her, saying, 'I must see your sister and the child.'

And now, leaving Liszt for the present, I return to

speak of my studies with Sgambati, which I pursued with great ardour, not as yet perceiving that the school did not suit me, however much I might admire it. The time for taking out the diploma drew near, and I had prepared as my solo piece Chopin's beautiful *Fantasia in F Minor*. Sgambati's kindness before the examination I shall never forget. He made me rehearse to him in the examination-room just before the examiners entered; he had advised me to play but little that day. All went well, as it ever has done with me when I have had to screw myself up for a great effort. I record it in grateful memory of 'the Italians,' and their warm and kindly feelings, that, as I came down the stairs of the academy after the examination was over, I found several of the students waiting to offer their congratulations on my success, and on reaching home there were three or four more of them in our drawing-room. I was very happy, but very tired, and instead of resting after all this fatigue and excitement, I set to work at Liszt's composition, and the result was that the following year, after suffering much from fever, I had to leave Italy, and return to my native country.

I think it but fair to state that it was not merely my studies for the diploma, nor, indeed, the Liszt pieces, which made me so dissatisfied and filled me with such a sense of failure. My sister and her little girl had been suffering from repeated attacks of very bad malarial fever, and I was a considerable sharer of the same illness, though in a milder form; and studying Liszt's works under such conditions, it was little wonder if the result brought me nothing but dissatisfaction and unrest.

Before, however, taking leave of Sgambati, it may not be out of place to relate one more anecdote about him—an anecdote which throws a pleasing light on the relations which existed then (and which, I believe, exist at the present moment) between him and the young students who were his pupils at the Conservatorium. The reader may perhaps recall the name of Signor R——; I have mentioned him more than once in the foregoing pages. He was a young Neapolitan, who had been recommended to me by Sgambati as a good reader at sight—one who, having met with a sad reverse of fortune, was looking out for the means of supporting himself; so that in engaging him professionally to come and play with me at stated times, I should be at once doing what was very advantageous to myself and helping a most deserving young fellow. Signor R—— inspired me with both sympathy and respect, and as he was aware that Sgambati had told me a good deal about him, he alluded at different times to his trials, his difficulties, his plans for the future, but all in a very general way, and without entering into any details. One day when he came to play, I could perceive, the moment he entered the room, that some unusual trouble was pressing on his mind. He not only looked ill and miserable, but he seemed to find difficulty in mastering his agitation. I would have liked to say something, but feared to make him break down by asking what was the matter. When we sat down to play, however, he was so absent, so unable to concentrate his attention on what we were doing, that more than once we had to begin afresh. It seemed cruel, under such circumstances, to let him go on, and I therefore told him that, as I could perceive he was either ill or in great trouble, I begged he would consider himself free, and not continue our reading for that day.

'I am not ill, signorina,' he replied ; 'nor am I in trouble in the way you perhaps imagine. But I am at this moment so unhappy about a friend of mine that I can think of nothing else. Ah, signorina, can you imagine what it is to look on at suffering and be unable to relieve it; to hear a person you love tell you that he is hungry, and even starving, and not be able to tell him that you can, at least, give him bread enough to satisfy his hunger?' As he pronounced the last sentence, Signor R——'s voice grew thick and husky, and I could see that it was only by making a great effort that he refrained from giving way to a burst of tears.

I entreated him to tell me who was in such pressing need, hoping to find some way of giving a helping hand in the matter.

He then told me that a young countryman from his own province (Naples) had, until within the last few months, held the foremost place among all Sgambati's pupils. He had supported himself by giving lessons; and such was his zeal, his deadly determination to conquer the keyboard or die, that he would play for hours and hours, and think of neither food nor rest. The result of all this was, that when he took a cold he had no strength to shake it off, and when he continued to cough for several weeks, by degrees all his pupils fell away, their parents believing that he was consumptive. Italians think this disease is catching, and they feared that in teaching their children he might communicate it to them.

'We all tried to help him as well as we could,' continued Signor R——; 'but we are ourselves poor —we could not go on supporting him; and he is now as nearly as possible in a state of starvation.'

'But Signor Sgambati—does he know of all this; and can he do nothing for the poor fellow?' I exclaimed.

'Oh yes, signorina; the professore has been very kind to P——; has helped him over and over again. But what can he do? It is not to be supposed that he can undertake to keep and support him.'

R—— and I talked a little more that morning about P——, and when R—— was leaving our house, it was with the understanding that he was to come back in the evening, to ascertain if I had succeeded in planning any possible way of helping his friend.

My first move was to try and see Sgambati, to whose house I accordingly set off at once. It was his dinner-hour, but though they had just sat down, I was asked to come in. Coming to the point almost immediately, I asked Sgambati if he could verify all that Signor R—— had just been telling me about P——. Was he so very gifted—so hard-working? Had he been able up to the present time to support himself by giving lessons? And had he lost his pupils because their parents feared he was consumptive? I asked Sgambati all these questions, not because I had the slightest doubt of Signor R——'s veracity, but because I had formed a plan, and in order to carry it out with success, it would be necessary for me to be able to refer to Sgambati.

Sgambati replied that all I had heard was, indeed, but too true. It was a sad case. Sgambati could see no way of procuring effectual help for the suffering and destitute young student. When he heard, however, that I proposed drawing up a statement of the case, and sending it in the form of a circular to our musical friends both in Great Britain and in Rome, he not only allowed me to use his name as vouching for the entire accuracy of the statement, but he also offered to stand second on the list of subscribers when the subscription-list should have been once regularly started. That was a happy and successful day! The first friend, to whom I applied in person, was an elderly English lady, well known in Rome for her benevolence. She immediately took a deep interest in the case, and consented to head the subscription-list with fifty francs. Sgambati followed with the same amount, and when R—— came to our house that evening, he went away with a joyful heart, carrying with him not only the means of giving his friend present help, but with the pleasing prospect of being able to send him into the country, where we hoped that pure air, entire rest, and freedom from all present anxiety, might restore him to health.

My friends both in London and in my native place responded most kindly and promptly to my appeal; the Italians gave a little, and Sgambati soon had the pleasure of telling his pupil that he need for the present have no anxiety as to the means of living.

P—— went off, accordingly, to the country (to the sea-shore, I believe) early in June, and in July, when the Sgambatis and I were at the Bagni di Lucca together, we used often to talk about P——. He wrote pretty regularly to Signor Sgambati; and we all hoped, from the cheerful tone of his letters, and the way in which he spoke about himself, that he was on the way to complete recovery. After three months, however, our funds began to run low. It was still too hot for P—— to return to Rome, and both Sgambati and I cast about in our minds what we should do next to replenish our now nearly empty exchequer. It had already been suggested that Sgambati should play one or two pieces in some miscellaneous entertainment, to which it was thought a numerous audience of summer guests might be attracted. This suggestion, however, never came to anything, not because of any refusal on the part of Sgambati, any holding back from associating himself with amateurs. Sgambati was altogether so entirely above such considerations, that he never made any difficulty about sitting down to play even on the worst of instruments, and would readily take the bass of a duet—and this not only with his own pupils, but also with persons whom he had seldom, perhaps never, seen before. And he knew well that in this instance the mere mention of his name on the programme of any entertainment would be quite sufficient to ensure its success. But the fact was, that in the first instance there seemed to be no one forthcoming who could set the whole thing in motion—decide what the entertainment was to be, find out the people who would be able and willing to take an active part in it, and bring all the different elements together so as to make some coherent whole.

Finally, however, three American young ladies, who with their mother were staying for the summer at the Bagni di Lucca, came forward and suggested a series of *tableaux vivants*, in which they offered to arrange everything—to allot the respective *rôles*, plan the scenery, and design with the least possible outlay costumes appropriate to the different characters. Bills were sent round, accordingly, to all the hotels, stating that on a given evening there would be *tableaux vivants* and other entertainments in the dependence of the New York Hotel; that the entertainment was given in order to raise funds for maintaining a poor student, who was gone away for his health; and though I am not quite certain whether Sgambati's name actually figured on the bills, yet I know the report that he and his wife would appear passed from mouth to mouth, until it was known all over the Bagni di Lucca. The result was that people thronged in from all the hotels, and from most of the villas, and if we had only thought of making the charge for admission higher, we might have realized quite a large sum that evening. But the room was small, and there were numbers who had to go away without being able to get even standing room, and half a franc was all we had thought of asking for entrance. The result was that, after paying for the use of the room, lights, and many other etceteras, the performance only left us a balance of one or two hundred francs.

One of the *tableaux vivants* depicted a scene in *Preciosa*, in which Sgambati appeared in the character of a bandit. I can still recall him, as he stood, gun in hand, on a high rock which frowned at the turn of a narrow mountain-pass. He was dressed in a very tolerable imitation of the bandit costume; with a knife slung from his loose and carelessly knotted sash, and a broad-brimmed high-coned hat, from which a tall feather waved, he quite looked the part he had chosen to assume.

In another *tableau* Sgambati and his wife took the parts of Coriolanus and his mother. The moment selected was that in which the women of Rome kneel before Coriolanus. How beautiful the signora looked in this scene! I shall not easily forget her.

We had not, as I have before mentioned, realized very much by this performance, but still there was enough to keep P—— for some time longer in the country. In October the Sgambatis returned to Rome, and I joined my sister in our pretty house on the Corso. P—— did not come to Rome until about ten days later. His first visit was, of course, to the Sgambatis, who told me that he looked quite strong and healthy, that he had grown stout—that, in fact, he would be quite able to do for himself; and I know they believed this to be the case. But that it was not so, the melancholy sequel but too plainly proves. Signor R—— was not quite so sanguine about his friend as the Sgambatis had been; but, still, he found him greatly improved in appearance, and quite, he believed, on the way to recovery, provided he could for a time be hindered from overworking himself. 'He will not come and pay his respects to you, signorina, until he is provided with a lodging,' said R—— to me; and it was not until long afterwards, when I myself had known what it was to mount hundreds of steps looking for a house, that I realized what 'being for a day and a half looking for a room' must have meant to a creature who, on account of his music, was always obliged to take a room at the top of the house. It meant simply being on a sort of treadmill for that day and a half. When the weary quest was over, he was to have accompanied R—— to supper at our house. The latter, however, to my surprise and disappointment, appeared alone, and his expressive face told me before he had uttered a word that there was something wrong.

'Well, but where is your friend?' was my salutation to him as he came in.

'Ah, signorina, he is very ill, and though the doctor has not said so, I believe that he is in great danger!' and then he told me how that afternoon P—— had, after finally securing a suitable room, met him by appointment at a *caffè*. He seemed much exhausted, but cheerful and full of hope, full of plans for the future. All of a sudden he was seized with an internal pain of such violence that he at once said he was dying. 'It became worse and worse until by his own wish,' continued Signor R——, 'I took him to the hospital. Various remedies were applied to relieve him, but he was not better when I left him, about an hour ago.'

'Are visits allowed in the hospital?' was my next query of Signor R——.

'Oh yes, signorina; but only by an order, for which one must apply beforehand. I have one in my pocket; and Sgambati, on whom I called on my way to you, has arranged to accompany me to the hospital at eleven o'clock to-morrow morning. When we are there I can get an order for you, and I will, if you wish it, call here immediately after your dinner-hour and escort you there. It will indeed cheer poor P—— to find that so many kind friends sympathize with him.'

Accordingly, at two o'clock on the following day. I was ready dressed so as to set out as soon as Signor R—— should arrive. A minute or two after the hour, the hall door-bell rang, and Signor R—— walked in. So ghastly was his colour, so sorrowful his expression, that I at once knew that there was no need for any further questions—no need for any more planning, any more anxiety, about the future of poor P——. He had been released in the night—in those still hours when even sick watchers grow drowsy and slumber. No one knew exactly when he closed his tired eyes, or when that throbbing, unquiet heart had ceased to beat. Thinking over the circumstances of the case, we could not but feel that it *was* a release. But that no one was near to hold his hand, and whisper some gentle word of hope, of consolation, was a thought of deep sadness to all of us who had taken an interest in the poor fellow. And even now, after he has lain so long in his lonely bed, I am only reconciled to that lonely, uncared-for passing away, when I look beyond, and remember that the deepest, the most tender human sympathy is, when compared with the Divine, but as a feeble spark to the glorious sun, a tiny drop to the mighty soundless deep.

Since the days when I studied the pianoforte with Sgambati he has given himself up more and more to composition, and his works have been slowly but surely winning their way in musical circles. Liszt spoke of his quintettes and concerto as 'nobles,' and this year a letter, or rather the copy of a letter, from Wagner to the head of the Schott firm, in Mayence, fell into my hands, in which Wagner refers to what Liszt thought of Sgambati both as a pianist and composer. With the permission of Sgambati, I here give that part of the letter which refers to him.

Second page of the copy of a letter which was written by Wagner to Dr. Strecker, principal of the Schott firm, in Mayence, November 23, 1876. (The original letter is in the possession of Messrs. Schott.)

'But to say the truth, my letter of to-day has another end in view, namely, to commend to you most earnestly for publication two quintettes (pianoforte and stringed instruments) composed by Signor Sgambati of Rome.

'Liszt had already, and in a most special and emphatic manner, called my attention to this distinguished composer and pianist. I recently had the genuine and extreme pleasure of, for once, coming into contact with the possessor of a truly great and original talent—a talent which, as he is in Rome [?!], and therefore possibly a little out of place, I would gladly be the means of introducing to the wider musical circle of the world at large.'

IV.

LISZT.

Before I left Italy, however, I had seen Liszt again. He was staying at a hotel in Rome, and he received me most kindly. I told him I meant to go to Weimar, and 'might I come to him'? He cordially assented, and just as I was saying good-bye, he said, 'Wait a moment—I will give you a little thing to recall me to you;' and going into the next room (his sleeping-room), he returned, and put into my hand a little medallion of himself, which had been struck off at the German Embassy in commemoration of his seventieth birthday. It was in profile. Need I say that I treasure it with care?

The year after I left Italy I went to Weimar; and after taking a room at the Kron Prinz (the best hotel there), I went off to wait on Liszt, who received me at once, and was so kind as to send his housekeeper round to inquire about some rooms close by, which he thought might suit me. They were engaged, and, worst of all, there was not a tolerable piano—not even an upright—to be had in the whole town! I tried all the different music-shops, but without success. I heard then of a musician in the town, who was Liszt's right hand; and I went to him, to see what he could do for me. He recommended me to advertise, which I accordingly did. The result was that I was offered a very nice piano on hire; but still I had no room in which to place it, for they had already two pianos in the hotel, and would not let another in! In my perplexity I went again to a *pension* which was, I knew, pretty full, but the lady had given me the impression of being good-natured, and disposed to oblige. When she saw me come to ask her advice as to the best way of getting rooms and board, she said it had just occurred to her that there was a family living close by who were looking for children to educate, and that, as they had rooms at their disposal, they might perhaps receive me temporarily before anyone else came to them. Armed with a few lines from this good-natured lady, I went to the house indicated by her, and was shown into a most charming *parterre* drawing-room, where a nice young-looking and very refined lady received me. She read the letter, and seemed surprised at the suggestion of receiving anyone into her home in so sudden a fashion; and, moreover, I felt bound to tell her at once that it was by no means certain I could stay very long in Weimar, for that I was feeling far from well. She said she would talk it over with her sister, and give me an answer in the course of the day. This was at ten o'clock in the morning, and having nothing to do, I went to walk in the park, where all was in full summer beauty. Returning to the hotel about noon, I walked into the little reading-room close by the entrance-hall, and was just looking over a paper, when the sound of Liszt's voice reached me, and in another moment he walked into the room, and I heard him say, 'Tell her that I am here, and I will go up to her rooms if she wishes it.' Little dreaming the visit could be to me, I remained buried in my paper, and made as if I neither heard nor saw anything; but the waiter who had ushered Liszt into the room perceived me, and when he said, 'The lady is there,' and Liszt came towards me, I was surprised and very much pleased and gratified.

Liszt asked me if I wished him to pay me a visit in my own rooms; but I at once told him that, as my room was very high up on the third floor, I could not dream of asking him to visit me there. He then sat down and talked a little to me, and Professor Zschocher from Leipzig coming in just then, Liszt introduced him to me. A minute or two afterwards a singer from the papal chapel joined us (having kissed Liszt's hand as he came in). The Meister then took leave, and the two musicians were falling into talk with me, when Fräulein Hummel appeared, to tell me that both she and her sister would be very pleased if I would make my home with them during my stay in Weimar. She had seen the act of homage done to Liszt by the young singer, and as we all sat there and talked a little, she inveighed against 'the Liszt worship' which was then going on in Weimar. By the profound silence that followed her words, she opined, I dare say, that she had confounded us all.

But no sooner was she gone away, than the singer burst out indignantly to the effect that he would have spoken, but feared that when he had once begun he would have said too much.

'And she is a woman,' he said, 'and I should not like to have been rude to her; but I had a mind to tell her that it would be an honour to her not merely to kiss his hand, but also his feet. Yes,' added Herr ——, 'I have seen Tausig kneel to him and kiss the hem of his coat!'

Laugh who will at me, I must own that my sympathies all went with the Liszt worship. And I was destined to see a good deal of it the next day, at the house of the two Fräulein Stahr, whose Sunday afternoon receptions Liszt nearly always honoured with his presence.

The way in which I made the acquaintance of these ladies will rather surprise English people, but it reflects a pleasing light on the Germans, and is but one among many instances of the frank, simple, unconventional spirit which prevailed amongst all those who belonged to the Liszt circle in Weimar. At the *table d'hôte* of the hotel where I was staying, there was a young American lady who, with her travelling companion, was chatting across the table with a gentleman whose appearance, manner, and conversation showed him to be an artist. I joined in the conversation, and hearing that both he and she were going to a reception the next day (Sunday) where Liszt was expected, exclaimed involuntarily:

'How fortunate and favoured you are!'

'But, *gnädiges Fräulein*,' said the gentleman to me, 'why don't you come likewise?'

'I do not know the ladies,' I replied.

'No matter; you are an admirer of Liszt, are you not? And if so, you have only to go and introduce yourself to them as such, and they will be most happy to see you.'

To my English notions this did seem a rather intrusive proceeding, and I at once said so to the young artist; who, however, sympathizing with my evident longing to be at the reception, and perceiving that I only hesitated because I was shy of pushing myself where I might not be wanted, offered finally to escort me there himself and introduce me to the ladies—who were, he said, old friends of his—as one who had come a long way just to hear and see all she could of 'the Meister.'

It was a beautiful summer day; and as we walked out of the town and wended our way towards the villa of the Fräulein Stahr. we came up with and were joined by numbers of young ladies and gentlemen, who were coming out in the same direction, and to the same house as ourselves. When we entered the villa all the rooms through which we passed were arranged as if for a *fête*, and beautifully decorated with flowers—a prominent object in the ante-room being a life-size bust of Liszt crowned with laurel. The two ladies, on hearing that I was a 'Lisztianerin' (the Weimar appellation for Liszt's followers), received me with great cordiality, showed me to a seat in the room where Liszt would be most of the time, and introduced me to all those near me. It was then about a quarter to four, and all who had access to these reunions were now assembled and waiting for Liszt, who both at these and the reunions held at his own house never appeared till all had arrived. It was, indeed, considered a great breach of etiquette to come in after he was in the room, instead of being there to await his arrival, as at the approach of royalty.

A minute or two after four the hum of voices suddenly ceased. 'Der Meister kommt!' was whispered from one to the other; and when Liszt immediately afterwards entered the room, everyone stood up, and all the younger people went towards him and kissed his hand. He looked as if he enjoyed all this homage, and his face lighted up as he glanced kindly at the eager faces which, from the moment he appeared, seemed to have no eyes but for him. Indeed, from the moment he came in, we were all listening to try and catch whatever he might please to say to those nearest to him. He did not play; but his expressive face showed the most cordial interest in all that was going on. Silotti, the distinguished young Russian pianist—a pupil of Nicolas Rubinstein (brother of Antoine)—played a Tausig-Berlioz piece with great *bravura;* Herr Reisenauer and Fräulein Emma Koch played some duets at sight; there was some singing, some violin-playing by a very clever little boy of eleven, and then a small slight girl sat down and charmed me by the ease and beautiful clearness with which she played one of Listz's *Rhapsodies hongroises.* As she concluded this, Liszt came over to the piano; and as she curtsied to him he kissed her on the forehead, his custom when the playing of a lady found favour with him.

'Who is she, and with whom has she studied?' I asked of a lady who was sitting beside me.

'She is my daughter,' was the reply, 'and the only pupil of his Excellency Herr von Henselt, of St. Petersburg.'

I cannot remember all that was played that afternoon, for, like those around me, I was far more occupied in watching the Meister's movements and trying to catch his words, than in either listening to the music or getting into talk with my neighbours. After about two hours and a half—during which time there had been one or two short pauses, when cake and wine and lemonade were handed round—Liszt rose to depart, and, as was the case when he came in, all the guests present rose, and remained standing until he had left the room. When he was gone I was conscious of a sensation which I am quite sure was shared by pretty nearly everyone in the room, whether they were quite aware of the feeling or not. Everything seemed to have become all at once flat and dull and uninteresting; conversation languished; it was as if a shadow had fallen on a landscape, and that which a moment before, when illumined by the sun, was a mass of warm and glowing colours, was now all gray, monotonous, and chill. We soon took our leave of the two kind sister-hostesses (the Fräulein Stahr), and each hastened back to his or her lodging or pension in the town or its suburbs. The young musician who had so kindly introduced me at these reunions accompanied me on the way home; and I opined from his conversation—an opinion which his playing later on fully proved—that he was a true artist. Yes, he was one in every sense of the word, and, but for his untimely death in London some two years since, would be now standing in the front rank with the younger generation of pianists—with Silotti, Reisenauer, Schönberger, Stavenhagen, and several others whom I do not name here.

The next day I took up my abode in the house of the two Fräulein von Hummel. The piano I had already secured was sent in, and placed in the front room opposite to that of the great Hummel (a fine old grand, on which it was understood that I was *not* to play, it being a precious family relic of their deceased grandfather). The rooms which they had let to me were, indeed, full of most interesting mementoes of the past. There was a lock of Beethoven's hair, cut from his head by the wife of Hummel, who, with her husband, visited him three or four days before his death. There was also a lock of Goethe's hair; and both of these were enclosed in glass frames, and hung on the wall like pictures. Another of these frames contained the last pen Beethoven's fingers had ever grasped; for on the same occasion when Hummel's wife had asked him for a lock of his hair, she had also begged leave to carry away a pen which was lying on the bed, and Beethoven, who knew he was dying, put it himself into her hand; and, as long as she lived, it was one of her most precious and valued relics.* At the time when the granddaughters received me into their house their grandmother had only been dead about three months; they were still plunged in the deepest grief for her loss. I could fill a little volume with all they related to me about this interesting and truly estimable woman, who had been a mother to them in the place of their own, who had died early—all that she had related to them of her beloved husband (Hummel), of his playing, of his manner of teaching, his compositions, his social and

* See note at end of chapter.

domestic habits. As it is, I only glance in passing at the curious fact that, going to Weimar to be under Liszt's influence, I found myself in a house where the current ran in a direction utterly opposed to all that was going on among the Liszt set. In art, I found there a taste severely classical and conservative; in the household, all was according to rule, and exquisitely refined; and their kindness to the English lady, whom quest of art-perfection had wafted into their quiet home, was as 'German and hearty,' as it was entirely free from any element of self-interest. From all I gathered from them about Hummel—for whom their grandmother had inspired them with the most profound admiration and respect—I could scarcely wonder if they had but little sympathy for the fervour which so often degenerated into fever; the spontaneity and *élan* which was said in so many instances to have overleaped the bounds which fence in domestic happiness. They did not dislike Liszt personally—indeed, far from doing so, they have on many different occasions narrated to me some of the frequent instances in which he had shown himself ready to do a kindness, to give a helping hand to the distressed, even at a cost of some personal inconvenience. It was, they told me, a common saying at Weimar, 'Liszt always helps whenever he can.' But they felt sore—they who were the descendants of one who has left us many noble and undying works, who had been beloved by a large circle, but whose heart had reserved its best for the home, in which he had left a memory so sweet that his widow would not leave the spot where his body was laid to rest—that *he* should be, to all appearance, forgotten and overlooked, while all the young generation were at the feet of a man who had been blameworthy in his life as an individual—sensational and 'emancipated' in both life and art! The grave in which Hummel's faithful widow was laid beside him, after a widowhood of nearly half a century, was kept by the two Fräulein von Hummel like a lovely flower-garden, and few days went by without one or other of the sisters, or else their old family servant, going to the cemetery with a watering-pot and all the implements of gardening.

Just as I had seemed to have got everything I could wish for in Weimar, all became clouded by the return of a physical trouble from which I had now been free for years. My breathing became so oppressed, even when not making any exertion, that my kind hostesses were much concerned about me, and believed that I was suffering from a bad form of asthma. I knew better, however, but in order to reassure them I consulted the best doctor in Weimar, and was told by him that if I did not avoid all excitement for the time being I should risk bringing on disease of the heart. To play at the Liszt reunions was thus for the present quite out of the question; and I felt it my duty to send a letter to Liszt, and tell him that I could take no active part in the performances then going on at his house. He at once wrote me a very kind reply in French on his visiting-card, telling me 'to come, at all events,' and listen. It may be imagined that the invitation so kindly given was gratefully and gladly accepted; and, in compliment, I believe, to Sgambati, he invariably gave me a seat near his own, where I could see his hands as he played, and catch every word he said. How I wish that I had written down what I heard and saw during those eventful weeks! All, however, that I can be sure of remembering quite accurately I shall relate as simply as possible.

The prominent pianists at the reunions during the weeks when I was 'a listener there' were Reisenauer, Katy Ranuschewitz, Silotti, Paul Eckhoff, Fräulein Richter, and Amina Goodwin (of Manchester). The first of these (Reisenauer) had for several years followed Liszt wherever he went, and it happened pretty often that when Liszt was himself disinclined to show some of the less-advanced pupils the reading he wished to be given to a piece, he would depute this task to Reisenauer. The same honour fell very often also to the share of Henselt's pupil, Mademoiselle Ranuschewitz. Silotti was evidently a great favourite with Liszt, and it was very pleasing to see how warmly the venerable Meister greeted the young artist after the latter had been a week absent at Baireuth. Liszt's whole face lighted up as Silotti came eagerly forward and kissed his hand; there exists a very charming photograph which represents Liszt as leaning on the shoulder of Silotti.

Miss Amina Goodwin came to Liszt with an introduction from St. Saens and several other Parisian musicians of note. The afternoon when she played for the first time among the young pianists, she seated herself at the pianoforte with all the ease of one who was quite at home on the keyboard, and played St. Saens' minuet and valse. She impressed me as having quite a style of her own—a most delicious staccato in octave-playing; a very marked, but not too strongly insistent, accentuation in her phrasing. The whole left the impression of great elegance, refinement, and charm. Liszt, who stood behind her, smiled several times during her performance and took her hand as she rose from the piano, bestowing on her some words of approval, which I cannot exactly recall. The day but one after, when the next reunion took place, Liszt again called upon her to play, but she had the ill luck to use an old and very worn edition of one of his concert-studies. She played most admirably, and was again very warmly praised by Liszt; but I had observed an ominous smile playing round his lips as he looked at the well-worn pages, and I had said to myself, 'The old Meister will pay you off for this.'

What took place when Miss Amina Goodwin next sat down to play at the afternoons proved that my conjectures were right. She had, at Liszt's own suggestion, if I remember right, selected an orchestral piece of Raff's, arranged for a pianoforte solo. Liszt had hardly heard her play through a page of the first movement before he said, 'I don't care for this; let us go on to the next movement.' The young pianist did not seem disconcerted by this first rebuff, and was playing, as desired, the second movement of Raff's composition, and, to my thinking, in a most finished and artistic manner, when Liszt, who must have been in a very ungenial and altogether unaccountable mood that day, lifted the piece from the desk, saying, 'I don't care to listen to such music as that.' Miss Goodwin had to leave the piano without having received one softening word from the Meister. She showed, however, admirable dignity and self-possession; but her aunt, who always accompanied her on these occasions, was extremely angry, and whispered to me, almost loud enough to be heard, as we were going downstairs, 'Is the old man doting?'

The whole thing had been manifestly the result of a whim on his part, for I had been watching all Liszt's looks and words during those weeks, and as I walked with her to the hotel, I gave the aunt the benefit of my observations. Liszt had a little bit of a grudge against her niece for possessing an antiquated edition of his studies; and, moreover, he was in a capricious mood, and it seemed to me that he very often made experiments on those who were playing to him, to see of what stuff they were made.

I have been told, by one or two who knew him well, there was nothing he disliked more than timidity and shyness—that pluck, and even a little boldness, were passports to his favour; and as I knew that Miss Goodwin had a perfect mastery over her powers as a performer, I told her that, if I were in her place, I would bring a whole roll of pieces the next afternoon, and instead of holding back, as if I had been either offended, or piqued, or rebuffed, I would just place myself right in Liszt's way close by the piano, and look as if I thought he would wish and expect me to play all the pieces I had brought with me. The result proved the correctness of my observation, for when Liszt saw Miss Goodwin with a smiling face and her roll of music, his whole face broadened into a most genial and pleasant smile. 'What a number of pieces you have brought with you, my dear child!' in a tone of good-natured banter; 'do you mean to play all these to me?' he said. 'Dear Meister, as many as you wish me to,' was the reply. He was delighted with the pleasant way she had accepted his rough-and-ready treatment on the last occasion, and allowed her to play two or three of the pieces, and she became one of his especial favourites.

There were several other very clever pianists at these reunions; and a good many likewise concerning whom one could not but ask one's self how they ever presumed to be there—how they ventured to think of playing before Liszt! I shall, of course, mention none of these latter by name, but I will relate one or two amusing and yet distressing scenes in reference to them at which I was present.

Before going further, however, the reader will doubtless like to know the usual order in which these interesting reunions took place. First, then, all those who were privileged to be there assembled three times a week, in the Meister's drawing-room, a little before four o'clock, and as each came into the room, he or she laid the piece which they hoped to play that afternoon on a large oval-shaped table which stood near a door leading into Liszt's sleeping-room. The Meister did not appear until it was fully four o'clock, and all were supposed to have arrived and to be waiting for him. The door was then opened, and when the Meister walked into the room all stood up at once, and moved respectfully towards him. The ladies kissed his hand. All then remained standing until he had motioned them to sit down. Liszt's next proceeding was to turn to the table, on which all the pieces were lying, and, looking towards the young people who were standing between the piano and the door, he would take up the pieces and look at them one by one until he had found something which he wished to hear. Holding it up and naming its title, he would say, 'Who wishes to play this?' The owner of the piece made a move, without coming forward, and then, if Liszt saw that it was one of his favourites who wished to play, or perhaps a new-comer whom he might wish to hear, he would say with a pleasant tone, 'Come over, then, and play it to me.' It was Reisenauer who usually put the music on the desk. Liszt seated himself beside the young performer, and all the others either sat close behind master and pupil, or else stood in a long close line all around the pianoforte. It was, indeed, a trying ordeal, and anyone who could pass through it and emerge victorious, might well face a concert-room with all imaginable *sang-froid!*

Being only a listener there, I was all the better able to give my whole attention to everything that went on; and out of a number of smaller and larger details which came under my notice during those weeks, I arrived (without ever consciously trying to do so) at certain general conclusions, which, be they right or wrong, have at least the merit of being unbiased by any spirit of either clique or school. Liszt was unvaryingly just in appreciating and encouraging all those who had really any 'talent'; but towards one or two who really had neither school nor talent he would, if their personality had pleased him, be so indulgent as to let the very worst faults, the greatest shortcomings, pass without any adverse criticism. On the other hand, woe betide either an incorrect and badly drilled player, or one who merely played the notes, and gave no musical reading of the piece, if his or her personality had made an unfavourable impression on the Meister! In the case of a badly drilled player, he would show his anger without disguise, and send the performer from the piano in a most summary manner; while in the latter case he would either get up from his seat, and walk up and down the entire length of the room, looking the very picture of an individual who is profoundly bored, but who has made up his mind to go through with it to the end, or else he would stand a minute or two beside the player, seeming to listen to the performance, and then, quietly observing, 'That is very nice, but I think we shall turn to something else,' he would take the piece off the music-deck, move away from the piano, and call on another pianist to come forward.

The following may serve as an example of how he treated a bungling and badly-trained player: A young man began to play one of the Meister's own compositions—a difficult *polonaise*—and in a few bars from the start came down with a jumble of wrong notes on a difficult chord, and when Liszt said in a loud voice, 'Begin again!' the luckless player, trying the piece a second time, made the same blunder over again. 'Shame, shame!' said Liszt, in a still louder voice; 'begin once more!' The unfortunate individual started off once again, came to the passage, and, for the third time, played the chord all wrong. Then, indeed, there was a scene which I cannot easily forget. Liszt's voice trembled with anger and scorn, as, flinging the music from the desk, he said more than once, in a voice which was calculated to terrify us all,

'Do you know to whom you have been playing? You have no business here. Go to the Conservatoire; that is the place for such as you.'

To my surprise, the young man did not leave the room, but merely moved back among the others; and if he was at all sensitive, he must have been conscious that he had spoilt that afternoon for the young girl who played next after him. She was a mere child, not yet sixteen, and was favoured by Liszt not only because of her youth, but for the sake of her sister, Fräulein Grosskurt, a most refined and charming pianist, who played Chopin's nocturnes exquisitely. On this day, however, Liszt absolutely clawed this poor little girl, to whom he was usually so gentle, that when there was any want of clearness in a passage played by her, he would stop her with the gentle reprimand, 'We don't want any neighbours here, my dear; play it again.' But the young man's performance had stirred up Liszt's bile, and after saying in an angry tone two or three times, 'We don't wash dirty linen here,' he pushed the piece into her hands and sent her away from the piano, and she got into a far corner behind the others, to hide the tears which she could not restrain.

An extremely handsome girl from the Leipzig Conservatoire then sat down to play one of Chopin's concertos, and seemed to be doing very well. Liszt sat down twice to give her his reading of a passage, and he did not appear dissatisfied; but as he stood by the piano, and I marked his eye, and the lines round his expressive mouth, I was not surprised when he said, after a minute or two, 'That is very good, but I don't care to hear any more of it,' and motioned her to pause and leave the piano.

On another occasion a fair youth, who wore long hair, and had a dreamy and artistic-looking face, began to play Liszt's own Fantaisie on Rigoletto, and having accomplished a page or two, in which he executed all the florid passages with faultless accuracy, Liszt made him rise, and, playing a page or two of the piece, then told him to go on. But after about half a minute Liszt lifted the music from the desk, with the observation, 'Das ist ganz pensionärisch' (a good *school* performance), adding in a satirical tone, 'and very maidenly playing.' This young man was at all the Liszt afternoons that summer, but did not get the chance of playing again. When Liszt held a piece in his hand which had been brought by someone whom he did not care to hear, he would just give a courteous nod to the individual who acknowledged its ownership, and, laying it down again, would take up another and ask whose that was. It has happened more than once that he has taken up several pieces in succession and asked who was going to play them, and put them down again before he came to one which one of his especial favourites had placed there. Sometimes, however, he did not wait for this, but addressing Reisenauer, Silotti, or Katy Ranuschewitz, he would say, 'Is there no piece here which you, or you, or you are going to play to me to-day?'

On the afternoon when Liszt had been so angry with the young man who bungled so in the *polonaise*, he recovered his good-humour as soon as Reisenauer began to play. As well as I can remember, this fine pianist played some of Liszt's *Liebesträume* that afternoon, and Fraülein Emma Koch, a pupil of Scharwencka (since then established in Berlin, where she has given concerts more than once with great success), took up the set in these charming pieces, and continued where he left off. Another afternoon a gentleman began to play a *polonaise* of Chopin's, and by the way Liszt's eye rested on him, as he seated himself at the piano, even a superficial observer could have seen that the Meister had taken a personal and, to my thinking, a most unjust antipathy to the player. The latter was young, and evidently very nervous and sensitive. There was no lack of swing and go in his performance, but his reading of the piece (to use a mild term) did not please Liszt, who twice impatiently motioned him to get up from the piano, and, playing part of the *polonaise* himself, he bade the young man to continue playing it in that manner. On the third time of doing so, however, Liszt quite lost his temper, and called out in an angry and imperious manner, 'What sort of playing is that? Playing indeed!' and so saying, he took the player's seat at the piano and played a few bars, just to show the unfortunate aspirant his reading of the *polonaise*. But instead of saying this time, 'Let me hear you play the rest of it,' Liszt stood up, and moving away from the piano, began to pace up and down, saying as he did so, as if partly to himself, partly to us, and in a voice calculated to strike terror in the bravest there, 'Such playing indeed; and to *me*, who have so often listened to Tausig! Ah, how *he* played this piece!' The discomfited young man stood beside the piano pale as death, seeming to be transfixed with terror. A profound and painful silence reigned among the students, and no one seemed to know what was coming next, until a young Belgian pianist—of whom I shall ever think with pleasure for the kindliness he showed on this occasion—managed by gestures, without saying a word, to make the discomfited young pianist understand that, as the Meister had not taken the music of the *polonaise* off the piano, the inference was that he should continue playing.

The mother of Mademoiselle Ranuschewitz never failed to accompany her daughter, and perhaps she may be some day induced to show me the book in which she noted down not only the title of every piece that was played to Liszt throughout the entire summer, but also the names of the different pianists by whom the pieces were performed (for the same piece might happen to be heard many times during the months when these *réunions des jeunes pianistes* were taking place). I remember that Reisenauer played, among other pieces, *Marche Macabre*, St. Saens; *Tarantelle* from the *Muette di Portici*, and Liszt's First *Concerto*. Silotti played the *Carneval de Pesth*, the *Zigeuner Reigen* (Tausig), Chopin's First *Scherzo*, and the *Pâtineurs*, while Mademoiselle Ranuschewitz seemed to have an endless *repertoire*, and a wonderful faculty of being always ready to play everyone else's pieces beside her own. Once, in playing the *Pâtineurs*, she broke her nail in doing the *glissando*, which Liszt told her to make three times instead of twice as it is printed. She made a wry face, and Liszt asked her what was the matter. She replied that she had broken her nail. He seemed highly amused, and said, as if he really enjoyed the notion of making us all see that a broken nail ought never to be an excuse for pausing in a performance, 'Well, what of that? Go on, my child.' Liszt was very fond of Katy Ranuschewitz, and was constantly laying his hand on her head, as if in affectionate paternal approval.

And Liszt himself, though he only played fragments of the pieces brought to him by the young pianists, and usually but a few bars of these fragments, was indeed a dazzling sun, that shone with a radiance before which all the younger talents, like so many stars, paled into insignificance. He gave one the impression of possessing an almost terrible mastery over every imaginable variety of passage—especially in leaping intervals so wide apart that to play them with ease is as nearly as possible like being in two different places at the same time. I have listened to him twice in the *Pâtineurs*, and a cold shiver has passed through me, not so much at what he actually bestowed on us, as at what he suggested as having still in reserve. To his interpretation of Chopin— three of whose Ballades, many of the Preludes, several Studies, three Polonaises, and one Concerto, I heard him play in Weimar—I have listened with delight mingled with awe. His sight-reading of difficult manuscript compositions, which were brought to him on different occasions, was simply marvellous. He would listen to the player for a minute or two with a smile which betrayed a sort of scornful sense of absolute mastery, and then he would sit down and execute the most intricate passages with as much ease as if they were the A B C of a language every syllable, every word of which was familiar to him. What astonished and impressed me most was, not so much that his fingers were responsive to every motion of his mind; I wondered at the *mind*, which one felt instinctively was gifted with the power of taking in at one rapid glance every possible variety of passage which has ever been written for the pianoforte. His glance seemed to be at once penetrative and all-embracing. He thought it out at once with clearness and rapidity; and instead of being any longer surprised at the almost adoring attitude of his followers, I was, though he knew it not, one of those who paid him homage with every single nerve and fibre of my nature. I think it is Lenz who, in the little book called *Beethoven et ses trois styles*, has called Liszt 'the apotheosis of the pianoforte'; and let me say that no words from any pen, were they ever so forcible, ever so suggestive, could give the most imaginative reader any adequate idea of what Liszt was all round. One felt as if one were standing at the foot of a great mountain, whose summit was veiled in luminous clouds. Whichever way you viewed him, there was immense variety. He was grand and colossal. He was a large nature, and yet full of grace and sweetness. His rendering of the middle part in Chopin's B Minor Scherzo (which Silotti brought him) will linger in my memory as 'a joy for ever.' On another occasion he played, 'with pauses' (in showing a young American lady his reading of the piece), the greater part of Chopin's Fourth Ballade, and on that afternoon, being in an especially genial mood, he spoke of the composition, and bade her observe how the composer, having wandered away from the opening thought, seemed afterwards to be as it were groping for it; and this groping, this seeking, Liszt pictured to us most wonderfully in his playing — when, without losing that which is the very life of a composition, its rhythmic beat, he seemed to waver and sway, as if uncertain whether to go on in that rhythm or not. During this wavering and swaying, he turned at intervals to the young lady and observed, 'He has not found it yet, but it is coming.' 'It is very near now,' he finally said, just before he struck a note of triumph, and came in with a full sweep on the opening theme.

When I had been about three weeks in Weimar, Liszt sent round one Sunday morning to say that he would pay me a visit after he came from hearing morning service in the chapel. At nine o'clock he came in, and I remember most of what he then said, as well as if it had happened but yesterday. He told me that no pianofortes lasted anything like so well as those of Broadwood—that the firm had been very generous to him, both on the occasion of his first visit to England, which took place when he was a boy, and his second, many years later on, when he had grown up to manhood. On the first of these occasions the Messrs. Broadwood sent a very fine instrument to his father, and when, on leaving London, his father asked what they were indebted for the use of the instrument, Messrs. Broadwood replied that the instrument was a gift which they felt pleased in offering for his acceptance. 'We left the instrument behind us,' said Liszt; 'and I am sorry to confess that having, as youngsters will do, got into debt a little while after, I sold it. Later on the Broadwoods gave me another instrument, and this I still possess. It is in the keeping of the Princess Witgenstein.' Liszt admired the charming rooms of the Von Hummels; and, casting a glance around at the different objects of interest which were there, went finally over to Hummel's grand pianoforte, and, opening it, sat down and played the whole of Hummel's Fantasia from beginning to end. When he had concluded, he stood up, saying, 'This is one of the pieces which will never die; and I am going to have Hummel's A Minor Concerto—also a favourite of mine — played at one of my *réunions des jeunes pianistes.*' When he went away I stood at the door, and looked after him as he crossed the street. He raised his hat to me, and smiled—a smile I still seem to see!—that smile of genial, kindly benevolence which has charmed and spell-bound so many, and won them to be his devoted and lifelong followers.

But my health obliged me to leave Weimar, and I spent the rest of the summer in the Engadine, where I had the great pleasure and comfort of being with old family friends. In the autumn my sister joined me in Meran, from whence I returned to Germany.

I naturally ruminated much over all I had heard at the Liszt afternoons, and the reader will naturally ask if I had by this time discovered what I was seeking for; and when I say, *not quite,* will probably feel extremely surprised. I had learned much, but there was *something* which I could not get at—something without which I felt dissatisfied; and yet I could not, even to myself, entirely explain the source of my dissatisfaction.

More than one critic observed, in reviewing my book, that if the Beethoven incident were true, it was an interesting contribution to the various details relating to this great musician which are being collected under the head of 'Beethoveniana.' When this half-formulated suggestion of doubt came under my eye, it was naturally my wish to prove that in this, as in every other fact related in the book, I had indulged in no flights of the imagination. The lock of hair and the pen had been shown to me, and by persons with whom I had lived in close intercourse for several weeks, without ever perceiving in them the slightest leaning to exaggeration, or the shadow of an endeavour to exalt their grandfather — for whose memory, nevertheless, they felt the deepest reverence — into a colossal figure. I wrote to these ladies accordingly, and they were not alone so kind as to answer my letter with little delay, but on a musical critic expressing a wish to have the date of the actual visit when Frāu Hummel obtained the lock of hair and the pen from the dying musician, they wrote me a second letter, giving all the particulars which we wished to know. The letters are given intact, because of the one interesting fact which they verify; and though I have not alluded to other relics contained in the Hummel house, there are, besides the lock of hair and the pen, many treasures which would interest those who seek for the autographs of great men, etc.

DEAR MISS WALKER,
   We have always preserved a friendly recollection of you, and we have ever felt pleasure in thinking of you. Beethoven's hair, which our dear grandmother herself cut from his head several days before his death, and the pen with which he wrote the last word, also the other named relics, are yet in our possession, and we hope never to part from these precious mementoes. We have been much interested in hearing of your book, and should much like to know how you have fared since you left Weimar.
   With kind greetings from my sister and myself,
                     Yours, etc.,
                        JOHANNA HUMMEL.

Weimar, *October* 29*th*, 1890.

MY DEAR MISS WALKER,
   It has been unfortunately impossible for us to answer your letter until now. The nearness of Christmas and so many festivities bring many delays into regular correspondences. I hope that even to-day my letter may reach you at an early date. As we understand from your letter, you are now again in England, and think of remaining there in future. We have felt such pleasure in hearing from you again, and have often talked to each other about you. Everything here is the same. We live in our house, having added new rooms for the young ladies. Up to this year we have always had our fixed number of pupils, but just now we have not been fortunate, and have three or four less. We have at present a young lady from Clifton, and a young niece of ours. We wish we could have a few more. For this reason I permit myself to enclose you one of our prospectuses. If you should chance to have the opportunity of recommending us, we shall take it as a kindness. I willingly give you information with regard to the Beethoven

8

relics, and my grandparents' visit to him. The existence of the relics is everywhere abundantly certified, and the visit in question took place on the 8th of March, 1827, the next on the 13th, and the last on the 20th. These dates will, I hope, be of use to your friend. You, dear Miss Walker, hold out to us the hope of seeing you again. How much would we rejoice at this, although, indeed, the special attraction, Liszt, is wanting. Still, I think it would please you to be with us. My sister asks me to remember her to you, in which I cordially join. And in the hope of once more hearing from you,

I remain, yours, etc.,
AUGUSTA HUMMEL.

Weimar, *November* 30*th*, 1890.

V.

DEPPE AND SCHARWENCKA.

It may be imagined that I thought much over all I had heard at the Liszt afternoons. Strangely enough, a certain conversation with Paul Eckhoff always recurred to me in a most persistent manner whenever my thoughts turned to Weimar. This talented young pianist had shown me some technical finger-studies of his own composition, which he said were so extremely difficult that but few could execute them. Looking at these, I played them at once (as I thought) with ease, and as I repeated them once or twice, I asked, 'Are these the very difficult studies of which you have been telling me?' To which he replied, 'Yes; they are the difficult studies which I have invented, and *you* will not be able to master them.' He said this very politely, but with an air of great conviction; and, on my continuing to repeat the *notes* of the studies in question over and over again several times, though he did not repeat what he had said,

I could perceive from his manner—his expressive silence—that he was still of the same opinion. This surprised, and not a little vexed me; but, not choosing to let him perceive my annoyance, I changed the subject by asking him to play a little to me. The fact of the matter was, that I had then not the remotest notion of what *technique* really was. All true *virtuosi* are well aware that it is one of the subtlest of all physical movements. Something at that moment, however, dawned on me, and the result of this very dim and faint surmise regarding the cause of my deficiencies in pianoforte-playing was that I resolved, on reaching Berlin, to seek out Herr Deppe, and get him to help me through the haze, which seemed to grow all the denser the more I thought on the subject. Miss Fay's book (which placed him as a teacher of the pianoforte above, Tausig, Kullak, and even above Liszt) had greatly interested me, but I had then so little notion of what was meant by 'a method,' that I actually thought that if there was a mechanical deficiency in my way of approaching the keyboard, a few weeks of good earnest study would easily remedy it. Having ascertained Herr Deppe's address, and heard that he lived in a small inn close by the Anhalter Bahnhof, I went there, and was told by the waiter to go up to the highest story of the building, where the Herr Kapellmeister had a suite of rooms. I set off up the staircase, and was on the first step of the stairs which led to the third floor, when I found myself face to face with a plain-looking, elderly gentleman, who seemed to be coming straight from the corridor on which, according to the waiter's directions to me, Herr Deppe's rooms were situated. I glanced at him just as he was about to pass by me, and probably my look suggested inquiry, for he asked me abruptly, but not rudely, what I wanted up there—if I were looking for anyone. I replied, 'I am going up to ascertain when it is possible to see Herr Deppe, and I have been told that his rooms are on the third floor.' 'I am Herr Deppe,' was the rejoinder, 'and if you want to see me, and speak to me, I must beg you to come back at four o'clock, that is my hour for seeing people; and I am now on my way to dinner, so please excuse me.' Saying this, he bowed slightly to me, and, passing on down the stairs, went into the dining-room of the hotel.

There was not the slightest pose about Herr Deppe —nothing remarkable in his appearance, his glance, or his voice; and yet he had at once impressed me, had inspired me with confidence in him. I seemed to see and feel that he was an individual such as one seldom meets with in a life-time. I came back to the hotel at four o'clock, and, going up the stairs, rang the bell at his door, and (German customs and ways being as yet unknown to me) was greatly surprised when he not only opened it himself to let me in, but, bringing me through the anteroom and into the music-room, pointed to a seat, saying as he did so, 'Now sit down and tell me all you have to say; I shall hear it quite well, though I must go on making my coffee.' He listened with a glance of kindly interest, which encouraged me to describe as far as I really was aware of them myself all my difficulties. When I had ended, he said he should like to look at my hands (Miss Fay relates that he did the same with her); and when I took off my gloves, and showed them to him, he at once said, ' You have a very good hand, though small; but the outer side of it is quite limp and flabby; it is undeveloped and untrained. Now, go over to the piano and play for me.'

I sat down accordingly, and attacked with great vigour Tausig's transcription of a Bach prelude and fugue. Herr Deppe seated himself at a little table, and began to drink his coffee as if my presence there counted for nothing. I played this piece with much energy and *aplomb*, and made quite sure that my performance would impress him with the idea that I had much mastery over the keyboard; but I had not played more than half the piece when, on glancing inquiringly at him, I perceived that he was highly amused—that, in fact, he was laughing to himself at my performance; and yet, strangely enough, it was not a laugh that acted like a damper on my energy, for I could perceive that he was fully as much interested as amused, and when I had ended the piece he said, 'Go on; play something more.' I played piece after piece, feeling neither nervous nor annoyed, though he was at so little pains to conceal his amusement that he once or twice laughed quite audibly. A tap just then was heard at the door, and on Herr Deppe rising to open it, a tall, pale, and singular-looking young man walked in without saying a word; and Herr Deppe having by this time finished drinking his coffee, the two gentlemen came over to the piano, and seated themselves side by side, a little to the right of me.

'Please go on playing,' said Herr Deppe; and when I did so, and glanced round at them both, I saw that the young man was just as much amused as Herr Deppe, and yet that, like the latter, his amusement was sufficiently leavened with interest to stimulate rather than to depress me. At length, however, I came to a pause, and, turning round to Herr Deppe, waited for him to speak. He did not do so for a moment or two, and then his words were addressed rather to the young man than to me. (The latter was Mr. Frederick Clarke, an American gentleman, who had some months previously married Anna Steinecke, Herr Deppe's best pupil.) 'She will never be able to give up all that—to lay it all aside from the beginning—nor could I expect it,' were Herr Deppe's first words. To which the other rejoined, 'Yet with such gifts, such a memory, such taste, such feeling, and withal so helpless! It is indeed a pity.'

But who could advise her to give it up?' said Herr Deppe again; 'for if she begins with me and has not the patience and perseverance to carry it through to the end, all her present enjoyment in piano-playing will be embittered.'

'What is wrong?' I asked very earnestly, but very quietly. 'I have not minded your laughing at me, because I had the feeling that there was much in my playing that not only amused, but also pleased and interested you; but it is scarcely fair of you to put me off like that with general statements. Tell me plainly where you think my chief deficiency lies, and whether it is of a nature which resolution, perseverance and patience can overcome.'

We all three looked full at one another for a few moments. The gentlemen hesitated. Herr Deppe still remained silent, and I think it was Mr. Clarke who first spoke, and addressed me thus:

'I tell you, then, that, to accomplish anything in the Deppe method, you must entirely lay aside every piece you have ever learned, and give yourself up to a physical drill of which you as yet have not the very faintest perception—and that, supposing you do this, and supposing you are unusually gifted in mastering this side of the school, in a year and a half, you who now play Schumann's *Concerto*, and Liszt's *Rhapsodies*, will at the most be only able to play some of Mozart's simpler Sonatas, and Moscheles' Studies.'

All this naturally roused and excited me. I did

not, of course, believe that I should be as long in making way as Mr. Clarke seemed to think. Turning to Herr Deppe, and assuring him that I had quite the resolve, quite the patience, quite the self-renunciation to give up all my present attainments, in order to attain that which I so much desired, that which I felt I so much needed, I entreated him to tell me what was the great want in my playing. He then replied:

'Your hand, to begin with, has never been properly worked—there has been little extension, and scarcely any muscular exertion; you cannot produce a succession of clear resonant tones. But you force me to say all this,' he added, 'and I warn you beforehand not to ask me to help you, and then grow weary of the slow progress you make, and leave off. If you do this, you will be unhappy. In one lesson you will have lost your innocence' (Herr Deppe's own words); 'for that one lesson will set an intelligent person like you on a track of thought, and as you will not be able without help to follow this out, and thus arrive at final and satisfactory conclusions, you will wish that you had never seen me, never come to me. And remember it will not have been my fault.'

At length, however, Herr Deppe was convinced that I was not only much in earnest, but that I *would* have the courage, the patience to carry through what I should begin with him. He named an early day for his first lesson, and I put aside all my programme, and came to him quite resolved to remain under his guidance until I had fully mastered his method.

And I had, after all, but one lesson from him! For a circumstance intervened which, much to my regret, hindered me from carrying out the plan of study which he had laid down for me. I at once wrote a courteous letter to him, and excused myself as well as I could for having occupied so much of his valuable time, having asked for his help with so much insistence, and yet not availed myself of that which he had so kindly given.

Although it is anticipating a little, I may add that when I visited Herr Deppe some years after this, I was received by him not only with courtesy, but almost with cordiality. I then told him that I had always felt myself to be his debtor for having given me his opinion in such a frank, unvarnished manner, and that even though I had not continued to study with him, yet in his one lesson he had done me immense service.

He was very kind and pleasant. He spoke of a young lady who, after Anna Steinecke-Clarke was gone to America, had taken her place as his 'best pupil.' This young lady was shortly to give a performance to a few friends in his rooms; and Deppe said that he would send me word when the day and hour were definitely fixed.

A few mornings after this interview with Herr Deppe, a young lady called on me about nine o'clock in the morning, and said she had come to tell me that in two hours' time Fräulein S—— was to play a long programme of pianoforte pieces in Herr Deppe's rooms. 'It seemed a short notice to give you,' said the young lady; 'but the arrangement was not made until the previous day, and I came round in the evening to tell you of it, but concluded everyone must have been out, as I rang several times at the bell, and had to go away without even seeing anyone with whom to leave the message.' I was very glad indeed to have this opportunity of hearing another of Herr Deppe's pupils, and one, moreover, whom he himself put forward as being an admirable exponent of his method. At the hour named I accordingly rang the bell at his door, and found myself, on entering the anteroom, among a set of young girls—all very quiet-looking, and all just as simply dressed as if there was nothing more in question than a walk into the country. The young lady who had opened the door to admit me ushered me into the music-room, where I found the genial musician sitting on a sort of ottoman-sofa, which was placed nearly opposite to the piano. A middle-aged lady (a person of rank, whose name I do not now recollect) was sitting beside him, engaged, as it seemed to me, in a very earnest discussion. When I appeared, however, Herr Deppe rose at once to receive me, and courteously asked me where I would best like to be seated I chose a seat so placed with regard to the piano that I could observe every movement of the player. It was some minutes before the music began—an interval which gave me an ample opportunity of taking in all around me. The large folding-doors between his sleeping-room and the one I was sitting in had been thrown open; some of the furniture had been moved back; and there were a good many girls and several young men (all, as I afterwards learned, pupils of the Deppe school) sitting both in the room and along the wall at either side of the doorway. There was a subdued hum of whispering voices, with which the Kapellmeister's presence did not seem in any way to interfere. There was something in the atmosphere of the room, in its arrangements, and, above all, in the manner of Herr Deppe, at once restful, stimulating, and homelike. I could have quite imagined any one of the school sitting down to play there just as if he or she were at home.

After a few minutes Herr Deppe called out, 'Willie, Willie, you may begin;' on which a young girl in a simple print dress, with her hair closely plaited, and brushed off a large and open brow—a gentle-looking girl, with a very slight figure, who looked as happy and free from all anxiety as if her task had been to decorate the room with flowers, or pour out tea for a school fête, instead of being the exponent of a 'method'—walked quietly into the room without making a bow, or looking around with the slightest air of self-consciousness. She went straight up to Herr Deppe and put a sheet of paper into his hands, on which was written a list of the pieces she was about to play. He, glancing at it, asked her which piece she intended to play first. 'Whichever you please, Herr Kapellmeister,' was the reply. He then named the piece with which she was to begin, observing in a very pleasant tone, as he took out his watch and looked at it, 'It takes just so many minutes to play.' Fräulein went over then at once to the piano and seated herself at it, laying, as she did so, all the music she was going to perform on the instrument beside her. She played most admirably —every single tone ringing out with delicious clearness—several of Bach's Preludes and Fugues, an Impromptu by Schubert, and a Sonata of Beethoven, etc.

The deep, simple, and genuine expression which characterized her reading of the *adagio* in the latter, inspired me with the most profound respect for the teacher who had such a beautiful conception of Beethoven's 'divine yearning towards higher spheres.' But I quite agree with Lenz, who more than once says, in his *Beethoven et ses trois styles*, 'Mais il y a des choses qu'on gâte quand on en parle;' and I refrain from going into any ecstasies about the music which I heard that morning. Suffice it that while the young girl was playing I kept saying to myself, 'That is what pianoforte-playing was meant to be, ought to be—a clear, unaffected reading of many lovely tone-poems, by turns soothing, stimulating, saddening, and yet as little insistent as the sounds in nature—the wind as it murmurs among the forest trees, or the sweet odours that exhale from the flower-spangled meadows in June.' And so thoroughly at her ease was the young pianist, that once or twice, before she commenced playing a piece (performed as if she were in her own room), she made some very curious movements with her fingers on the keyboard. On playing the first movement of Beethoven's Sonatas she took up the music-book that lay beside the desk, and seemed to be noting some point in the *adagio*, for she looked at it carefully for a moment or two without betraying the slightest flurry or anxiety, and then, laying it down again, she gave the reading of this movement to which I have already alluded as giving me so high an idea of what Herr Deppe's musical conceptions must be.

Returning now, however, to the time when I had seen Herr Deppe only three times, and had, after one lesson from him, been drifted away, I come to speak of Xaver Scharwencka, who is regarded as one of the leading teachers in Germany, and one of the highest authorities on *technique*.

The one lesson I had had from Herr Deppe had so far helped me, that I had reached the conviction that all the practice in the world never gives anyone perfect mastery over the keyboard; (that it is only reached by getting inside of certain lines, which should be as clear and definite as the first principles of drawing and perspective.)

But now the question was, 'Where should I find a master who would be able and willing to guide me to these lines?' And turning over the matter in my mind, I remembered that Scharwencka was in Berlin, and that three of his pupils—Miss Stephens (an American), Fräulein Richter (now married and settled in London), and Herr Paul Eckhoff—had all taken a prominent part at the Liszt afternoons. I went then to Scharwencka, and told him that I was anxious to get a thorough training in *technique*. I said that I had heard that he was a great authority on this point, and I begged him to give me lessons. (I had then between thirty and forty pieces thoroughly under my fingers, which I could play by heart, besides a considerable number more which I was quite able to play when I had the music before me. When I went to Scharwencka, I put a list of these into his hands, and he stood opposite to me as I played, and called for a Rhapsody of Liszt's, for the Tausig-Bach Prelude and Fugue, for Chopin's Third Scherzo, and some of Chopin's Studies. His comments on my mechanical deficiencies were, that I did not work the small joints of the fingers, and that I did not use the *hand* sufficiently in pressing out the tone. He told me to bring him for the first lesson his own staccato study, and Liszt's transcription of Bach's Organ Prelude and Fugue in A Minor. In the former, he took great pains to show me how to form every single tone, using both finger-tips and wrist; and in the latter, how to practise the prelude with displacement of accent in order to give strength to the fingers. He told me that I should do very well; reminded me again to bring my finger-tips well into action, and sent me away feeling very much pleased.

Scharwencka's Conservatorium is looked on in Berlin as a school of virtuosity, and many of the pupils who had taken out their certificates at the Hoch-schule went to him to get the last finishing touches, and learn the effects suitable for concert-playing. He was a very interesting teacher, and I not only had private lessons from him, but I also played in the large evening class, at which there were not many performers, but many listeners (*hospitanten*), who occupied seats which were placed close by the wall all round the room. Scharwencka is a most extraordinary reader, and seemed to have the power of playing off at sight and in the most masterly manner any piece one might bring to him. A gentleman who had been his fellow-student in the Conservatoire of Kullak, told me that when he ceased to study under Kullak, he had set himself with a most iron determination to conquer every imaginable difficulty which the pianoforte might present, and in three years he had never flagged or faltered until he had accomplished his purpose. His playing was, as compared with Sgambati's, as sculpture when compared with painting. There was an element of great and massive grandeur, a tremendous force of will, and a fervent glow of imagination, which told even more when he played *en robe de chambre* in the Conservatorium, when he was just enjoying himself among those who looked up to and admired him, than when he was in the concert-room, weighted with responsibility attaching to his name and his position. He had a very interesting class on teaching, harmony, method, etc., which he himself conducted in person every week. And his manner of imparting knowledge was most clear and full of suggestion. He had his own special way, too, of stimulating his pupils, and calling forth their powers. When he said, 'Vorwärts!' it seemed to inspire the most timid pupils to push forward at all hazards. Liszt greatly admired and esteemed him; and to have come from under his guidance was a passport to the Meister's favour.

I naturally rebelled rather at Herr Deppe's uncompromising condemnation of all my pieces—I should rather say his demand that I should give up all the pieces which were part and parcel of my life, and start afresh—and here I had the pleasing prospect of a shorter and more pleasant road to the goal. And so, for the first few lessons, I was really charmed with Scharwencka; but then Deppe's prediction began to verify itself. I grew restless and anxious, and, in addition to my studies with Scharwencka, I began to try and feel my way through different books on methods for getting the mastery over every possible difficulty. Groping my way thus (if I may so phrase it), I came on Ehrlich's edition of Tausig's 'Daily Practice'; and in reading his observations on some of the finger-studies I was much struck by his commenting on these as 'demanding great muscular exertion.' Now, I was able apparently to play these very studies without being conscious of making any such exertion. I would have liked then and there to have gone to Herr Ehrlich, and asked him to tell me what was the cause of this apparent ease, which I then—naturally connecting it with what Paul Eckhoff had said to me in Weimar—began to fear meant that I was still getting no nearer to the object of my desire.

But I was with Scharwencka; he was giving himself great trouble with me, and I felt it but due to him, before making another move, to try if he could or would help me. I therefore brought the Ehrlich-Tausig Studies to him, and said, 'Why does Ehrlich speak of muscular exertion, and I feel none whatever? I wish you would sanction my going to Herr Ehrlich and asking him to help me in the Tausig alone, for I wish to continue my lessons with you.'

He replied that he would go through them with me himself; that such studies needed to be approached with much thought and much care. But I never had a single lesson from him in which these studies were the subject-matter. Meanwhile, something strange and unforeseen had occurred—something which was

to bring me again, though indirectly, *en rapport* with
Deppe and his school.

I lived in a pension where only ladies were received
as boarders, and the fact that there are so many of
such pensions in most German cities renders a stay
in that country most convenient and pleasant for both
young-lady students and older ladies who wish to live
abroad. Mr. Steinecke-Clarke had introduced his
wife to me the very next day, I believe, after he and I
had met at Deppe's. I had found the pair very sympathetic and interesting, and they had asked me to go
and see them. I had paid them one visit; but when
I left Deppe, and when, later on, instead of returning
to him, I had consulted Scharwencka, I did not
believe the Clarkes would care to see me again; I
therefore did not seek to renew the acquaintance,
and it was by no means agreeable to me to hear that
they were coming to spend a few weeks in the same
pension with me. Their plans were, it seems, a little
unsettled; they were moving out of a house in which
they had lived since their marriage, and they were
undecided whether to remain in Berlin or go to
America. The ladies of the pension had known Anna
Steinecke all her life, and they told me that they were
making an exception in her favour by admitting a
gentleman. They told me it would be only for a very
short time; but, still, I was not at all pleased at the
idea, for though I liked them both greatly, yet, knowing that they looked on everyone outside their school

'as being in the outer courts of art,' I did not much relish having them for such near neighbours. A little reflection, however, suggested to me that as my quarters were shut off from the rest of the pension by double doors, they could hear but little of what I might be doing. We need not be neighbours at table, and whenever we did meet there was no reason why we should approach the subject of pianoforte-playing and the Deppe method—no reason, indeed, for my becoming in any way intimate with them. I thought all this, and arrived at these conclusions; and yet the Steinecke-Clarkes had not been a week in the house before by the wish of all three I sat beside them at table, and it seemed to us quite a matter of course that, instead of retiring to my own room after supper, I should turn into theirs (which adjoined the Speisesaal), and that we should spend the evenings together in a frank and simple interchange of our thoughts and feelings. Need I say that the subject which we discussed most frequently, the one in which we all three waxed most eloquent, was music, and, above all, pianoforte music? Mr. Clarke was one of the greatest, the most ideal enthusiasts I have ever met with, and the intercourse I had with him and his gifted wife was the nearest possible approach to what one might picture the intercourse of primitive yet cultured men and women ought to be. None of us attached any value to externals. Anna Steinecke wore short hair, and did not try by pressure to give any conventional symmetry to her large and by no means ideally proportioned form. Her dresses, indeed, both in cut and colour, gave one at once the impression of a woman who never troubled herself to do more than buy the first suitable stuff which might offer itself to her when she entered a shop; and that she never did more than just let her measure be taken for a dress, and then step into it, without any afterthoughts on the matter.

But it will be of course asked, What was her playing like—was it beautiful, peculiar, masterly? To which I reply that it *was* all these, and that, moreover, it had a special quality of simple unobtrusiveness, which at the first hearing prevented one from fully realizing all that was in it. Mr. Clarke had irritated me greatly the first time I heard her play, by saying, 'If you are smart, you will see that there is a sincerity, a simplicity, and an unaffected sweetness in her playing which you will scarcely ever find approached.'

I could not, and I would not, in the first instance, accept this judgment of his; but living in the same house with her for several weeks, and hearing her practise as I went up and down stairs, and walked along the passage which led to their room, I came insensibly under the charm of her truly unaffected and unobtrusive depths of expression; while as I stood beside her when she was playing, and perceived, from the expression of her face and the ease of her position, that she was in a state of the highest possible enjoyment, I was forced to acknowledge her great mastery over the keyboard.

One evening we all agreed to tell each other the history of our musical aspirations, and it was on hearing Mr. Clarke relate his that I arrived by a sudden leap at the fullest and clearest idea of what it was (as regards the pianoforte) that I had been longing for all my life, and yet had been unable to express in so many words.

Mr. Frederick Steinecke-Clarke's life took three successive evenings to relate, for we were all sufficiently primitive to feel sleepy long before the hour when most people retire to rest. We were, moreover, all working hard during the day, and we agreed, when we first arranged to spend our evenings together, that we would not allow our sociable instincts to tempt us into encroaching on the hours which we needed for rest. Accordingly, as soon as the clock struck ten, Mr. Clarke would break off in his narrative, and we wished each other 'good night.'

I give the following as nearly as I can remember in the narrator's own words.

'My family,' he said, 'had been for one or two generations settled down in one of the loneliest and most isolated spots you could possibly imagine. They had cleared a tract of land in the heart of a great American forest, built a homestead, and reared a large family there. I was the youngest. One or

two of my sisters had been sent for a year or two to
relations who lived far away, and while there had got
a little smattering of pianoforte-playing—just enough
to bungle through waltzes, pots-pourris, and the like.
My parents bought an old piano for them, and
when I was still a small child, I used to listen with
awe-stricken admiration to their performances on it.
It was to me quite enchanted ground, and as I grew
bigger it was the greatest joy of my life to be allowed
to try and learn some of my sisters' pieces. Having
made these my own, I began after awhile to hunger
for more. Several odd chances so favoured me at
different times, that I gradually got hold of many
pieces by Bach, Mozart, Beethoven, and Mendelssohn.
When I was about twelve years old my parents began
to turn over many plans in their minds for my future,
and finally deciding that I was to learn the book-
business, sent me for the purpose to a distant town,
where I would have the advantage of living in the
house of a near relation during the years of my
apprenticeship. It was then that I first heard of
Liszt, and, some of his compositions falling into my
hands, I threaded my way through them, and actually
believed that I was on the road to playing them so as
to astonish the public. I say I believed myself to be
on the road to excellence,' continued Mr. Steinecke-
Clarke, 'but my musical instincts told me that I
should not reach the goal to which I aspired without
help. In Germany, the land of music—in Leipzig,

at that time regarded as the first musical college in that country—there alone was that which I needed in order to realize my dreams! But it seemed hopeless to wish—to think of ever getting there. I thought and thought, however, planned and planned; the upshot of all this thinking, all this planning, being that I resolved, by doing various jobs out of working hours, to earn the money which would bring me to Germany—to Leipzig. Once resolved on this, it was my thought by day and night for several years. I gave music-lessons in the evenings, did a good deal of copying, and finally, at the age of sixteen, in counting up all I had put together, believed the sum total would enable me to travel the whole way from America to Leipzig, and there I hoped my talents—of which I had no mean opinion—would gain me free instruction at the Conservatorium of Music. I knew my parents would never have given their consent to such a step; and, therefore, without saying anything to them of my purpose, I left my country and came to Hamburg in a steamer. When I reached this city, I found that I had only a few marks in my pocket, and there was, therefore, nothing for it, if I ever wished to reach Leipzig, but to travel there on foot.'

Mr. Clarke must have had an admirable memory, for he described each day of this journey, and every little incident that marked the various days. He was deeply religious, and he told us that he prayed earnestly that people might be kind to him. He was thankful to sleep in stables and haylofts, and people were sometimes so kind as to give him a good meal for nothing, while there were dreary days, when he was very thankful if he had succeeded in getting enough of dry and stale bread to satisfy his hunger. One day it had been raining hard for hours, and he had been trudging on, footsore, and weary in body, but brave and hopeful in spirit; but, as he himself said in relating the incident, 'I was but a boy, after all; and when night came on I was worn out and very wet, and as I walked on, I prayed that I might find some sheltered corner in which I could lie down and rest myself. The country all round was open and bleak, and it seemed as if I would have to trudge on all night; my clothes were soaked through, and I was in the greatest state of exhaustion. My courage gave way at last, and flinging myself on the ground, I cried, 'Father, is it possible that you have no pity for your poor child?' Just as I had uttered these words, my glance lighted on a haystack, which was quite near, though I had not before perceived it. How glad and how thankful I felt as I saw it! And how I chid myself, and, kneeling down, prayed to be forgiven for my want of faith! How sweet and refreshing was the sleep I enjoyed that night in the shelter of that most opportunely discovered haystack!'

At last, however, he reached the long-wished-for goal—he arrived at Leipzig. 'You may imagine,' he said, 'after the exposure and fatigue of that long, weary journey, what I must have looked like when I presented myself as a candidate for admission to the Conservatorium! I had, however, immense belief in my own talent, though I noticed that the professors looked at one another and shook their heads, when they heard, in reply to the question, 'Where have you studied music up to the present time?' 'I have studied by myself—both at home, and in the city where I was learning the book-business.' 'But your teacher, or your teachers, who were they?' 'I have never had any teacher, but have studied by myself.' I saw them shake their heads at these replies; but I was no whit daunted by their looks, and was quite ready to show them what I could do. Need I tell you that, even before I had left America, my playing was nothing—could, indeed, have been nothing—but a wild chaos, especially in the mazy intricacies of Liszt's compositions? You may imagine what it must have been when want of practice and extreme fatigue were added to all the other drawbacks! Yet, so little was I conscious of my own deficiencies, that, instead of choosing for my trial-piece before the examiners a piece of any ordinary difficulty, I attacked a difficult polonaise of Liszt's, and, with all the presumption and foolhardiness of unblushing ignorance, would have played it on to the end, had not the examiners angrily called out to me to stop—that I knew nothing —that they had heard quite enough, and would not listen to any more! I begged them, however, so earnestly not to send me away without one more trial, that one of them—who, it seems, had from the first moment felt an interest in me—asked if I was able to read at sight. And when I said that I could, he induced his professional colleagues to give me another trial. Mozart's Sonatas were placed before me, and my reading, or rather my attempt at reading these, immediately influenced the board in my favour, and I at once perceived with joy that I would be admitted into the Conservatorium. But before all this was finally arranged, my ideal conceptions about musical Germany, and, above all, of the world-renowned Leipzig Conservatorium, received a cruel blow. I had fondly believed that such musical genius as I supposed myself to possess would, even in the crudest possible state, have at once gained me admission—that, in fact, I should be admitted into the Leipzig Conservatorium, have all my expenses paid, and have my musical education free. I was, therefore, thunderstruck when the question was put to me, "Who is going to pay the fees for your instruction, and the cost of your living here?" I was overcome with sorrow, for it seemed as if, after all I had gone through, my plans were to end in nothing. But my great earnestness, my firm belief in my own powers, and perhaps, still more than these, something in my bearing which showed them that under my shabby attire there was one who had come of well-principled and worthy parents, won them so far in my favour, that they said I should remain there at the expense of the board until I should have written to my parents, and ascertained whether they were willing and able to promise to supply the funds during my stay there. My parents were good enough to forgive the runaway and guarantee all that the board required. In two years and a half I took my diploma,' continued Mr. Clarke, 'and, returning to America, sought for and obtained a position as organist, which, giving me a small income, relieved my good parents from the burden of supporting me. In America I continued to study with unflagging industry and zeal during the next three or four years. I gave several concerts, at which I played nearly all the pieces which form the programmes of the leading pianists. But I was restless and dissatisfied with myself; there was a want in my playing, which went far deeper than a mere inability to master a difficult passage. Not only did I fail to produce the quality of tone for which my nature was always craving, but I never could be certain that when I laid my hand on the keyboard I could produce an even succession of rich clear tones. The consciousness of this feeling gradually increased, until it became so intense that even in my sleep it let me have no rest, and I have dreamed that the piano played of its own accord, and in tones whose delicious timbre thrilled me with delight, and with a deep satisfaction which was at once physical and spiritual. At last I could bear it no longer. I felt I could not rest without trying to discover if there was any way of producing tones similar to those which haunted my dreams; I must try to realize what I heard in my sleep. I tried, but it was like being in a labyrinth, in which I could not see my way to any possible outlet. At last I was unable to bear this strangely mingled physical and mental strain any longer. I once more saved up a little money, and, again crossing the ocean, returned to Germany. There I had almost at once the singular good luck to hear of Herr Deppe, and to be introduced to him. The moment I heard my Anna play, I knew that my quest was over. I was at the goal of my desires; these were the tones of which I had dreamed! If I had gone on,' continued Mr. Clarke, ' giving concerts, and refusing to listen to the voice of my musical conscience, where should I be now?'

Anna was the next to tell her life. She described how she had been admired and *fêted* as a fine pianist, and had thought herself one, until undeceived by Herr Deppe; and yet how—though it had cost her a severe struggle, and the loss of all prestige and position for several years—she had given up all her previous acquisitions, had ceased to play either at concerts or in society, and had surrendered herself wholly to Herr Deppe's guidance.

When my turn came, and I spoke of my past, and of St. Cecilia, and related what I was doing at the present time, Mr. Clarke, who was utterly unworldly and unconventional, burst forth with all the fervour and all the heart of one who feels that vital interests are at stake : 'My Anna there has not a tenth part of your natural gifts—for I have been listening more than you can surmise to your practice since you came here. Ah! how conscientiously you go to work, and how you toil at the keyboard; and yet, alas! it will result in nothing but pain and dissatisfaction with yourself!'

'I must wish you "good-night,"' I said; 'there is not the slightest use in your speaking thus to me.' And so saying, I turned to go; but this strange, simple, unconventional, and really noble being held my hand, and detained me quite against my will.

'No, no,' he said, 'you shall not evade me; if you never hear the whole truth in your life again, you shall hear it now, and hear it to the end; and you may be as angry just at this moment as you like at the freedom which I take, yet I know when we are in different parts of the world, perhaps never to see one another's face again, you will forgive me—you will say it was a true, deep, and tender interest in your welfare that made me thus insist on detaining you against your will. I repeat once more, and repeat it in the presence of my wife—in natural gifts you stand far, far above her; but this makes it all the sadder, that in art she—ah! she is up there,' and, suiting the action to the word, he raised his hand as if he were pointing to something towering above us, 'and you are down there;' and he brought his hand down lower and lower as if he were directing our attention to some yawning depth. 'You know it in your inmost heart,' he continued; 'but you won't listen to your conscience and give in. You will not strip off all these rags of pretension, and become like a little child. I could weep for you,' he continued, with ever-increasing fervour, 'for your aim is ideal, and you will suffer cruelly when you at last discover that you have never even been on the road to it.'

Such was the force of his eloquence that, although I would not at once tell him so, he had nearly won me over to return to Herr Deppe, and thus become truly their comrade in art. But a friend at whose house I was a constant guest never ceased to influence me against Herr Deppe and his followers. I, moreover, did not like the idea of offering a slight to Scharwencka, whom I liked and admired, and who had taken great pains with me, and was in many respects an admirable teacher; I therefore decided that when the summer came, and I should be away from all personal influences either for or against Herr Deppe, I would think it out for myself, and decide whether I should join his school. When I said good-bye to the Steinecke-Clarkes early in July, it was, therefore, quite with the idea that we should all three be much together during the following winter.

This is, I think, the best place for quoting some

very interesting observations of Anna Steinecke's on pianoforte-playing, of which I made a memorandum at the time in my note-book. She was a woman who had thought profoundly on this subject.

'The question is not whether we study very many subjects, nor, as regards art, whether our knowledge extends over a *large surface* of the special department or section in which we work. No; the question is, to select certain points which we feel to have special value for our special individuality, and dig and delve *there*, until we get all that can possibly be got *there*, deep down below the surface. We must live ourselves, as it were, into a musical composition before we can *reproduce it*, give it again that life and pulsation which it has lost, as it crystallizes into *mere* notes and passages on the page.'

With regard to slow practice she says: 'People talk here and there of a person reading off anything at sight, as if that were the *sine quâ non* of a finished artist; but what can there be to interest in such sight-reading? When the performer begins to work at a sonata, or a concerto, or such-like, he must play every passage, so as to observe, without hurry or anxiety, all that is in the composition, and all that is in his or her performance of it—touch, phrasing, etc. With every several repetition the observations are more rapidly taken in, and after awhile, without any strain or effort, the whole develops just as calmly, as silently, and as harmoniously as a flower.'

My readers may possibly remember that it was Miss Fay's book which sent me to Herr Deppe in the first instance. And if they have read her book, they may feel rather surprised at the different ways in which he expressed himself to her and to the writer of this little book, and may conclude that the present writer was very little advanced, as Herr Deppe permitted her so very little latitude. It is pretty clear to me that, at the time when I went to Herr Deppe, in the Anhalter Strasse, his system must have become much more formulated than it was when she paid her first visit to him in the Königgrätzer Strasse. For he allowed her, even in her first lesson, an amount of freedom which at the present date is never granted to anyone. It is not so much for my own sake, as for that of the schools in which I had studied, and of the musicians under whose guidance I had worked, that I anticipate the probable rejoinder to what I have just now said about Deppe. It will be said, and very naturally too—Miss Fay must have been far more advanced in pianoforte-playing when she went to Herr Deppe than was the writer of this little book.

But I will take Mr. Clarke as an instance. He had been a concert-player in America; and when I first knew him, he had been working under Deppe for a year and three months with all his might, and during a third at least of that time he had had the advantage of constant help from his wife. He had great musical facilities, and was very gifted; and yet he had been allowed to advance so slowly, that he was then only beginning to work at Moscheles' Studies—they had hitherto been too difficult for him to play in the *technique* of the school. I can perhaps make this last observation more intelligible. On the day before I left Berlin he played to me, for the first time, one or two of the Moscheles Studies at which he was then working, and I must confess that, in the first instance, I was far more taken up in observing his hands and fingers, which to me looked like claws on the keyboard, than in analyzing any special quality of tone in his playing; for, as I have before often said, my perception of tone was as yet very undeveloped.

After he had played several of the Moscheles Studies to me, Mr. Clarke changed the position of his hands, and then began to play most brilliantly and with great force several grand concert pieces, saying as he did so, 'I am not now playing in the Deppe *technique*, but in the manner which I had before I ever went to him.'

'But you are playing very well,' I replied; 'most brilliantly, and with great effect.'

'But don't you observe the difference of tone? Don't you perceive that, although I am playing much louder now than I did before, yet the tone I produce has little or no timbre, no ring?'

I remember feeling in a sort of maze as I looked at him and listened to him; and yet, in just a year from that date, I was myself making something like the same reply to a friend who sat beside me as I played to her in St. Petersburg. I had then been several months in another great tone-forming school, in which I was almost entirely restricted to Cramer; but having had a large programme of pieces when I began to study in that school, and Henselt not having, like Deppe, desired me to give them up, I used for a long time to play them occasionally for myself or others. But the more I set myself to the delightful task of seeking to produce a clear, telling, and *cantabile* tone, the less was I satisfied with any piece in which this tone was not present. I said so to the friend to whom I was playing on this particular occasion, adding, 'I shall play them no more, but drop them all, and this with a conviction which comes from the very centre of my being.'

'Is it possible, my dear friend,' she replied, 'that you can bring yourself to commit what I cannot help calling "un suicide moral"?' and as she said this she actually burst into tears!

'But do listen,' I said to her; 'don't you note the difference?' And then I played the studies of Cramer which I had studied according to Henselt's method, afterwards giving her once more some pieces of my old programme, and she was in a measure convinced that the latter performance was in truth unsatisfying, though far more brilliant than the former, far more calculated to impress the hearer with the idea that the player was doing something masterly and wonderful; she felt at length that the apparent mastery was mastery on a comparatively low plane; it was, in fact, not on the plane of true art at all, but on that of a gigantic dilettantism, while Henselt's method was leading me on, slowly, perhaps, but none the less surely, towards the true heights of art. Whether I should be able to climb very high, or indeed to climb at all, was not the question for me; I had rather be on the lowest step of Art's ladder, than on the highest pinnacle of dilettantism.

But I have anticipated my narrative, and I must return once more to Herr Deppe—just to observe that he is, to my thinking, one of the most sagacious beings I have ever come across. He tells his pupils to 'live a child's life,' and keep much in the open air; to wear no gloves, not to go to many concerts, and (most of all characteristic of the man) not to associate with people who are either not worth being listened to themselves, or do not possess the faculty of listening with attention to others. 'Chatty people,' said he to me (at a later date than the time of which I have now been speaking), 'get often into a habit of not listening, and this habit carries itself into all they do. A person who gives way to this habit will lose by degrees the power of concentrating his attention, and without concentration advance in any study is simply impossible.' This observation tallies admirably with what I have often heard from a valued friend, whose life-work was science, and not art. He puts it thus: 'Better inaction than a half-effort—for in the former you rest; and if you have a conscience, you will finally tire of inaction, rouse yourself up, and push vigorously on; whereas in the latter case you may indeed be moving, but you are not advancing, and every one of these half-efforts tends to relax the mental system, and to deprive it of the energy to focus its powers for an effort in a given direction.'

And now I must relate how it came about that, somewhat early in the winter, the first link was woven in the singular chain of circumstances which brought me at last under the influence of Adolf von Henselt. Many of Henselt's compositions were already known to me, and I had heard vague rumours here and there of his extraordinary powers as a *virtuoso*, but it was not until I listened to the playing of Mademoiselle Katy Ranuschewitz (the young lady who had taken such a prominent position at the Liszt afternoon reunions) that I became aware of his greatness as a teacher, and discovered that he was recognised among musicians as one of the greatest authorities in *technique* the world has ever seen. The way by which I was brought into contact with Henselt was curious enough; it was by a seeming chance, and it came about simply because on one particular Sunday morning I had taken a rather longer sleep than usual, and consequently had set out for church fully half an hour later than I was in the habit of doing. I always went to the Dom—not only because one was sure of always hearing a good sermon there, but also attracted by the famous choir of men's voices, and the further advantage of the museum being close by, into which I often turned after service, to spend a quiet hour among the early Italian masters. It was always necessary to be early at the Dom Kirche, if one wished to secure a good seat, and it is a curious fact that I never remember having been so late in setting off for church as on the eventful morning which was to prepare the way for bringing me into personal contact with Henselt. Looking at my watch when seated in the tram-car, which was going in the direction of the Dom, I saw that by the time we should arrive there I should be far too late to get anything like a good seat; and as I observed a hymn-book in the hand of the lady who was sitting beside me, I thought she might possibly be on her way to some other church which we should reach before service had commenced. Turning to her, I asked if there was any church nearer to us in which the preaching was good. The lady whom I had addressed did not at once answer me; but while she seemed to be making up her mind which church to recommend, another lady whom I had not before observed, and who was sitting right opposite to me, said in a pleasant tone, and with a glance of kindly interest, 'My husband and I are just getting out of the tram to attend service in a church close by; perhaps you would like to accompany us? I assure you the preaching there is very good.'

The tram-car stopped in a minute or two after this. The lady, her husband, and her son got out. We all went into church together, and sat in the same pew. There had been no opportunity for us to interchange more than a word or two before we entered the church; and when the service was over, we all came silently out until we had reached the door. There we paused and looked at each other for a moment, and she it was, I believe, who took the initiative by asking me whether I intended to walk or drive to my home. The friendly drift of her question being pretty evident, I replied that, as the day was fine, I thought a walk would perhaps be more agreeable. Perhaps our respective ways home lay in the same direction? This happened to be the case, and we agreed to walk together, and soon got into such an animated conversation, that we found ourselves near our homes, which were in adjoining streets, not five minutes' distance from each other, much sooner than we could have imagined possible.

We had not taken very long to discover that there existed between us one of the strongest reasons for becoming intimate, *i.e.* that we both had had all our life long an infatuating, all-engrossing love for music. I told her that I was a wanderer from my country in search of a perfect scientific method for acquiring mastery over the pianoforte; and she told me that she was by marriage a favourite niece of Adolf von Henselt, of St. Petersburg, who was, according to her, the greatest pianoforte authority of the age.

When I parted that forenoon from Frau Mila, it was settled that I was to go with her the following evening to hear some very good pupils of the late Herr Vogt play in Kullak's Conservatoire. That evening cemented our intimacy, and before long I almost invariably spent my Sunday afternoons with Frau Mila. We used to talk about Scharwencka, Deppe, the Steinecke-Clarkes, and what they said, and then of the musical labyrinth out of which I was vainly trying to find my way. She would often say to me, 'If you could but see my uncle, and be under his guidance, he would soon smooth away all your difficulties.'

VI.

HENSELT.

Time, meanwhile, had sped on. I had arranged to join some friends from my own country at Hombourg in the month of August, and fully intended to remain on in Berlin until then. The summer that year was, however, intolerably hot; and feeling myself quite unable to work any longer, I went off to a little bathing-town on the Baltic Sea, of which I had heard a most charming description from a friend who had once or twice passed her summers there. I arrived the second week in July, meaning to stay until my friends should have arrived at Hombourg. I immediately found a room in a small hotel, where they took people *en pension*, by the week or the day. Though I did not mean to study much during the great heat, yet I wished to have a piano; but I found, on inquiry, that the only means of procuring one was to order it down by the railway at great expense. As this did not seem worth while, I resolved to content myself with playing occasionally for half an hour on a very tolerable upright pianoforte which stood in a small salon—a sort of a marine drawing-room, which belonged to the hotel. I was very careful to select the hours when the rooms were empty, for I naturally wished neither to be disturbed myself nor to disturb others, and for two or three days I flattered myself that I was playing wholly and solely for my own benefit, without having any audience. But it would seem that in this primitive little spot musicians must have been somewhat of a novelty, for it was not more than four days after my arrival at S——, when the owner of the hotel sent a waiter up to my door, to ask if I would kindly see two gentlemen who were downstairs asking for me. They had sent up their cards to me, and I perceived that one of them was a colonel. I was all in a flutter to know what they could possibly want with me. Addressing the waiter, I told him there must be some mistake, for that I knew nobody in the place. 'The gentlemen do not know you,' replied the waiter, 'but they have asked a good many questions about you. They are in the parlour, waiting to see you. Will you not descend for one minute?' Great was my surprise when the gentlemen, after one or two preliminary polite speeches, informed me that, being aware I was a musician, they sought to enlist my help in a concert which they wanted to get up for the benefit of the district charities. The concert was to take place in the following month, and a prince had placed his spacious rooms at their disposal for the purpose. I told the gentlemen that I did not play in public; that I had come there for bathing and rest; that they would surely have no difficulty in finding someone who would be willing to do all they asked. They were, however, most persistent, and said so much, that at length I said I would help in concerted music, if they could find any one who could play fairly well on the violin or violoncello; that if both one and the other were forthcoming, we might play a Beethoven trio; and I would also, if necessary, accompany the singing.

On the following day, one of the gentlemen who were trying to organize the concert called on me at the hotel, bringing with him a tall, awkward-looking youth. The latter carried a violin-case, and was introduced to me as a promising pupil of one of the best violin-players, himself a pupil of Joseph Joachim. The youth did not look very intelligent, nor did his replies to the one or two questions I put to him as to the pieces he had been studying give me the idea that he was an advanced player on the instrument. The name of Joachim, however, carried with it a weight which quite overruled my first impressions, and when they asked me if I would not come and try over some duets in the marine salon, I at once put on my hat, and we three set off there together. But scarcely had we begun our duet (musical natures, whether amateur or professional, will sympathize with me in the following experience) when I made the embarrassing discovery that my coadjutor could neither play in time nor keep in tune; that I was associated, in fact, with such a player as would not have been tolerated in any educated circle, even in unmusical England. I saw, however, that the poor young man was extremely nervous; and his nice, gentle manners so far enlisted my sympathies in his favour, that I continued to play with him for two or three days, venturing to hope that when he had become a little more used to me, and his shyness had somewhat worn off, he would keep in better time, and not play so deplorably out of tune. My hopes, however, on this head were doomed to disappointment, and the situation became perplexing in the extreme. The youth fully believed that he had a career before him, and looked forward to being able in the future to do much for his parents, to whom he seemed greatly attached. They had made great sacrifices in order to give him the means of developing the talent which both he and they were fully persuaded that he possessed; and was I to tell him that, instead of being full of promise, his playing was pitiable, and often most excruciating? But it really was labour lost for me to go through such a penance day after day; and then would come, as the wind-up, a performance which even pleasure-seekers must feel to be ridiculous. So I tried to persuade him in the first instance that he was not sufficiently advanced to play before a large audience; and even ventured to allude to his nervousness as a reason for his giving up the idea of the performance. But he was so obtuse, so innocent, that he actually said he relied on me to hide all his shortcomings!

I would not tell the gentleman who had made us acquainted that he was nothing but a bungler; and, after turning over in my mind for another day or two what was best to be done, the only way of escape that suggested itself to me was to leave the place before the programme of the concert should have been definitely settled. As soon as I had arrived at this conclusion, I packed my box, and, leaving letters for both the violinist and the colonel, expressed regret at my inability to stay at S—— until the date at which the proposed concert was to take place.

I left S——, and surprised the lady, in whose pension in Berlin I had been staying all the winter and spring, by reappearing there after an absence of only ten days. She handed me a letter, which by some unaccountable oversight had been laid aside on a shelf, instead of being forwarded to me—a letter, too, which, had I remained in S—— until the end of July, and then gone on to Hombourg, would in all probability have never reached me. And it was this very letter which was to bring me into a personal contact with Henselt; and this meant that I must go to the far, far north.

My friend (Henselt's niece) had left Berlin, and gone down to Görlitz, where she and her husband and son always spent the summer holidays, in a country home which the family had owned for more than one generation. She had seen her uncle, who had just come to Warmbrunn (not far from Görlitz), where he was accustomed to spend from June to September with his wife; and she had excited his interest in me by talking to him about me, but still more, I believe, by showing him a letter in which I had compared my passion for music to an unrequited love, which, however it might sadden one, yet one never could wish it out of one's life. Henselt, reading this letter, wished to see the writer; and the letter which the lady of the pension in Berlin handed me on my arrival there was from Frau Mila, and enclosed some lines of Henselt to her, in which, alluding to me, he thus expressed himself: 'Tell your friend that if she comes down here, I will help her with word and deed' ('mit Wort und That'). My friend urged me not to be tardy in availing myself of an offer made with such hearty goodwill; and the whole plan chiming in admirably with my own wishes, I made no delay in Berlin, but set out the next day but one after my return thither for Warmbrunn, in a state of the greatest expectation and delight. It was pouring in torrents of rain when I reached the post station in Warmbrunn, and I can vividly recall the pleasure which I felt when I saw my friend's kind face looming out from under a big umbrella, as she looked into the coach to see if I was inside. So little had I dreamed of asking her to come and meet me, that I had not told her whether I should come on that day or the one following. And there she was, so pleased and so cordial, all affectionate anxiety to have me under her uncle's guidance, and to make me feel happy and at home in Warmbrunn.

She took me at once round the village to look for rooms, but we did not then succeed in finding any that were quite suitable. Then we had some dinner at a restaurant; and I suspected that our search for rooms would recommence after we had rested ourselves a little. But I found that Frau von Henselt had invited me to take coffee with her; and though I had not the least wish to be seen for the first time in my very plain but comfortable travelling-dress, and though I urged that I was very untidy—having spent the whole of the previous night in the train—my friend laughed at me, said I looked very nice, was pertinacious, and finally marched me off to the Villa von Henselt. All I here beheld was entirely different to anything I could have pictured to myself beforehand. Frau Mila had spoken as if her uncle occupied a palace in St. Petersburg; and having never been before in a small German watering-place, the only ideas I had were of places like Hombourg and Baden-Baden. Warmbrunn was quite a deliciously primitive village.

We soon reached the Villa von Henselt—a one-storied and unpretending, though very cosy and homelike dwelling—with a jutting-out veranda in front, up which the roses climbed in luxuriant festoons. It was with a feeling of relief that I heard the servant say to my friend, 'The *gnädige* Frau is alone, for his Excellency is spending the afternoon at a whist-party given by some friends.' We went in, and Frau von Henselt came forward and received me with much kindness, and even cordiality. We sat down to coffee, and I took many a glance round at the room and the portraits on the walls. After an hour or more of pleasant chat with Frau von Henselt, her niece and I set off once more in search of rooms, and after looking at several in different directions, we finally decided on some very homely quarters, consisting of a sitting-room which opened into a tiny sleeping-room. They had the great advantage of being in a simple but very clean *Gasthaus*, where I could have all my meals either served to me in my own room, or else in the open air, under a large covered veranda which ran along the front of the house. There was the still further advantage of being in the country, and quite among the fields, which were smiling in all the beauty of summer; it was, moreover, not five minutes' walk from the Villa von Henselt. After taking the rooms we went at once to the post, where I had left my boxes; and I remember my amused surprise when the porter—

whom I engaged to carry my box and several large
parcels to the hotel, which was at least half a mile
distant—only asked sixpence for his pains, and seemed
much obliged when I handed him twopence extra.
His Excellency had kindly secured a piano for me,
which was sent in early the following morning. But
eager though I was to begin work, I did not touch the
keys that morning, for I was to hear Henselt giving
a lesson at twelve, and I could do nothing but wander
in the fields round the house, wishing it were time for
my friend to arrive—for I was to go there under her
auspices. How I fumed when, instead of fetching me
at a quarter before twelve, as she had promised, she
never came until the clocks of the various village
churches were striking noon!

When we reached the villa we could hear the
piano; the lesson had therefore begun, and I half
feared we should have to content ourselves with what
we could hear from the adjoining room, into which
the servant had ushered us. Frau von Henselt,
however, pushed aside the heavy curtains which were
drawn between the two rooms, and, with finger put
to her lips, signed to us to come in. We accordingly
stole in very noiselessly, and took seats a little behind
the chair where the Meister was sitting with his
pupil. My friend told me that the young lady played
extremely well, and yet that she had no special talent
for music. It had fallen to her lot to enjoy the
enviable privilege of being Henselt's pupil during

many successive summers. In his absences from St. Petersburg he missed his winter occupation, that of teaching, for which he had a passion. A family of good birth, who were on intimate terms with Henselt's wife, happened to have a daughter who had just left school, and was trying to get on with her music by herself. This young lady had the good fortune to come under the notice of the Meister, and it was a lesson given to her this day at which I had been invited to be present. Under Frau von Henselt's auspices, we stole softly in and ensconced ourselves noiselessly behind the Meister and his pupil; but though we had made scarcely a sound on coming in, Henselt had noted our approach, and, turning right round, he looked full at me. His glance met mine, and in silence, and without a word of introduction, he held out his hand and closed mine in a firm and friendly clasp. The young lady was playing Weber's Sonata in A Flat; and Henselt made her pause over and over again in order to show her how he wished her to play, and to phrase various passages in this piece. He did not on that day play more than a page or so at a time, and yet he had scarcely seated himself at the piano, scarcely played a few bars, before it was clear to me that I was in the presence of one who united in himself all the rarest excellences of a musician and a *virtuoso* of the highest order.

His naturally short, fleshy hand, with short fingers, had been so widened and developed by studies which he had thought out for himself while yet a mere boy, that he was not only able to play the tenths—of which there are so many in the *finale* of this sonata—but all the notes that lie between these extreme intervals, without any semblance of effort. His touch was deep, and yet he seemed to have the power of nipping out, whenever he chose to do so, a *pianissimo* the timbre of which was at once most penetrating and yet most exquisitely delicate. In the left-hand accompaniment of the *finale* of Weber's sonata his phrasing was most charming, and he was at great pains to make his pupil understand exactly what he wished. Just as this lesson was over there was another arrival—a gentleman, who walked in silently and took a seat close by me. I glanced round at him, and perceived with some amusement that he was the very Professor Zschocher whom Liszt had introduced to me on the day he paid me a visit at the Kron Prinz Hotel in Weimar. We just smiled a recognition at each other; and Henselt, in rising from the piano, perceived him, and, after exchanging a very cordial greeting, they got at once into a most animated discussion. It was about a new edition of Moscheles' Studies, which Henselt was eager to see in print without delay; and he worked himself into a state of the greatest excitement as he inveighed against the slowness and *nonchalance* of his publishers. As he seemed to have entirely forgotten that I was there, I had all the more opportunity of observing him closely and taking in every detail of his personal appearance. His fine head was quite bald, excepting a slight fringe of silver close by the neck; beard and moustache silvery white; eyebrows which reminded me of Liszt's; a prominent nose, and a very harsh and combative-toned voice. The eyes were the most noticeable feature. As I looked at them I thought that, except those of Liszt, I had never seen any that were so large, and so ablaze with light; but Liszt's eyes were gray, and these were the darkest shade of brown; and, in alluding to their brilliancy, I have been told that when he was a younger man no one could bear to meet the glance of those eyes when they flashed in anger or in scorn.

Professor Zschocher and I chancing to meet the next day on the promenade, we naturally fell into talk of Liszt and Henselt. The professor was surprised to find me in Warmbrunn instead of Weimar; and it was easy to see that he had more respect than love for Henselt, at whose 'pedantry' he began to rail in no measured terms. For all this, before we parted he said, 'Nevertheless, now that you are with him, Fräulein, try, if you can, to get at the secret of his wonderful touch—that touch of which Liszt has so often spoken to me, so often said, "Niemand weiss es ihm nachzumachen"' ('No one can imitate it').

To speak of this wonderful touch, so as to convey any idea of what it was like to those who have never heard him—now, alas! will never hear him—is, I feel, a hopeless, an almost absurd task; and yet I shall try by just one or two imperfect metaphors to give some idea of it, however faint and dim.

Henselt's touch suggested a shelling—a peeling off of every particle of fibrous or barky rind; the unveiling of a fine, inner, crystalline, and yet most sensitive and most vitally elastic pith. With this, it suggested a dipping deep, deep down into a sea of tone, and bringing up thence a pearl of flawless beauty and purity; something, too, there was of the exhalation of an essence—so concentrated, so intense, that the whole being of the man seemed to have passed for the moment into his finger-tips, from which the sound seemed to well out, just as some sweet yet pungent odour from the chalice of some rare flower.

In justice to Professor Zschocher, I feel it but right here to explain that the exclamation, 'He is a terrible pedant!'—which irritated me and led me to imagine that Professor Zschocher had more respect than love for Henselt—must have been made in one of those passing moments of ill-humour to which all of us are more or less liable. After the Meister was gone he wrote warmly and lovingly of him to the afflicted widow, telling her that he should never cease to miss one who had ever been a true and kind friend to him. And when I visited him (Professor Zschocher) at his own house in Leipzig, the following year, one of his first thoughts, after we had exchanged a few words of greeting, was to place in my hands a sketch by La Mara, which forms part of the addition made to the present volume.

When Henselt had finished giving his lesson, I returned to my rooms, had an early dinner, and in the afternoon was practising with great energy, when, to my great pleasure, a servant from the Villa von Henselt brought me an invitation to dine with their Excellencies the following day (Sunday). My friend and I had a long talk that evening. She told me that I should be welcome to sit in the pew which her uncle and aunt had in the village church; and then, anticipating a question which I had meant to put to her before she left—'And now, my dear friend,' she said, 'before we say good-bye to each other, let me say what I was very near forgetting to tell you. Do not on any account suggest the idea of a fee for the help my uncle is going to give you. He is doing it for me, and it is entirely complimentary.'

On Sunday morning the Von Henselts' nice little housekeeper called upon me, in order to show me the way to the church, and where to find the family pew. We had it all to ourselves, and I rather wondered at this, for Henselt's niece had spoken of him as one who never absented himself from church. Frau von Henselt had, I knew, a slight cold, which accounted for her non-appearance. My surprise was even greater when I heard that, though Henselt scarcely ever missed going to church, yet he never sat in the pew, which belonged to him and was in a prominent place in the aisle. He had a seat in the gallery, where he liked to feel as if he were alone.

When we were coming out of church, the housekeeper, with whom I had got on rather pleasant terms during our somewhat lengthened walk to church, brought me to see the grave of the Von Henselts' only child—a young officer who had died about five years before. We were standing there— I was reading the inscription on the tombstone, 'Die Liebe dauert ewig' ('Love is eternal')—when I perceived Henselt coming towards us. I felt very, very awkward, for I asked myself what right had I, a stranger, a foreigner, to be standing there? He did not seem to mind, however, for he came up to us, just nodded to his housekeeper, shook hands with me, and saying, 'I shall see you at dinner to-day,' went off with the stride of a sturdy old warrior who finds no one who can keep step with him.

At one o'clock that day I dined at the Villa von Henselt, and was so charmed with the old couple, that as I looked at them the tears came more than once into my eyes. They were both aged, and I knew I could not hope to have them for very long; in fact, I half wished that I had not come to know them. I had lost many friends, and I shrank from making friends only to lose them.

Each of this venerable pair drew out my sympathies, though quite in a different way. Frau von

Henselt was distinguished-looking; she had a manner suggestive of court circles, in which she must have been a prominent figure; and there was beneath all this a tender pathos, an air of intense repression—the reserve of a proud soul that will not confess its pain. Henselt, looking at him quite apart from his genius, at first reminded me of a blunt, unpolished country gentleman. Later on, I always saw in him the type of a splendid, tough, sturdy, and uncompromising old general; a hater of all shows and shams; an enemy to all roundabout speeches, which not only involve loss of time, but cloud our perceptions of the truth; a foe to the knife of all compromises and half-measures, of all veneer and pretension.

The portrait of their only child (the young officer at whose grave I had been standing an hour before) faced me as I sat at the dinner-table, and in each of the three sitting-rooms which opened one into the other there were portraits of Henselt, which represented him at all the different periods of life. At twenty-two, when he was singularly handsome and attractive-looking; at forty, when the loss of youth was compensated for by the depth and intensity of the glance—the wave-lines of pathos which told that sorrow and disillusion had been his, and in no scant measure; then the recent likeness of the 'old lion,' with a look of war, and an attitude suggestive of one accustomed to rule—yes, even to the very verge of despotism.

After dinner Henselt went at once upstairs to his sanctum, which consisted of three rooms *en suite* on the first floor. The first of these (the ante-room) was a little salon, where he often had one or two gentlemen in the afternoon to play whist with him—his one special recreation during the summer interregnum from his professional duties.

The grand piano, which stood in the middle room, had been *mute* for years, he having had a sordine put on it; for he said he did not choose the neighbours to know what he was doing. And here a word on the subject of dumb pianos.

Sterndale Bennett had years before expressed, both to my mother and me, his unqualified disapproval of them. Sgambati, however, thought very differently, and I have often heard him say that a dumb piano ought to be used by everyone who aimed at playing with perfect finish—his opinion being that no one who can avoid it has any right to inflict on his neighbours the annoyance of listening to that amount of passage-practising from which no talent can dispense any individual player. Henselt always used a dumb piano for conquering technical difficulties; he said that doing so spared the nerves, and advised his pupils to do the same. In St. Petersburg all the lady-professors of his school with whom I became acquainted invariably practised on instruments for which they used two sets of sordines; one which so deadened and softened the sound as to render it inaudible outside the room, while the second made the instrument a complete dummy.

To return, however, to my narrative. When Henselt had, after dinner, gone up to his sanctum, his wife retired to her sleeping-room for a short siesta; and I sat in the drawing-room and occupied myself in taking in all around me, and looking out into the beautiful flower-garden. It seems to me, as well as I can remember, that his Excellency had a whist-party that afternoon, for coffee was sent up to him and his friends, while Frau von Henselt and her housekeeper were chatting with me in the drawing-room.

About five o'clock I left the Villa von Henselt, and went home to my simple rooms in the hotel. Much did I speculate that evening as to when Henselt would send for me to play to him, and what kind of help he was likely to give me.

On Monday morning I half expected to have a message from him, but the day passed on and still I heard nothing. In the evening, about six o'clock, I was in the middle of practising Scharwencka's fine variations in D minor, when there came a tap at the door, and when I rose and opened it, who should be there but Herr and Frau von Henselt! As they were coming into the room he glanced towards the piano, and said bluntly and without any preamble, 'Where is your music? I want to see all you have brought down with you.' I hastened to lay it all on the table before him, and there was a goodly pile of it. He seated himself, and Frau von Henselt, saying to me, 'You and I can chat while my husband looks over the music,' sat down beside me on the sofa, and we got into talk. Henselt, meanwhile, seemed to be turning over, piece by piece, all the music I had laid before him. All of a sudden he broke in on our conversation with the question, 'Who is your favourite composer, mein Fraülein?' I answered without a moment's hesitation (for that year I had lived myself much into Schumann), 'Schumann.' When I said this he made no further remark, but to my thinking he seemed to scowl at me. When he and his wife were going away, he arranged that I was to come to him at twelve o'clock the next day; and on Frau von Henselt asking him what music he wished me to bring to him, he gave the characteristic reply, 'She shall play nothing with *me* that she has played with anyone else; I will not help her in anything over which there has been any other influence than mine.'

The lesson fixed for the next day did not take place until Wednesday; a note had in the meantime informed me that his Excellency had forgotten, when making the appointment with me, that both he and his wife were previously engaged to a birthday reception at the house of old friends. On Wednesday, then, I betook myself to Villa von Henselt, carrying with me a portfolio full of the pieces which I could play from memory—Schumann's Concerto, the Kreisleriana, several of Chopin's Polonaises, two rhapsodies of Liszt, Beethoven's Sonata in E Major, Op. 101, and several other pieces. To my surprise and mortification, however, Henselt, who came in looking cross and ugly, with one side of his face all covered with wadding (he had been suffering from toothache), just took the portfolio out of my hands, laid it on the top of the piano, and then pointing to a piece of music that was lying open on the music-desk, said imperiously and without any preliminary remarks, 'You are to play that.'

I looked at the piece and perceived that it was a sonata of Hummel's, and one which I had never seen before. I therefore replied in a tone of remonstrance, 'But I don't know this piece; I have never seen it before.' 'No matter,' was the reply, in a short and surly tone; 'play it, or try to play it, in whatever way you can; if you cannot manage to play the two hands together, you may play the left or the right alone.' I was not afraid of him, but rather wound up and excited by his downrightness of [manner; therefore, after looking attentively at the piece for a moment or two in silence, I began to read it very slowly, and, as I thought, with tolerable correctness. I had not, however, gone very far, when, to my surprise, Henselt stopped me and told me to pause, and asked me in a very loud voice why I did not *bind* the notes, and carry the tone on to the following bar. He seated himself, and began then to show me what he meant by *legato* and 'binding'; and one may perhaps ask whether I was much surprised—whether my consternation was not great on hearing something which I was utterly unable to follow 'even afar off.' And I reply that my surprise, my consternation—if you will have it more strongly, my despair—did not come until I had been for some time under the Meister's influence. To feel one's own impotence—to appreciate the last fine touches of art—one must one's self be on the quest of the unattainable; and since I have known Henselt this has dawned on me, and more and ever more do I appreciate him. I tried hard to follow out Henselt's intentions in this first lesson; and he was very kind to me—looked at my hand, which was, he said, a good one, though rather small in size; he showed his hands to me, and pointing to the palms, which were quite flat, the result of extension, he said, 'Just look at the hand—leather—how it is stretched!' He gave me on that day a study for widening the hand; and in spite of the blow given to my *amour propre* by his choosing to ignore that I had a large repertoire, and would have liked to play if only one piece to him, I was on the whole far from being dissatisfied at the prospect before me.

His wife came in just as I was rising to go, and observed to him, 'She has a very sweet touch, has she not?'

'She has no *fleisch*,' was the reply, in a surly tone.

It was not for months afterwards that I understood what he meant by *fleisch*. He meant *technique*—the body through which the spirit reveals itself to our senses.

After an hour's lesson he dismissed me, putting the Hummel sonata into my hands, saying, 'Go home and work at this, and when you are ready to play it to me you can let me know.' And I did work away constantly and vigorously for several days, having in the first instance not the least doubt of being able to master it, and thus show him that I could do a great deal more than he seemed to give me credit for. But the more I studied the more clearly did I become aware that to get it in any degree approaching to what he had demanded would be the work, not of days, but of weeks. When I was quite convinced of this, I wrote and told him so. The characteristic lines in which he replied to me are still in my possession.

'I did not expect you to conquer the Hummel sonata, but you can come and show me how you have been working at it.'

I went to him accordingly the next day, and he received me most kindly, heard me play two movements, and was rather more encouraging than I had ventured to hope. I was, however, intensely irritated by a sort of growing consciousness that he regarded me as a mere dabbler in art, and that he would not and could not give me all he had to give, because he had 'a system,' and I was quite outside of it, and he would not have anything to do with *patchwork*. Still, he seemed interested in me, sent me Raff's lovely *Fileuse*, edited by himself, with my name written on it, and told me at the next lesson that on his way to take a walk in the country, in passing by the little inn where I lived, he had paused a moment to listen to me as I practised, and that he was pleased with the way I had set about studying the *Fileuse*. He then gave me his own extremely difficult cadenza from Beethoven's C Minor Concerto, and the lesson on this was the first regular drill I ever had from him.

'Why, you are playing that just like a fly,' he growled; 'no tone!'

'But I cannot play it louder,' was my rejoinder.

'We shall soon see that,' was his reply; and so saying he called out in a loud and imperious tone, 'Begin, and with one hand only,' and calling out, 'Again — again — again!' and 'Louder — louder — louder!' he made me repeat the passage in question at least twenty times before he said, 'Now you may go on.'

He did not frighten me with his rough manner and loud voice; but I was greatly excited, and Frau von Henselt came in when I was going away, and, patting my cheek, said, 'You are all in a flame, my dear.' I went away from this lesson with the impression that Henselt was interested in me, and really anxious to help me. Between this and the next lesson I drew a little nearer to him from having chanced to meet him in a walk which we both were taking across the country outside Warmbrunn.

The manner of our meeting and joining company on this walk is so amusingly characteristic of Henselt, that I pause for a moment or two to give it to the reader in detail.

I had one evening set out for a country walk, and had not gone any great distance, when, on pausing for a moment to take in the view, I perceived a group of persons not far behind me, amongst whom Henselt's form was most unmistakable. The group, however, dispersed in a moment or two; most of the persons composing it went off in different directions, and I saw that Henselt was by himself, and was walking on towards me at such a rapid pace that he must soon overtake me. And what would then happen? was the query which at once suggested itself to me. I was afraid of having a *tête-à-tête* with him; for he had none of Liszt's charming ease of manner, none of that delightful *bonhomie* which enables one to slide at once into topics of general interest. I knew instinctively that he could be hearty, cordial, outspoken with those whom he knew well, but that he had no small coin for general acquaintances! And so, like a coward, I tried to evade an embarrassing encounter by making a side-cut into a field which ran parallel for some distance with the path on which I was walking. The fates, however, that evening were very propitious to me, though just at that moment it seemed to my thinking to be quite the other way. I had not gone very far in the field, before I found all further progress impeded by the awkward fact that I was getting into a marsh. There was, therefore, nothing for it but to turn back; this I accordingly did, taking care, however, to keep as far as possible from the path, along which Henselt was now advancing with rapid strides. Just then it occurred to me that he was said to be short-sighted. I reflected, therefore, that if I could regain the path before he came up, I might cross into the fields which lay on the other side, and so avoid a meeting, which would be otherwise almost inevitable. The first step, however, which I made to regain the pathway plunged me nearly ankle-deep in water. I tried a second, and sank even still deeper. All the space between the pathway and the edge of the field where I was standing had been flooded by recent heavy rains, and was, though covered with grass, quite like a marsh. No use, therefore, in trying this mode of escape! By this time Henselt was very near, and, as a last desperate resource, I walked along without looking round, in the hope that perhaps he might not observe me. But the old general could see further than his friends imagined. He had seen me, and had probably thought that I was trying to regain the pathway in order to come up with him. Be this as it may, in a moment or two more he paused just opposite to me, and pointing to the marshy ground lying between us, he called out, 'You won't be able to get across there. If you want to get to the pathway, you must go a good way back;' and so saying, without another word and without any offer of help, to my great relief he continued his walk.

A lady, however, who was quite a stranger to me, came up at this moment. She had been an amused looker-on at the whole scene, and possibly thought that I wished to join 'his Excellency,' for she directed my attention to a moss-covered rock which ran right through the marshy ground close up to the path. I would have gladly continued my walk in the field, thus going further and further from Henselt, but I could not call out to a stranger that I had changed my mind, and did not now wish to get on the pathway. I therefore went where she pointed out. We interchanged a few remarks, and she then observed, 'You want to join that gentleman, and he is waiting for you. I will not detain you any longer.'

Yes, there he was, a little way further on—actually waiting for me! There was clearly nothing for it but to pluck up courage, and go to meet the danger with a brave face. As well as I can recollect, when I came up with him, he neither shook hands with me, nor uttered any of the usual words of greeting, but just took it as a matter of course that I was to walk with him. This simple acceptance of my companionship, this absence of all forms and preambles, at once put all my shyness to flight, and in five minutes after I had joined him, I was feeling quite at home with him—indeed, I had rarely if ever been so much at my ease with anyone in my life before.

For the first part of our walk he spoke but little, but he seemed to be enjoying both the brisk exercise and the fresh balmy evening air. I can recall as if it were yesterday the turn by the corn-field, where we both stood for a few moments, and gazed in silence at the setting sun. He asked me, when we continued our walk, how I liked Warmbrunn, and seemed rather surprised when I told him that I felt it lonely.

'Have you not your work, and the walks in this beautiful country?' was his rejoinder. 'I never feel lonely, for my ideal is always with me. My ideal, which I shall never, never attain—*in der Ewigkeit nie erreichen werde*—is more to me than anything or anybody in the whole world!'

A few days after this he was taken ill, and was for a fortnight unable to see anyone but his own family, and though I had only known him for about a month, I was in the deepest state of anxiety about him; indeed, there were times when I firmly believed that he would die—that I was doomed to lose one whom I had already divined would be to me a sort of musical father.

The only consolation I had during these first few days of Henselt's illness was in talking to his housekeeper, Fräulein Helmuth, when she took out her Excellency's two pug dogs for their evening walk. These high-bred and handsome animals were a present from Henselt to his wife; he brought them from St. Petersburg to Warmbrunn himself a year or two before. One of them had a very harsh and unmusical bark, and after this summer he was, in consequence, put out to board at a little distance—far enough off for the Meister not to hear his bark. It must not, however, be imagined that the Meister disliked the banished one.

Two days before his return to St. Petersburg I went to his house for my lesson, and was waiting, when I heard his voice in the next room, speaking with singular and unusual tenderness. My curiosity was so much aroused that I ventured to say when he came in:

'Who were you speaking to so kindly, dear Meister?'

With a grim smile, and rather a pleasant voice, he replied, 'Oh, I was talking to the pug.' This was the banished one, now permitted to return, as his master was about to depart.

'I never heard you speak like that before, dear Meister,' I observed.

'You never thought I could have softened my voice so much,' he replied, with a sort of grunt, not displeased.

The housekeeper told me a good deal about the

Von Henselts, with whom she had lived, with one or two interruptions, over thirty years. She related to me many anecdotes about his Excellency, for whom she had the greatest affection. Indeed, I never should have understood him so well had it not been for the various traits of his character she gave me. She told me on several occasions that she always thought of him as a Nathaniel, without guile—'*ohne Falsch.*'

Great was my joy when the Meister recovered; and when he sent for me to play to him, I brought him his own arrangement of Chopin's E Minor Concerto, at which I had worked so hard in the fortnight during which I had not seen him, that I could play the whole piece from memory without the slightest hesitation. And here comes in an amusing instance of the way in which the intentions of composers are often misunderstood.

The room in which I practised adjoined that of an extremely cultivated and refined old gentleman, who professed to have heard Chopin play very often, in a country house where they both used to visit for weeks together. He had heard me play many of Chopin's compositions; and assuming the privilege of age, and (as he himself said) of superior knowledge and experience, he commented freely on my rendering of Chopin, as being far too strictly in time, and he often told me that Chopin played his compositions with much freedom, and many variations in the *tempo*. Whilst I was practising the Concerto which I was preparing to play to Henselt, my self-constituted mentor has come more than once in the course of a morning, 'just to offer me suggestions,' as he chose to term them. The result of all this well-meant but unsound advice was, that I tried to turn the Concerto into a sensational piece, something in the style of the Liszt *Rhapsodies Hongroises;* and when I went to play it to Henselt, I had not the slightest doubt that he would be much pleased at what my self-constituted master called 'a very spirited and genial interpretation of the composition.' Hardly, however, had I begun playing the piece, when Henselt moved away quietly into the next room, saying as he did so, 'You may play on, for I can hear you just as well in the next room as here.' I accordingly did play on, and reached the end of the piece, having, as I imagined, accomplished something for which I should have some cordial words of approval! But little did I dream of what was in store for me—little did I anticipate what would happen when the piece had come to an end! It was a scene I never shall—never can forget. Henselt rather rushed than walked into the room, and addressed me in loud and angry tones. 'What sort of playing is this? And whatever can you mean by all these changes in the *tempo?*' I was beginning to answer him, I believe, by saying something about 'tempo rubato;' but he motioned me imperiously from the piano, and, sitting down to it himself, played the Concerto in a manner which, better than any words, demonstrated to me that, in seeking to give a warm and poetic reading to that over which I had no real mastery, the result was but 'a complete caricature.' Still I had courage enough left to ask him if I might try to play it to him just to show him that I understood what he wished. 'No, no,' was the angry reply, 'I won't listen to you; you have studied it all wrong, and you cannot in a moment make it all at once right. I see, I see! if I were to give you thirty or forty lessons' (his own words), 'I should still have to begin afresh, for you are not in my school.' At that moment I luckily bethought me of Bach's fugues, some of which I have always had under my fingers, and I asked him if he would allow me to play one or two of these to him. He consented, but it was only to say repeatedly in an angry tone as he listened to me, 'To be able to play these so well, and yet do so badly in the Concerto! I will now try what you can do with Cramer.' He left the room for a moment, and returning with some music in his hand, said, 'Here, take that,' and gave me the first book of the Studies, and told me to come to him again as soon as I was prepared to play three or four of these to him. This whole scene had greatly excited, harassed, and perplexed me, and on leaving the villa of Von Henselt I carried the music up to my rooms in the inn, and going off to take a walk, remained out for hours, quite oblivious of the fact that I had not eaten any dinner.

The question which I debated with myself was, What was to be done? and the answer was not easy to find, for, look round where I would, it was pretty clear to me that, for what I just then wanted, Henselt, and Henselt alone, was the man. But, then, he lived in St. Petersburg, and only came to Warmbrunn every summer; and, moreover, he had told me over and over again that I was not in his school (inferring by this expression that I was not in a fit condition to receive all that he wished to impart). At first I thought of remaining in Germany, and getting some pupil of his to drill me; but I heard from his wife that there was no one in the country who was, in his opinion, qualified to initiate one thoroughly into the school; and so I let the matter rest for a few days, and after preparing four studies of Cramer, went again to Henselt.

This time I had worked just as if I were studying Bach's preludes and fugues, and was myself by no means dissatisfied with what I had done after but four days of practice. Henselt heard me play the first study without interrupting me or making any remark, but when he sat down and played it himself, I was in utter despair at my own miserably unsatisfactory tones; and when he not only played No. III., but gave me a lesson in the left hand of this study, I caught such a glimpse of possible perfection that I was at once crushed and enchanted—crushed with an overpowering sense of my own utter dilettanteism, and enchanted with what was presented to me as even a distant possibility.

Setting off again for a long walk after this lesson, and turning all possible plans over and over in my mind, it all at once flashed on me that Mademoiselle Ranuschewitz (the young lady already alluded to as having taken such a prominent position at the Liszt afternoons) lived in St. Petersburg, and that if I went there she might be perhaps induced to drill me into the school. I said nothing to Henselt about what I thought of doing until I had fully made up my mind on the subject, and I did not do so for nearly a week after the idea had first occurred to me. I went then to his house, intending to ask him for the young lady's address; but I heard that he was out walking with a granddaughter of Frau von Henselt's, who was staying just then for a few weeks on a visit. The postman, whom I met as I left the villa, handed me some music for which I had written to St. Petersburg a week or two before, and, holding the parcel in my hand, I came back to the little inn where I lived, and found to my surprise that Henselt and his granddaughter were sitting outside in the porch. He saw the parcel of music in my hand, and asked me to open it, and on my asking him for the address of Mademoiselle Ranuschewitz, he at once wrote it with a pencil on the cover of one of the pieces (which I still have), and then said, 'Why, what do you want with this address?'

I told him that I had quite made up my mind to go to St. Petersburg in order to make a thorough study of his method with Mademoiselle Katy Ranuschewitz, provided only that I could be sure of having a suitable home when I arrived there.

Henselt, who was at all times chary of speech, and, except on rare occasions, very undemonstrative, merely observed, 'You are doing the right thing.' Then, after a few minutes, he added, 'It is not to Mademoiselle Ranuschewitz, but to Mademoiselle Heinrichsen, that I should wish you to go, if you indeed follow up your plan. She is, indeed, no artist like the former, but she has taught for twenty-five years in the Imperial Institutes, and she is, of all my teachers, the one who understands my method best.'

I wrote, accordingly, to this lady, and asked her if it would be possible to find a nice family who would give me rooms and board, for that by Henselt's advice I wished to study his method under her guidance. I also asked her if she could arrange to meet me at the railway-station on my arrival in St. Petersburg; for, as I did not know a word of Russian, I should not be able to direct the coachman where to drive me.

Henselt must, I believe, have written to her about me, for she replied without any delay, and all she said seemed most clear and satisfactory. She promised to meet me at the railway-station, and to accompany me to a hotel, where I could remain until I had seen and decided on one among the various lodgings which she hoped to have found for me.

All this time, curiously enough, I had never dreamed of becoming Henselt's pupil in St. Petersburg; for the mother of Mademoiselle Ranuschewitz told me that her daughter was the only private pupil that Henselt had ever had, and on my repeating this to Henselt one day in Warmbrunn, with a view to feeling my way with him, he had said, 'It is true.' From this I had naturally got the impression that Henselt only taught in his official capacity as Inspector of the Imperially-endowed Schools, and that Mademoiselle Katy actually was the only one who had ever had a private lesson from him; whereas what both the mother of the young lady and Henselt himself meant to say was that she was the only one who had ever been from first to last Henselt's pupil, without the intervention of a preparatory teacher. It had been Henselt's custom in all other cases to let a preparatory teacher give the pupil a grind, and thus smooth the way for him, and obviate the necessity for his descending to the level of the pupil. Of this I knew nothing whatever, and, going to Russia to study the Henselt method, the utmost I had allowed myself to hope was that he might possibly allow me to play to him now and then — at the most, perhaps, once in six or eight weeks.

Being under the impression, therefore, that I

might not for a long time have an opportunity of again playing to Henselt, I was very anxious, before I had the last lesson at Warmbrunn, to show him that I had in a measure understood both what he wished me to lay aside and what he wished me to aim at. I took, therefore, his beautiful study, *Entschwundenes Glück*, practising each hand by itself, very slowly, note by note, for nearly a fortnight during the time that I was also playing Cramer's studies. He was kind enough to let me play it to him the day before he left Warmbrunn. At the end of about a line he called out, 'Rosalie, Rosalie!' and when his aged wife came in he bade her in a pleased tone 'Stay and listen to the Miss,' and when I had concluded, he said that he was sure Scharwencka would be very much pleased with what I had been doing. Both he and dear Frau von Henselt were as hearty and cordial to me that day as if they had been my own relations; and, as I was going away, both kissed me, and he said, with a ring in his rough voice, which I now recall with a glow of pleasure, '*Solche momente machen das Leben angenehm.*' Yet this was not my good-bye to Henselt, for their housekeeper told me that he received all friends who wished to say good-bye to him early in the morning, about an hour before his departure.

It was the habit of his friends in Warmbrunn, as well as in St. Petersburg, to bring him a bouquet as a parting greeting. I happened to be the first to arrive at the villa, and was shown in while he and his wife were sitting at breakfast. One could see that Frau von Henselt was much moved, notwithstanding her firm self-control. She must have felt that I understood her, and she pressed my hand in silence, and took the opportunity of his Excellency rising for a moment to ask the servant some question about a parcel, to whisper to me, 'Have I not great courage?' After a minute or two I heard noises outside, and perceiving that a group of friends was coming up to the door, I thought that it was high time for me to depart. But the bouquet, there it was, still in my hand; I had not the least idea in what way I was expected to present it. I rose, therefore, to take leave, and would have laid it down on the table and gone away without saying any more, but the Meister had, I suppose, noticed my embarrassment, and came to my rescue by saying, '*Nun, mein Kind, reichen Sie mir doch das Bouquet.*' Then the old couple wished me good-bye in the most affectionate manner, and I left the villa.

I went up to Berlin from Warmbrunn, and spent a few days in providing myself with all I could possibly need for 'a winter in the north.' Henselt's niece (my friend) and I talked by the hour about all that I was to see and find there; and on the night I left for St. Petersburg she put round my neck a pretty little snow-white fleecy muffler, which was the work of her own hands. She also put into my hand-bag a nice sandwich of chopped meat, well seasoned with various sweet herbs, saying to me as she did so, 'This is one of my uncle's (Henselt's) favourite dishes.'

I had not, through all the rush and whirl of these days, forgotten the Steinecke-Clarkes. On reaching Berlin, I at once went to look for them. I wished much to tell them all that had happened to me since we had last seen each other—wished to show them that I was coming very near their school. Even at that early stage of my tone-perceptions I felt that Herr Deppe's method had some points of analogy with the school of Henselt. They, however, had gone to live in Charlottenburg, and, much as I desired to see them, I could not give an entire day to going out there. I wrote, therefore, to them—told them I was going to St. Petersburg on a given day, and begged of them to come and see me before I started. They, however, did not realize that the journey was quite a settled thing. I suppose my letter had not been sufficiently explanatory, for they did not reply for a day or two, and it was not until the morning of the day I left that I had a card from them to say 'It was impossible I could have so suddenly decided on going so far,' and begging me to wait a little—to come out and see them. For the next few days they would not be able to come into Berlin; but surely I could not be in such a hurry to go to Russia. Though they were too busy to come to Berlin for the next day or two, could not I come out to them?

But the day of my departure could not be altered. Mademoiselle Heinrichsen had arranged to meet me at St. Petersburg on a given day, and if I put off my journey she could not have found another leisure time for ten days at least; so, to my intense regret, I was obliged to write and tell the Steinecke-Clarkes that I could not possibly wait. Meanwhile Henselt had written me a very long letter, which I was obliged to ask his niece to decipher, as his handwriting resembled nothing so much as Egyptian hieroglyphics. His niece was very much pleased with this proof of her uncle's cordial interest in me. No father writing to a daughter about to take a long journey could have given more minute directions. He omitted nothing— even to an exhortation to avoid much hand-luggage. He also told me what to do on the frontier, where, he said, my baggage would be somewhat minutely examined. He described Mademoiselle Heinrichsen as '*eine hohe Erscheinung*.' And then, anticipating all possibilities, he enclosed me the address of a hotel, and also a card, addressed to Mademoiselle Heinrichsen in the Russian character, telling her where she would find me. This, of course, was to provide for the event of her being unable to meet me.

Before I speak of my arrival at St. Petersburg, I hope there is no harm in relating what the Steinecke-Clarkes thought of my journey to Russia. I had hardly been a week in St. Petersburg when I received a long and very interesting letter from Mr. Clarke, written in the heat of great indignation at what I had done, and great disappointment at his having failed to win me for their school. Mr. Steinecke-Clarke was, as I have before said, a burning enthusiast; but he was more than this—he was a fanatic who neither would nor could recognise any possible salvation for anyone who was outside his musical creed. His letter (some expressions of which I shall quote as characteristic of the earnest and downright nature of the man) did not, however, in the least disturb or disquiet me, for I could quite understand the way in which he viewed the matter. I had, moreover, my own firm conviction of being about to make the right start, and I felt sure that when we again met, he would not be able to refuse me some partial recognition of this. Finally, the letter, from first to last, showed me that he believed I had been actuated in my decision by motives which were just as foreign to my nature as they would have been to his own.

I had, he said, 'found a pearl of great price,' and had passed it by for the sake of getting in amongst people of rank and fashion; for he had, somehow, like many others, got the notion that Henselt lived *en prince* in St. Petersburg, and that he was in constant intercourse with Russian princes and princesses. Mr. Clarke had most absurdly taken it into his head that I was to be introduced into these circles as an Englishwoman of birth, and have my attainments lauded and praised up to the skies. He said I had disdained to become as a little child, and enter the kingdom by the 'strait gate'; and he wound up his exordium by applying to me the words of Holy Scripture, 'Many are called, but few are chosen.'

To this letter I replied by telling him that I believed he had understood me better. I hoped he would at least have given me credit for an unalloyed and pure devotion to art for its own sake—a love into which not an iota of worldliness or calculation had ever entered. I said that, so far from having the prospect of any social pleasure, I was likely to lead when in St. Petersburg a life of seclusion, which might be almost compared to that of the monks of La Trappe. I told him Henselt was advanced in life, and had for many years withdrawn himself from court circles and general society, and that he lived wholly for his vocation as teacher, in a circle of intimate friends, none of whom I might ever know; that before going to Russia I had seen enough of Henselt to feel sure that, as far as he was concerned, I need never reckon on seeing him except when he gave me a lesson, and that as yet I was not far enough advanced in the school even for this. I finally begged him and his admirable wife to reserve all they chose to think against the Henselt school until we should meet again.

The next time I passed through Berlin, however, they were no longer in Charlottenburg, but had gone with an infant son born after I went to Russia to Chicago.

When I left Berlin, in the first week of October, I was quite under the impression that when I reached St. Petersburg I should find myself in the midst of a northern winter. My friend (Henselt's niece) had the same idea as myself, and she had been very urgent with me to wear every imaginable garment, both visible and invisible, which should render me impervious to the cold, which both she and I imagined would be intense. This very natural miscalculation on her part and mine very nearly, however, prevented my being discovered by Mademoiselle Heinrichsen.

I had heard from Henselt's housekeeper that Mademoiselle Heinrichsen was no longer young, and that her hair was getting gray. Accordingly, when I got out of the *coupé*, and could see no one on the platform whose appearance at all answered to the above description, I became very anxious. Once, twice, thrice had I paced the entire length of the platform, and I knew not what to think, what to do. The porters, too, were very officious, and every time I laid my hand-parcels (against which his Excellency had warned me so earnestly) on a bench, I found them being carried off by one of the fraternity, who made signs to me that he was willing to find a cab into which to put them and their owner. I had to rescue my parcels, indeed, more than once, not only by gesticulating at the man, but actually taking hold of him.

When I had nearly given up all hope of seeing Mademoiselle Heinrichsen, I observed that a lady had once or twice passed and repassed me, and after half pausing, as if uncertain what to do, had walked on again. I imitated her movements. The next time she passed me, I too stopped, looked, and seemed to hesitate. She then addressed me, and asked me if I was looking for anyone.

'Yes,' I replied; 'can you be Mademoiselle Heinrichsen?'

She echoed my words with a change of name at the end of the query, and we both were not a little surprised and amused to find each other quite different from the description which our mutual friends had given of us. Henselt's housekeeper had spoken of Mademoiselle Heinrichsen as I have said, and as she had been twenty-five years teaching in the Imperial Institutes, I was prepared to see a settled-looking and middle-aged person, instead of this tall and young-looking lady, whose black hair only showed a silver thread here and there when she had her hat off, and sat near one indoors.

She had heard of a lady in a black hat with a crimson feather, and she saw one clad in fur from head to foot; for not only had I on a fur-lined mantle which completely covered my dress, but my face was fenced in with a large brown felt bonnet, also trimmed with fur. As I have said, I had expected to find myself, when I reached St. Petersburg, in the midst of frost and snow. It was, however, still quite like summer, and my reader can picture my sufferings in all this winter gear. My first thought, on reaching the hotel to which Mademoiselle Heinrichsen brought me, was to open my boxes and get into some lighter attire.

In spite of Mademoiselle Heinrichsen's promise to seek for me a suitable home, she had only been able to find three families willing to receive me, who all, however, lived in flats, where the rooms were so small and the accommodation was so limited, that I felt it would not be possible for me to settle down quietly to work in any of them.

I was much disheartened by this discovery, and returned to the hotel much perplexed as to what should be done. The next day, about noon, I was writing letters in my room, when the waiter came up to ask if I would see a young lady who had asked for me. When I looked at the card which he handed me, and perceived that the name Heinrichsen was written on it, I told him to show her upstairs at once: it was not, however, the Mademoiselle Heinrichsen whom I had already seen, but a younger sister who had come, she said, to show me some other quarters which her sister had heard of that morning. My hopes accordingly rose, and putting on my things, I sallied forth with Mademoiselle Nadine; but our quest on this day proved just as great a failure as on the previous one. We spent three or four hours in a most unsatisfactory manner, and saw nothing that was in the least suitable for me. My cicerone and I were both very tired, and she proposed our going to rest a little at her sister's, and telling her how we had fared. We accordingly got into a tram-car and drove, and it seemed to me a long, long distance before we reached the house where Sophie Petrowna lived. The servant told us that her mistress was at dinner, and showed us into a pretty drawing-room.

Sophie Petrowna presently appeared, and seemed much surprised to hear that I had not cared to engage any of the rooms we had seen that day. 'You must be tired,' she said kindly: 'will you not come in and have something to eat?' I assured her that I was far too anxious and worried to have any appetite; but she would take no refusal, and opening the folding-door, she brought me into the dining-room, saying as she did so, 'Now I am going to give you a great pleasure.' And there sat the Meister! And though he did not greet my appearance with any special word, I could see that he was pleased, and I quote here, as very characteristic of him, that when Mademoiselle Heinrichsen again asked me if I would not eat something, he broke in, before I had time to reply with, 'Can't you make her take it, and don't be asking it?' I was, however, not disposed to eat, but took a little coffee when it was brought in.

Mademoiselle Heinrichsen then asked me if I would be able to direct the cabman where he was to drive me, and if I knew how to pronounce the name of the hotel and street in which I lived. On my replying that I could not, she uttered some strange sounds, which I did my best to imitate; but it would appear that my attempts were not very successful, for the Meister stopped all further repetition with the exclamation, 'No one will be able to understand that; the Miss will never be able to go home by herself.' Then, with a sudden thought, addressing me across the table, 'Now, look at me, and pronounce slowly after me what you hear me say.' Then, syllable by syllable, he pronounced the address of both hotel and street; and whether it was the influence of his will, or his extremely distinct articulation of the sounds, or both combined, I cannot say; but after imitating him two or three times, he said, 'That will do very well.' And the two sisters laughed and said, 'You will make her do anything.' I then got up from table in order to put on my things, which were in the other room; and Henselt, rising from the table a minute after, was much amused at finding me repeating to myself the new and strange sounds which I had just acquired from him.

In wishing me good-bye he only uttered one word; but that one word was better to me than a dozen of the current commonplaces. That word was '*Willkommen*,' and was accompanied by a cordial grasp of the hand and a glance of warm and kindly interest. I had naturally not liked to make my difficulties a subject of conversation at the dinner-table; but when by myself once more in the hotel I began to feel very worried and perplexed. Mademoiselle Nadine had suggested my living in the hotel—a thing I had never thought of doing; for it was not only expensive, but miles away from where her sister lived, and also from Henselt; and I felt pretty sure that, for anyone who wished to practise much, the hotel would not be a suitable place to reside.

There seemed no chance of anything, and I had been already three or four days in the hotel, when I made the discovery that there was a German paper published in St. Petersburg, and, going to the office of this paper, I advertised. The family of a retired officer answered my advertisement, offering me two large airy rooms and board in their house. Mademoiselle Heinrichsen accompanied me there, in order to assist me in making the necessary arrangements. I was charmed to find that it was only ten minutes' walk from the street in which Henselt lived. I at once decided on going there, and on the following day I arrived, preceded by a grand piano, and settled myself down.

Before I had had my first lesson from Mademoiselle Heinrichsen, a little *contretemps* occurred which, had I not spoken out my mind then and there, would have materially damped the energy which made my studies with her so successful.

As I have said, I had come to St. Petersburg without being aware that Henselt had a large number of private pupils, and imagining, as I have already said, that the most I might hope or expect from him was an occasional examination as to the progress I was making in his school. I was, therefore, utterly confounded to hear a young lady whom I met in a house to which I had gone with a letter of introduction from Frau von Henselt observe that she must go away now, for she had to play to Henselt by-and-by. She played very nicely, but it was the playing of a young, and not by any means a gifted, girl; and when she told me that she went to his Excellency every fortnight, I was astonished, and somewhat hurt that he had not offered to teach me.

I did not know that this young girl (a teacher) had not only been taught from her childhood by one of Henselt's best lady-professors, but that, like all the pupils who had not reached a certain standard, she always had one or two preparatory lessons from a lady in the interval between each visit to Henselt. Knowing nothing of all this, I ran home in a state of great agitation, and wrote a long letter to Henselt, to the effect that, in coming to St. Petersburg to study his method, I had indulged in no hopes of being in any way specially favoured by him; but if he gave lessons to Fräulein B——, he surely might give them to me. That, whether he did so or not, I meant to carry out what I had planned to do in coming to Russia, but

that I feared it would not be with real energy and
spirit if I felt that I was to be left outside, whilst
others were having that which I so much prized. I
posted this, and then retired to rest. But it was not
until morning that I closed my eyes, and when I
woke up, and the whole thing came back to me, it
was with a feeling of alarm that I recalled my letter
to Henselt, for I had written in a state of great excitement, and I dared hardly think how he might take
it. I wrote it alternately in French and German.
When my German failed me, I fell back on French,
and *vice versâ*. Henselt did not, however, leave me
long in suspense; he walked in himself quite early in
the morning to see me, and his first words of greeting
were :

'Such a long letter, my dear, and so many needless
words! You shall, if you like to do so, have regular
lessons from me in three weeks' time. But, believe
me, once you have begun to study with Mademoiselle
Heinrichsen, you will so thoroughly understand my
reasons for insisting that all who study with me shall
first pass through her hands, that you yourself will
scarcely wish to leave her in so short a time.'

Impressed, convinced, and consoled by his words, I
went off with a light heart on the same day to have
my first lesson from Mademoiselle Heinrichsen. She
asked me to show her how I practised the scales, what
finger-exercises I used, and how I set about practising
my pieces.

In going to her I had not the slightest doubt of my ability to accomplish all I wanted, at least so far as comprehension went, in a few lessons. But how soon did I learn my mistake! For genuine *technique* is full of subtle problems, and all *virtuosi* will bear me out when I say that no one, however intelligent, can pretend to give an authoritative dictum as to the merits or demerits of any school or system, unless he has himself put his neck into the yoke, and submitted himself with a child's docility to the regular drill of that system.

After I had shown Henselt's drill-mistress how I was accustomed to work, she placed Henselt's *Études préparatoires* on the music-desk, and said, 'Now we are going to tire, and perhaps to hurt, your fingers.'

I laughed at the notion, and said, 'I don't see how you will manage that, for my fingers never tire, not even if I play for hours; and my hand, as you see, is just like a piece of indiarubber.'

Her reply was to place my hand and my fingers in a given position on the keyboard; and telling me to keep them so, she pointed to certain studies, and made me play them many times in succession. I began doing so, and being conscious of no fatigue and no strain of any kind for the first few times, I met her inquiring glance with a smile. After a few more repetitions, however, I began to feel it; it became more and more of an effort to keep on. After a moment or two this effort became so distressing that, though resolved not to give in, I was obliged to stop at last, and say, 'I cannot go on any longer!'

This was the beginning of my initiation into the Henselt *technique*. I learned that day how to practise scales, octaves, thirds, etc. Then opening the first book of Cramer's Studies, my instructress showed me how to begin, and step by step to build up—a process which, when faithfully and patiently carried out, must result in a comparative mastery of these fine studies. As this book is not intended as a guide, either to *technique* or to the right method of practising pieces, I shall not enter into details regarding my lessons with Mademoiselle Heinrichsen. Suffice it that, after going to her two or three times, I was deeply interested, and entirely satisfied that I was getting something definite—something which would enable me to develop my hand, and help me to approach all pianoforte compositions in such a manner that, if I only had strength and patience to persevere, I should succeed in taking, at all events, the first step towards artistic perfection.

I now recognised that all that I had done heretofore had been mere dilettantism. In thinking it all over, I felt that it was extremely probable that, in descending from the height on which I had stood as a *dilettante*, I might never be able to get up to an equal height as an *artist*, but I resolved anyhow to be *on the road* thither; and thus

I so fully appreciated what Mademoiselle Heinrichsen was giving me, that I cordially acquiesced in her wish that I should not go to Henselt until I had been with her at least five or six weeks. She herself, however, was so pleased with the result of a few lessons, that she spoke warmly to Henselt about me, and excited his curiosity to know what I had been doing.

Meeting me on the staircase of a house where I was visiting, he stopped me and said, 'Well, when are you coming to me?'

'No hurry for that, dear Meister,' I replied. 'I am full of my work.'

But when I came home the next evening, after having had a long lesson from Mademoiselle Heinrichsen, what was my surprise to hear that Henselt was sitting in the drawing-room, chatting with my host and hostess!

I thought, as they were old acquaintances of his, the visit was probably meant for them, so I went at once to my own room. The daughter of the house, however, who had opened the door for me, came in a minute or two to fetch me; she said, 'His Excellency has come here to see you, and has been waiting for you a whole hour!'

How fresh and vivid it all seems now!—my hurry to get off my wraps, and not lose one of the precious few minutes which the Meister would still have to spare after waiting an entire hour!

He looked so genial, so vigorous, as he rated me

for taking a sleigh on my way home from Mademoiselle Heinrichsen instead of making use of the tramcars! I told him I could not, like the natives of the country, get in while the car was in motion—that I had never been accustomed to such feats. 'Nonsense!' was the reply: 'I am seventy years of age, and the trams have only been running for about ten years. I was sixty when I first made use of them. You who are so much younger—why should you say you can't do such a thing?' Thus encouraged, I felt bound to try, and in about a month's time I thought nothing of overtaking and getting into a tram-car, even when it was in rapid motion. To get out of it was not so easy, but after awhile I was able to accomplish this likewise.

After chatting for a few minutes longer, Henselt rose and took leave of my host and hostess. I thought he was going away, and would have accompanied him to the door. When we had reached the hall, however, he turned round and said he should like to see my rooms and piano. Almost his first words when we were alone were, 'Scharwencka is in St. Petersburg, and there is some talk of his getting an appointment in the Conservatorium, and so remaining here permanently. Perhaps you might wish to study with him again, and if you have such a wish, I shan't take it one bit amiss. He has paid me a visit, and has impressed me with the conviction that he is a very able, very gifted man.'

'I did not come all the way to St. Petersburg to study with anyone but yourself, dear Meister,' was my reply.

'Good,' he said; 'then we remain together—*dann bleiben wir beisammen.* But now I wish to hear you play, and you are to come to me on Friday next.'

But I respected my teacher's wishes, and at once said that although I was, of course, eager to begin with him, yet, since Mademoiselle Heinrichsen had taken such immense pains with me, I felt it right to consult her wishes, and to wait at least ten or twelve days more before coming to him.

He said with an amused look, 'I told you it would be so;' and after a little friendly chat he went away.

In about a fortnight after this I wrote to the Meister, and said I was ready to show him the result of my work with his teacher; and he at once named a day for giving me the first lesson, as to one belonging regularly to his school. I had worked during those weeks as I never believed that I could have worked again, since the days when I was preparing to take out the St. Cecilian diploma. But the work of getting into the Henselt *technique* and into the Henselt method of practising had not tired me, except in a very healthy way. My fingers often ached, and there were days during the first weeks when I could not have held the pen to write a long letter.

In this my first lesson with Henselt in St. Petersburg, I heard him for the first time in all his unveiled radiance as a *virtuoso;* for the reader may remember that it was on an upright Seiler that he had given his lessons in Warmbrunn, and though, even on a poor instrument, a great artist will make himself felt, still, it is as if he speaks through a mask. I can still recall the delight with which I listened to him as he played Cramer's Studies on his pet instrument (a concert grand Becker). He played Study No. 1, which I have heard him play many times since, and each time with increasing admiration and delight. Indeed, any piece which the Meister 'professed to play' always made me feel as I have done with no other artist—that the whole essence of a lifetime lay concentrated there for the moment, and that if—supposing such an *if* possible—he had played no other piece except just that one, he stood just by that one performance on a height where none could approach him. Study No. 1, as played by him, was simply a marvel of lovely elastic tones—pearls of unflawed beauty—and the whole floated in an atmosphere of poetic charm. In No. 3, where the left hand plays a two-part canto-firmo, the delicious fluid song of the treble floated and wound itself round the canto like some delicate arabesque round the shafts of a fluted column.

Henselt was as much pleased with what I had been doing as if he had received some rich gift for himself, and I was very happy that day. As I was going away he put into my hands Chopin's Study on the black keys, No. 9, Op. 25. This charming study has been much handled by Henselt, who has turned most of the single notes in the right hand into octaves, extended some of the chords in the left hand, and lengthened the close with a few bars, which are so delicate, so aerial, so fanciful, that they seem like a sort of ecstatic reverie on what has just gone before.

And here I must observe that if *anyone* might presume to add to or alter the 'written letter' of any composer, especially of Chopin, Henselt, who was inclined neither to diffuseness nor to self-glorification at the expense of art, might be allowed some little latitude in this direction. But I have convictions on this point which are very strong, and not likely to change. It is, I hold, a sacred duty to give back the thought which has been bequeathed to us by poet, musician, or painter in the exact form in which he left it behind him.

But to return to my studies as a pupil of the Henselt school. I valued Mademoiselle Heinrichsen's teaching so highly, that I went to her several times after my first lesson with Henselt; and then, with his sanction and approval, wished her good-bye, and worked on with him alone.

That first winter was chiefly devoted to Cramer and *technique;* but before the summer came, I had played some of Henselt's own Studies, one or two *Nocturnes* of Chopin, and many of Bach's preludes and fugues (in which Henselt made me play all the shakes), and some of Moscheles' Studies.

The reader will, I fancy, like to have some description of Henselt's house and of his ways; and he, I know, would not have objected to my giving this somewhat in detail, for he was much amused when a German periodical described the castle in Görlitz, where many years ago he and his wife lived in palatial style. This paper even quoted conversations in which he had taken a prominent part, and made no attempt to conceal the names of the persons who were referred to.

I fancied that Henselt, when in St. Petersburg, lived in a large mansion, that he had an equipage and a retinue of servants, and I was much surprised to find that he had only a first floor, consisting of five or six rooms. Going through the hall and up to the first floor, one read in Russian characters, on a plate at the right-hand side of the outer door, 'Excellency von Gensel' (there is no *h* in the Russian language).

On ringing the bell, his servant-man, if it was in the winter, helped you to take off all your outdoor attire—goloshes, cap, etc.—and then ushered you into the ante-room, a small, one-windowed room, where all the furniture was covered with holland of spotless whiteness.

On a grand piano, which occupied the entire length of the wall between door and window, several kinds of outdoor caps lay ready for use; and his Excellency's gloves, varying in texture and thickness, were placed in the greatest order beside the caps. On the wall opposite the piano all Henselt's outdoor wraps were hanging, and in the pocket of whichever he was going to wear there would be a pocket-handkerchief, which his housekeeper had placed there, having first scented it with eau-de-Cologne. She herself showed me all these details during one of the occasions when her master was absent from St. Petersburg, on a journey of inspection which his official duties as inspector-general obliged him to take through Russia. Leaving the ante-room, one entered the master's sanctum, where he worked, wrote, and lived, but in which he very seldom gave a lesson. Two grand Becker pianofortes stood side by side, near the windows. There was a cosy fireplace, an armchair, with side-rests for lamp and books; and on the walls hung the portraits of various friends in very different walks of life, which by the style in which they were done, and the frames in which they were enclosed, all gave me the idea of 'long, long ago.'

Indeed, the first impression one felt as one entered the rooms, was that everything there, and the very way that everything was arranged, was just what one would have found there more than half a century ago. Chairs, pictures, mirrors, and their mouldings, all were 'out of date,' but all was in the most perfect order; everything shone as though not a particle of dust could ever be tolerated there.

To the right of the music-desk on each piano was a small oval tray, containing several pencils cut ready for use, indiarubber inserted in wood, and last, not least, a piece of pumice-stone with which Henselt used to file his nails—for he never used either a pair of scissors or a knife to cut them.

Everything in his rooms was for comfort, convenience, and work; there was nothing merely elegant, nothing superfluous. His favourite instrument was still in splendid condition, though it had been over twenty years in his possession. He never worked upon this instrument; he only played on it the pieces which he had conquered upon the other. On the other, rendered mute by means of a sordine, he wrestled out his tone-problems. It was by labour such as this that he approached the great ideal of perfection towards which his whole life was one continued striving.

From the Meister's sanctum one passed into his sleeping-room, of which the housekeeper insisted on showing me every detail during one of his visits to Moscow. Here, too, all was old-fashioned, simple, and solid; but here, too, all was in exquisite order. His brushes all in a row; his reading-glasses by themselves; his writing-table, his drawers, and all their contents so systematically neat, that even in the dark he could lay his hand on anything that was wanted without a moment's loss of time.

And now that I allude to order, I feel bound to say that all who studied with Henselt found that they were learning from him a good deal more than music. If there was a spot or even a crease on a cover of the piece brought to him, a new cover had to be supplied. No pupil ever dared to lay one piece inside another on the desk when playing to him; the first piece was to be removed before the other was laid on the music-desk. This precision was carried into all that one studied. The shakes, for instance, and their fingering, must be all written out, and likewise any passage in which there was a difficulty in the fingering; and he insisted that all this should be done so clearly and with such exactness, that anyone who took up the piece on which this was written out could make no mistake as to what was intended.

Some of Henselt's friends and pupils were inclined to turn me into ridicule for saying that to be under him was to be in 'Die Schule der Demuth'—the school of humility. But when the Meister heard the expression, he gave a cordial smile of approval and looked well pleased. He did, indeed, stimulate his pupils to strive and aim at virtuosity, yet the special tendency of his teaching—a tendency which should be the true end of all earnest study—was to awaken and intensify in those who came under his influence a perception and appreciation of an excellence lying beyond their reach—a perception and appreciation which are more to its possessors than any degree of personal attainment.

This first winter in Russia I did not quite understand the Meister, and often thought him rude, when he was really trying to help me, and doing me the best service one human being can ever do to another, by speaking out the truth without putting on any gloss or varnish to make it pleasant. He expected one to start the time of a piece in a very decided manner, and to come in with the greatest exactness in the middle or end of a bar before which there had been a rest or a pause. Everything that he ever said on these points remained indelibly impressed on my mind, because he had been so severe in his manner of pointing out the delinquency, that the blow to one's *amour propre* left an ineffaceable mark behind it. When I knew him better, I used to tell him it was giving one a moral 'box on the ear,' when he would say, 'That has been studied like a dilettante;' or, 'What would the orchestra do if you came in with such an uncertain beat?' or again, if there was any deviation from a fingering which had been fixed on, 'Yes, it is the same to *you*, I suppose, what finger you put there.'

Besides this, he often seemed to go out of his way just in order to come tilt against one's *amour propre*, and tear one's self-esteem into shreds. He would say, after himself recommending a piece, and knowing perfectly well that it had been only studied for a week or ten days, 'Such a piece one may make a study of; but to *play* it—no, that is the work of a lifetime;' and then he would sit down and play it two or three times in succession, each time working himself more deeply into it.

Summer came at last, and though I meant to return to Great Britain and see all my friends, yet I was deep in the charm of the school, and the only consideration that hindered me from at once going to Warmbrunn was the fact that it would be only on the old Seiler that I should hear Henselt play, and have any lessons he might be pleased to give me. I thought of going to Liszt, who had, I was told, expressed much interest in me; and Mademoiselle Ranuschewitz and I had almost arranged to go off together. I did not, however, think it quite the thing to carry out this plan without consulting Henselt. Accordingly, at my next lesson, I asked him whether he would approve of my studying with Mademoiselle Ranuschewitz during the summer, as we thought of going to Liszt together. He did not say much, either for or against, that day; after the following lesson, however, he rather surprised me by the quaint question, 'Warum spekuliren Sie auf Fräulein Ranuschewitz, und nicht auf mich?' I replied that I had been rather spoiled in St. Petersburg, always having my lesson on a grand piano, and that he must know it was not quite the same thing to hear him play on the old Seiler as on his own beautiful Becker. He then told me that the Bechsteins had offered to send him down one of their grand pianos for the summer, and that his wife had been trying to persuade him to accept. 'But,' he said, in quite a cross tone, 'if I have a good piano, people will be asking me to play.' 'Asking you!' I said. 'Why, dear Meister, who could presume to take such a liberty with you?' 'Well,' he said, 'they'll be wishing me to play.' 'Who could blame them for that?' I replied. Then he said, in a very tough manner, 'Sie wollen die letzten Lebenskräfte eines alten Mannes, und die will ich ihnen gar nicht geben.' I saw, however, that he was undecided; so, waiting till the last moment, I summoned up my courage for a bold stroke, and just as I was saying good-bye to him I made the audacious speech, 'If you will comply with your wife's wishes, dear Meister, you will see me at Warmbrunn.' Then I was so frightened at my own boldness that I ran off, without giving him time to make me any reply. I knew that if he had once said 'No,' nothing would induce him to change his mind afterwards.

Before my next lesson I heard, to my great delight, in an incidental manner, from Mademoiselle Heinrichsen, that the Meister was going to have a Bechstein sent to Warmbrunn for the summer.

Upon this I, of course, decided to go to Warmbrunn. Mademoiselle Ranuschewitz was much disappointed at having to go to Weimar without me. I left St. Petersburg at the end of May, about the same time that Henselt set out for Warmbrunn. I went to stay with some friends in Berlin for a week or two on my way to Warmbrunn, and, while sitting out in the garden, my ankles were so bitten by mosquitoes—which are very troublesome in Berlin—that I could scarcely move the day before I left. I made light of it, however, and started. But when I reached Warmbrunn, after travelling all night, my ankles were so much inflamed that I was obliged to send a message to Frau von Henselt, begging her to send me a doctor. This gentleman arrived in the course of an hour or so, and told me I would have to keep my room for some days, as I was suffering from blood-poisoning, which had brought on erysipelas.

He was not long gone before Henselt and his wife appeared in my room, asked me what the doctor had said, and looked all round to see what might be possibly wanting for my comfort. When they went home, Frau von Henselt sent her maid round to me with a large hair pillow, her own cosy dressing-slippers, and her own handbell; for in Warmbrunn, bells, as we have them—rung by wires through the walls—are, if not quite unknown, looked on as a luxury in which every householder does not indulge.

Next day I felt very ill, and had to keep my bed, and the Von Henselts came again to see me; the

Meister also came by himself quite early in the morning, to hear how I had passed the night.

The following day was Sunday, and I was still very ill and feverish, but, in spite of this, was rather enjoying a condition which brought into play so much affectionate sympathy from the dear old pair. Henselt came in on his way to church, and, without sitting down, began to fumble in his coat-pocket, and slowly drew out from thence a clumsy-looking parcel; and while I was in wonder as to what he could be bringing me, he opened the paper with an air of importance, and out came a bell, which he put on the chair beside my bed, saying as he did so, 'This is my own bell, child. The one which my wife sent you does not ring very loud, and I was thinking this morning that you might ring it more than once without being heard.'

That bell, when I had been long convalescent, and even when I moved out of the hotel into lodgings, still remained in my room. And one day, when Henselt had called to see me, I said to him, 'Your bell—don't you want to have it back?' But he looked dreamy and abstracted, and I confess that I felt very reluctant to part with it, and delayed to return it until the summer was over, and Henselt was about to leave for St. Petersburg. I then asked him one day, as we were walking in the 'promenade,' if I might keep it.

'The bell? Oh yes; but why do you want to keep it?'

'Well, dear Meister, I am afraid you will think me very silly, but——' I paused, and seeing that he, who liked everything to be clear and definite, was getting angry at my hesitation, I grew bold, and said, 'You looked so kind the day you brought the bell in your pocket and put it beside my bed, that I long to keep it—as a better memento of you than anything else you could ever give me.'

He looked kind, and grunted rather than gave an assent to my keeping the bell; and it has travelled with me twice since then from Germany to Russia, and back again, and then from England to Italy, and through Germany back to England.

That summer I had rooms in the house of a Polish lady, whom family troubles had led to seek rest and retirement in country life. She had a magnificent concert grand Steinway pianoforte in her drawing-room. Like many whom I have met from time to time, she had aspired towards art in her youth, and had been checked in these aspirations by the most natural circumstance in the world—marriage, and the care for and devotion to her husband and children—and yet, like all art-natures, that something in her being that was repressed and had not found an outlet, stirred and throbbed at times, and though it did not actually make her unhappy, yet it sometimes filled her with unrest. It was singular that she and I should chance to come together.

When she had heard me working for a few days, she came up to me, and in the sweetest and simplest way imaginable, said, 'How I long to do as you are doing! And,' in her simplicity, thinking that she was offering me an equivalent for what she now asked, 'what I came to say is—there is my piano; you will not find its match, even in Berlin, for hire. Do pray use it as much as you please, if you will but show me a little of this beautiful method.' She was rather surprised when I replied that I did not care to play on her grand pianoforte; that if she really had such an earnest desire to get an insight into the Henselt system, I would most willingly help her—on one condition, but only on one, *i.e.*, that she should begin right 'from the beginning,' which, as I was aware that she had a good deal of irregular facility, I feared, after all, she would scarcely like to do.

This Polish lady had, however, more power of self-renunciation than I had given her credit for; and she put her neck so thoroughly into the yoke that, after a few weeks of study, Henselt, on hearing her practise as he passed by the house, thought that I was recommencing some of the work I had been doing with him in the earlier part of the winter at St. Petersburg, and, meeting me out walking, said in a tone of remonstrance, 'Why do you begin again to work at that in which you are already pretty far?' He was surprised and much pleased when I told him it was not I whom he had heard, but a lady who had been only a few weeks in his school. I used to run down to her drawing-room from my quarters upstairs to set her right whenever during the first days I heard anything go wrong, and I gave her leave to come and listen to my practice.

That summer, besides playing much of both Moscheles and Cramer with Henselt, I played Chopin's Nocturne in C Minor, one in F Sharp Minor, the Ballade in A Flat, and two of his own concert studies. But if I had built up hopes of hearing him play on the Bechstein, I was doomed to be disappointed. He took a most violent antipathy to the little instrument almost from the first day he played on it, and during the whole summer it was only on two occasions that I heard him play an entire piece on it.

On one of these occasions I met two friends of his, who told me that he had promised to play some Cramer studies for them that morning. Though I had not been invited by Henselt to come, these old and privileged friends of his asked me to join them, telling me that, as I belonged to the inner and more intimate circle of the Villa von Henselt, I should no doubt be welcome there. But the old Meister was a strange being. When he saw me come in with the gentlemen, his salutation was, 'You here! I am going to play a few of Cramer's studies for my friend and these two gentlemen.' It was a delightful morning; ensconced quietly in the embrasure of a large bow-window, I heard that sweetest of all singers on the pianoforte play for more than an hour and a half. He began with Cramer, then he passed on to Moscheles, Weber, Chopin, and some of his own lovely studies.

The second time I heard him during this summer was at the invitation—I may say by the connivance—of Frau von Henselt, who invited me to come, but not to let myself be seen. Henselt had promised to give a lesson in 'si oiseau j'étais' to a lady who lived in Hirschberg, and his wife felt pretty certain that he would play a little for this lady. She brought me into the porch until he began to play, and then allowed me to come into the room close by, where there was no door, no wall—nothing but a curtain between us and the musician. There was a sad tone in his playing that morning, and when he began he was not up to his usual tone-plane. By degrees, however, he rose in all his greatness—suggesting to me a city rising by enchantment out of the dust of ages. It was a wonderful morning!

When it was over I stole away, and went off to walk and muse, and as I was returning homeward through the promenade, I met Henselt, who had come out to have a little walk before dinner. When he saw me he said (he knew that I usually dined at one o'clock, while his hour was two), 'What, not at dinner yet?'

'I have been listening at Villa Henselt, by the

permission of your wife,' I replied; 'and I felt that I must walk off a little of the excitement caused by your playing before being able to eat.'

'I am not pleased,' he said, 'that you should have heard me in my weakness; for,' he added, 'I have not been in the mood to-day — *heute war ich gar nicht aufgelegt.*'

'How can you say so, dear Meister,' I ventured to say — 'even though I can perceive that you vary, that you are not always on a height, that you have your low moments. But this only shows that you are human. You demand from yourself that which is given to no mortal being.'

He was not displeased at my frankness, but allowed me to stay and talk with him; and from day to day he and his wife grew kinder and more accessible to me.

A London friend, deeply interested in pianoforte-playing, who used to write and ask me many questions as to Henselt's method, told me he had heard, many years before, from Herr Schachner, that Henselt advised him, in playing, to imagine that he was sinking his fingers into warm wax. On my repeating this to Henselt, he said he had not spoken of warm wax. 'But I believe I have,' he said, 'told pupils to think that they are going to sink their fingers in dough.' This is but one instance of Henselt's abhorrence of anything inelastic. 'An ass,' he said once, 'can give the notes a knock like that!' And another time, when a pupil had come down with too hard an emphasis, he exclaimed in anger, 'You just come in there with the tramp of a trooper!'

It was a truly instructive summer, for besides having a lesson from him once every week, I had the advantage of being present at the lessons of two other pupils who also played to him every week.

He taught one lady Weber's *Concert Stück*; and I have heard him play it several times, though never the whole at a time.

His playing of Weber's *Momento Capricioso* was a marvel of delicate elastic tones, and he observed himself, after playing it (I entered it in my note-book at the time), 'It is not a question of hearing either nail, or bone, or flesh, but pure tone.'

It was one of Henselt's peculiarities that he would listen to the practice of a pupil, if he got the chance of doing so, and if he considered that the work was being done without conscience, he would observe the next time the pupil was playing to him, 'No wonder that you have not conquered that difficulty; you have been working with so little method.'

If you had practised the piece with both hands at the same time, instead of studying with each hand separately, he invariably perceived it, and would tell you so, and that in very plain language. If technical drill had been relaxed even for a few days, and yet the pieces seemed to be going well, he would suddenly surprise you with the observation, 'It is evident you have been of late giving your fingers but little nourishment.'

When the end of September came, and Henselt returned to St. Petersburg, I paid a visit to Great Britain, and had the gratification of convincing all those on whose opinion I set any value that in going to Henselt I had followed a true instinct, and that in the few months I had worked under his guidance I had got a very solid footing in the domain of true art. But I had not yet played any of the great concert concertos with him; and it was with the feeling that, even if I did not intend to play these in public myself, yet that it was imperative I should study them in order to be able to direct others, that I returned to St. Petersburg in the first week of the next January. On this my second visit I was received with great cordiality by various disciples of the Henselt school, with whom I had grown intimate during my former stay there.

I now looked upon Henselt as a sort of father, and being obliged to take temporary rooms while waiting to get something more suitable, I did not at once hire a piano, but went to practise at the Meister's house twice a day, in the morning from about twelve to two, and again between half-past five and eight or nine o'clock—for he was always out at these hours. On the third of these evenings, however, he happened to come into his rooms without my being aware of it, and after listening for a little to my practice, he startled me by walking in and saying, 'You are a little out of step, my child, and must come to me tomorrow.' I had been working at one of Moscheles' most difficult studies on the shake.

This winter I made an entry after every lesson of what I had played, and every single observation of Henselt's, whether favourable to me or not, stands recorded there.

He still insisted on my playing much of Cramer, for he held that to anyone who can play Cramer really well, everything else comes easy.

In February of this year I studied Mendelssohn's First Concerto with him, and had the great enjoyment of playing it three times on his grand Becker, he playing the second piano. His lessons on this composition were highly instructive, and I have noted down all that he said. He then told me to study Hummel's grand Concerto in B Minor, and before I had had a lesson in it he went off to Moscow for ten or twelve days. On his return I went round at once to ask when he would give me an hour; and I may mention as one of Henselt's characteristic traits, that although he *never* received a visit, yet when there was work in question he was always accessible, even if only for a moment, and would come out into his ante-room, notebook in hand, and saying without any preamble, 'Well, what do you want?' would at once settle to give the hour, note it in his book, and dismiss you without losing any time in complimentary salutations. But to return to Hummel's B Minor Concerto. When I went to play it to Henselt it had not been quite a fortnight under my fingers, and I knew quite well that I was only playing *notes*, and not music. But in a way specially and provokingly his own he observed, 'Yes! study that piece one may, and long enough too; but to play it—that is another thing!' And then he motioned me from the piano, and, a wonderful artistic mood coming over him, he played it as I knew full well that I should never hear it played again. That day he also played his own beautiful concert-study, *Danklied nach Sturm*. There was in Henselt's playing an element of pathos so deep, so tender, that in hearing him play the *Danklied* I was quite overcome by emotion, and being, like all English people, very averse to showing my feelings, I was very angry with myself, and tried to move away from beside the piano without being observed by the Meister. He, however, having no idea why I was moving away from beside him, called out in an angry tone, 'Stay quiet, please; stay where you are, and don't move away.' When he had finished he turned slightly round, and as I was looking right away from him, I felt rather than saw that he smiled to himself, and, beginning the piece again, he played it right to the end once more, thus giving me time to recover my self-possession. Those sweet and clear and most thrilling tones seemed to come right from his very heartstrings; an enchanting spell of beauty pervaded the whole. It was an old man who was breathing out a whole lifetime of sadness and disenchanted illusions in song. He said, indeed, once to me, in speaking of art, 'It is a compensation for the many disillusions with which life abounds.'

My next piece this winter was Beethoven's C Minor Concerto; and it was when studying this that I had a misunderstanding with Henselt which made me stay away from him three weeks, during which I neither inquired after him nor had a lesson. He sent his servant to me several times to say that I was to come and play to him; and each time I wrote back a courteous line to say I was not quite ready to go to him. To his wife, with whom I constantly corresponded, I wrote, however, a full account of the whole —the why and wherefore; and she, dear woman, wrote me a letter which I still possess, telling me that they both loved and valued me much, and that I must not mind her husband, I must bear with him, for it was *his way*. But I could not in a moment recover from what Henselt afterwards called 'a fit of touchiness.'

The two lady-professors who stood nearest to him, and were my friends, remonstrated with me more than once, and assured me that I was venturing on what they would never have dared to do; but it was not until I met the Meister on my way to church, after three weeks had elapsed, that the difference was smoothed over, and that in a very characteristic manner.

In passing Henselt's house on my way to church, I rather divined than actually saw that he was in the hall, and just coming out at the door. Knowing him to be short-sighted, I hoped by hurrying on to avoid a meeting. He had, however, seen me, and called out my name quite loud enough to attract my attention. I made, however, as if I had not heard him, and had nearly succeeded in entering the church door, when a lady who knew me (one of his lady-professors) came up with me, and saying, 'You must come and speak to the Meister, he is calling after you,' she put her arm through mine, and brought me back to the church gate, where Henselt had paused for a moment.

When I came towards him, slowly and reluctantly, his first words were, ' You have been very candid with my wife; why could you not have been the same with me ?'

'But are we not just going into church, dear Meister?' I rejoined, in a tone which suggested that here was neither time nor place for a discussion.

'True,' he replied; 'but mind you come to me the minute you come out of church.'

It was a curious interview that Sunday morning; for when I came into Henselt's sanctum, he pulled over a chair, and placing it opposite to his own, and as near as it well could be to him without touching him, he bade me sit down right opposite to him, and looking straight at me from under his bushy eyebrows, he said in a grave, but not an imperious manner, 'Now tell your grievance, and come to the point at once, without any rounds.'

I had, when in church, made up my mind that, as he seemed to wish for an explanation, I would speak, and tell him what I had touched on in my letter to his wife. And though his great eyes flashed more than once when I was speaking, he listened to all I said, and did not once interrupt me.

I began by telling him that I did not believe that anyone more fully realized than myself *who* he was, and to what an immeasurable height he towered above his *best* pupils—among whom I did not rank myself—but that I had my individuality, and had a right to have an opinion of my own, though my respect for him might hinder my expressing it audibly in his presence. I said that, if he told me a piece had been badly played in his hearing, I should never dream of calling that dictum in question; nor, if he said to me, 'Your ideal is not very high, or else you would not praise that'—even then I should not feel I had any right to feel hurt or vexed for his trying to set me right, if he thought me in the wrong; but, woman though I was, I would not bear to be told that the greatest *virtuoso* of the age had played Chopin's Study in C Sharp Minor below all criticism, on the bare word of a 'professor' (Henselt was not himself present at the concert). I fear I shall be thought very bold when I confess that I went on to say, 'If I don't know the difference between good and bad playing, especially in the performance of a piece which I have just been studying with you, dear Meister, the obvious conclusion at which any person with sense can arrive is, that I am a fool. But I do know the difference,' I said, 'and for this reason I am your disciple; and I fear not to say that the man who had the impertinence to criticise that beautiful reading of the Chopin Study was not worthy to hear it, and I still further venture to assert that it was envy that made him say it. You are our king, dear Meister,' I finally said; 'but surely you would not care to reign over slaves, but over those who have some faculty of thinking and judging for themselves.'

He listened to all this and never interrupted me; indeed, I believe he at least 'half' felt that I was in the right, but, of course, he would not say so. I had, he said, pushed his words to the most extreme conclusion possible—I had taken them in a much more personal sense than he had intended; I was very touchy. Then he turned the subject, and said quite pleasantly that he was coming the next day to give me a lesson. Everything seemed to have been smoothed over, and I greatly enjoyed his masterly suggestions and drill in Beethoven's C Minor Concerto, and many of Chopin's Studies; I quite believed that he would never again refer to what he had been pleased to call a whim—a touchiness on my part. But I was mistaken, and the Meister had a little score against me, on the ground, I believe, of his having troubled himself to send for me several times. His man who took back my replies had become aware that I was neither ill nor discontinuing practice, but was simply not disposed to go to his master. I was, as the phrase goes, 'to be paid out for this,' and that in a manner very characteristic of Henselt.

The next lessons were most delightful. Henselt was most kind, but the following incident will show that he was bent on 'being *even* with me.' Just a little more than a fortnight before the time when Henselt was to leave St. Petersburg, and when I calculated on having at least four or five lessons more from him, he said as he stood up from the piano to go away, 'We have but one lesson more this season.'

'One lesson more!' I exclaimed, in surprise and consternation. 'Are you going away earlier this year, dear Meister, than you usually do?' He had the previous year given me a lesson the very day before he left.

'No,' he replied, 'I am not going away just yet; but if you choose for a mere whim to throw away three weeks in the middle of winter, is there any reason why I should push myself to the last moment for you?'

I would have expostulated, would have asked him to reconsider the matter, but he hurried downstairs;

and though he turned to wish me good-bye before he passed into the street, his face told me that he was not in a yielding mood, and that for that day at least I had better leave the matter as it stood. But the same evening I ran down to Mademoiselle C——, one of his lady-teachers, the one who, after Mademoiselle H——, held the highest place in his favour and confidence.

'Don't worry about it,' said this kind and intelligent woman to me; 'but wait a day, and then go to his house at the time when you know he is just getting up from his breakfast, insist on getting in somehow, and seeing him for a minute; and don't be too proud—remember *who* he is. And you did really hurt his *amour propre*, when you stayed away those three weeks in the winter. I believe that he means to make you entreat him before he gives in, and I am sure that, as he really is fond of you, he himself will be very glad to do so; but you must show him that you want it very much; and, as I said before, you must not be proud, or so shy that you let yourself be rebuffed by his first words of refusal.'

Fortified by her kindly counsel and sympathy, I went to his house on the next day but one, at the hour she had suggested, and saying to his man, 'I must see your master, just to ask a question,' I was at once told to walk into his sanctum. He was standing putting on his coat, while both the housekeeper and man busied themselves in helping him.

'What do you want?' were his first words of greeting to me.

'Just a word,' I said—'a question which will not take a moment.' I hoped as I said this that he would, according to his usual custom on such occasions, have either gone with me into another room, or sent the two servants away. But I believe he felt it was due to himself that they should witness what followed, for he said:

'Speak out; ask your question—and quickly, please, for I am just going out.'

Seeing, then, no help for it, 'Dear Meister,' I said, 'I want you to unsay what you said the day before yesterday.'

'Unsay what?' was the gruff rejoinder.

'Unsay that the next lesson will be the last you intend to give me this season,' I replied.

'You have had your answer; and, what's more, I have just told a gentleman whom I have known for years that I could not spare him an hour, and that this time I do not intend to give lessons up to the last moment before I set out for Germany.'

This last speech of Henselt's would have left me unable to utter another word on the subject (for I never chose to presume that he would give me what he refused to others); but Mademoiselle C—— told me that he had promised several more lessons before his departure to a young and, as I was aware, a very mediocre player, and I did not feel I was so *very* presumptuous in asking him to do the same for me. But it was not easy, for he looked resolved; and saying, 'I am in a hurry—can't wait to hear any more,' he was moving to the door, when I summoned up what for me was extreme boldness, and, running before him, I took his hand, which I pressed to my lips, and with great earnestness begged him to pause just one moment—just for one moment reflect on the distance I had come to be under his guidance; and granting that it *was* by a 'whim,' 'a fit of touchiness,' that I had stayed away three weeks in the winter, who, I asked him, was the loser by it? I said that I had been really worried by it at the time more than *he* could imagine; that I believed him to have forgotten it all; and now that we were going to part for many long months, surely he was not going back on old grievances? I ventured to add, 'I presume to ask nothing which you are not likewise giving to others.'

I know full well that the venerable Meister enjoyed having me in the position of a suppliant in the presence of the two servants, one of whom had been sent for me several times; for he said, in a less gruff tone: 'Well, child, you must let me run off now; but we shall see.' I knew he was mollified even more than I had ventured to hope, for his man brought me a letter the next morning to say he was coming round in an hour or two, and I could tell him then whether I should like to have four more lessons.

When Henselt left St. Petersburg—which he always

did some time between the 26th and 30th of May—he liked to say good-bye to his most intimate friends and pupils at the railway-station. On these occasions we all used to bring bouquets, which his servant-man arranged all round the inside of the *coupé* in which the Meister always travelled alone. Everything was arranged for him by the two ladies, who were quite like daughters—and very devoted ones, too. Well-filled provision-baskets, fruit, cigars, all were in the carriage, and so arranged as to give him no trouble in getting at them. Perhaps you will think they spoiled him—and you are quite right, for even he himself said so. From his youth up he had resolved to know nothing of what he called ' *les petites misères de la vie.*'

Wherever he turned in his house, whether in St. Petersburg or in Warmbrunn, he expected to find his wishes had been anticipated. In the families with whom year after year he dined on stated days, what he liked was known, and in many cases they would beg him to order his dinner beforehand ; and he would do so, for he knew they were pleased in being thus treated as if they were actually related to him. On such occasions, too, he liked to be allowed to avail himself of the usages of St. Petersburg hospitality, by which, when asked to join the family dinner, you are not bound to remain for the evening. Henselt was so thoroughly at home in all the houses where he went to dine, that if he fancied a siesta he would take it *sans cérémonie;* and then he would usually go off to inspect one of the great Imperial Institutions, over which he had had supreme rule ever since the year 1863. The title of *Excellency* and a patent of nobility accompanied this appointment; and when one takes into account that in St. Petersburg alone there are five such Imperial endowments, three in Moscow, and one or more in most of the larger cities throughout this vast empire, and that, furthermore, some of these institutes count their students by the hundred (that, for instance, of Nicholas, in St. Petersburg, numbers six hundred pupils), we shall then be in a position to realize what an enormous influence over pianoforte-playing throughout all Russia was thus placed in Henselt's hands. It is not, indeed, too much to say that never before has a single musician had so wide a sphere of activity opened to him; and though that influence only extended over one single department in music's vast domain—that of pianoforte-playing—still, if we consider that it was these institutes which trained all the governesses and female teachers throughout Russia, that all the musical instruction in them was (and is still, as I write this) given by teachers who had either been actually pupils of Henselt, or else had been thoroughly drilled by his lady-professors, it is not too much to assume that for more than a quarter of a century his influence has been felt more or less in every home in Russia where there was a pianoforte.

A quotation from the brochure, entitled 'Observations, resulting from long years of experience, on Pianoforte-playing, and intended as a guide for teachers and pupils in the Imperial Institutes over which I am placed, and to be observed by all such as are therein engaged,' signed Adolf Henselt, will enable us to form some idea of the nature and extent of this authority. Henselt begins his observations by saying that what many people, especially teachers, are pleased to cavil at and call 'Henselt's method,' and to describe as so special and peculiar as to be neither possible nor desirable for all, is only a simple and thorough carrying out of those fundamental and absolutely incontrovertible principles of true art which all musicians and all teachers are bound to know and follow, and which are contained in every sound pianoforte school. He then goes on to define what good teaching should be; and in many interesting examples, taken from pieces with which we all are more or less familiar, he exposes the superficiality and inaccuracy which characterize the opposite. The brochure closes with the authoritative mandate that all teachers of the pianoforte in these Imperial Institutes shall provide themselves with a copy of these 'Observations,' and to the very utmost of their ability teach according to the principles laid down therein. But not only were the pianoforte-teachers (whether men or women) theoretically supposed to teach this system thoroughly and conscientiously, observing in all points the dictum of the 'Inspector-General,' but their doing so was secured. In fact, they were fenced in to obedience by the fact that at stated times of the year the pupils entrusted to their charge were examined by Henselt himself. It was an anxious hour, even for those who stood highest in the Meister's regard, for it was no personal question with him; his one idea was that the thing should have been done, that the pupil should have been taught thoroughly and well. And as the lady-directress of the institute, and all or most of her assistants, are always present on these occasions, woe betide the teacher whose pupil did not play her piece as if she had been drilled with all the care and thoroughness which (according to Henselt) must always result in a comparative approach towards artistic excellence.

To return to my narrative. Henselt came, and was most hearty and genial. I had, I believe, five instead of four more lessons, for he now often gave me two 'hours' in the week (the only special favour he ever showed me in our relation as master and pupil). He left St. Petersburg at the usual time, and in company with others I went, bouquet in hand, to see him off. I then went to spend the summer in Courland, with a lady who had become a dear friend of mine some two years before in Germany. And here, before going on further, I must pause to say just one word à *propos* of the Germans, against whom so many in this country have such an unreasonable prejudice. I can speak from personal experience, for more than one family of distinction have received me into their homes, and made me feel that I was a loved and honoured guest.

The husband of the lady I have mentioned belonged to the ancient order of the knights (*Ritterschaft*), which dates back some hundred years, and he had a fine estate some distance from Riga in Courland. She had made me promise that I would some time or other pay her a long visit, and it was with her that I spent the summer of this year. Whilst there I witnessed the celebration of St. John's Eve, and as few in this country have the opportunity of knowing much about the people of those parts, or the customs which prevail amongst them, I feel tempted to give a little sketch of what interested me so much.

I must, however, first tell my readers that the aborigines of Courland are *Letts*, not Germans, nor do they speak German. A simple-hearted, intelligent, and very musical race, they live on the estates of the German nobles, do all the field and artisan work, and are paid in kind, not in money—*i.e.*, they grow flax, for which the proprietor gives them a slip of land; and they not only spin their own flax, but weave their own linen, fashion winter garments for themselves out of sheepskins, and in many instances make their own shoes.

The first thing I noticed on St. John's Eve was the stir in the household to have a sufficient number of small cylinder-shaped loaves piled up in large baskets, which were placed in the veranda or front entrance to the dwelling. A small-sized cheese went with each loaf. Beer and *schnaps* were being brought down to a barn, in which the people, by the light of two or three big tallow candles, danced nearly all night long. In Russia the sun does not set at midsummer until half-past nine, and after sunset all the lovely tints seem arrested as if by enchantment; and when they do change, instead of fading into soft gray, they dissolve into a transparent blend of all colours; and the light does not wane, but grows so sweet and tender, that when I first saw the May twilights in St. Petersburg, I said to myself, 'This is what I should imagine the night might be in heaven.'

The home of my friend was situated on a gentle rising-ground, and as there was no wall round it, and the surrounding country was flat, it was possible to see for a very long distance. It had been a lovely day, and after sunset the entire country was all in a glow of warm yet mysteriously soft light. I retired to my room, which had three windows, and was in the front wing, and on the first story of the house. By-and-by strange sounds of men and women's voices could be heard in the distance, rising and falling with many weird changes, and becoming more and more audible, until at last a long procession was seen winding its way along the road. As the singers came nearer, I could see that they all wore wreaths, and as they paused in their song the sound of their glad voices told that this was a night of merry-making and festivity. I ran downstairs and seated myself in the veranda, where the master and mistress of the manor, with their children, and the governess and tutor, had already taken their places. On came the procession—men and women, girls and boys—and winding up the pathway that led through the lawn to the house in regular order, the foremost halted in front of the veranda, and made a speech in the Lettish language to the master and mistress, wishing them every blessing life could bestow. At a motion from the latter, each person went singly over to the baskets, and took his or her portion of bread and cheese; and as he retired, took off his wreath, and laid it at the feet of the hosts. And what a motley pile of these we had the next day! Some were simply made of two or three large fronds of fern, twisted and bound together with little art; others were made from the branches of trees, and many were most fancifully fashioned of the loveliest wild-flowers. As they retired towards the barn, which had been arranged for dancing, one or two of the leaders stepped forward, and wished each member of the family some special form of the sort of good luck which occurs to simple hearts as the best. Their delicate little girl was to grow strong and tall; the boy was to be like his father; the tutor was to marry the governess; and as I was the loved friend of their lady, I was by marrying the owner of the next estate to be planted near her for the remainder of my life! How they did enjoy the dance in the barn, where, to my astonishment, there were only a few tallow candles to light up the scene!

And now again returning to music and Henselt, I have to tell that, although I intended after the summer was over to spend the early part of the winter in St. Petersburg, this was not to be. Courland lies low, and in a place where I had everything to make me happy, and where we rambled in fields full of wild-flowers, in woods where all was song and all disposed for summer reverie, summer enjoyment, I grew so ill and languid that I had to seek in the Engadine renewal of health and energy. In January, however, I wished to go to Henselt; but the friend who had the most leisure to seek fit quarters for me failed to find exactly what suited. We corresponded and discussed all the pros and cons of the various quarters which she suggested to me. At last, when March came, I decided on waiting in Germany until Henselt came to Warmbrunn, and spending my summer there.

It was on an afternoon early in June that I found myself once more in Warmbrunn; and as I knew that there was a great shadow over the Von Henselt household, instead of going directly to greet the family and announce my arrival, I took temporary quarters in a nice *hôtel garni* close to the promenade (park), and spent some hours in looking about for rooms for the summer.

As it grew later, I naturally wished much to greet the venerable pair; but I knew Frau von Henselt had been very ill, and I thought it better to see the Meister in order to know how best to approach her. Henselt was, I just then remembered, very fond of the theatre, and often went to it evening after evening, so I resolved to try and get a glimpse of him on his way thither, and hear how all went on at the villa, and find out if I might call on his venerable wife.

Setting off to the promenade for this purpose about half an hour before the time the theatre generally began, I watched the Warmbrunn folk and the summer visitors enter the leafy alley from various sides, and walk up the steps of the theatre. It was just seven, and I began to wonder whether he could have gone round by a back entrance, or whether he was indeed coming that evening. Speculating thus, I forgot for a moment to keep my eye on the sidepath by which he usually came, and on looking again, there he was—the old general whom I had not seen for a year and a month. I knew the peculiar swing; but, ah, how bent and aged! He was walking quickly, and was close to the theatre, and, laugh who will, from a hurried walk it became a run with me, just to get up in time to have one shake of the hand, one word of greeting, before he got into the theatre. Until I saw him there before me, I did not know how glad I was to see him once more. He was pleased when I reached him, quite out of breath, and said, 'Meister, Meister, just stop a moment!' and then he went in, and I had a lovely walk through the leafy alleys and out into the open country until it grew quite dark, and I went home to my *hôtel garni* and retired to rest.

At seven the next morning, while I was taking coffee in my room, the maid came to tell me that 'Excellency von Henselt' was downstairs, and asking for me; and when I ran down, there was the venerable Meister, looking so kind, so genial, so hearty, that I was in great delight, and augured on the spur of the moment—what turned out afterwards quite the reverse—a very happy summer. The trying state of Frau von Henselt affected the Meister's spirits so much, that it was all one could do to keep him from falling into gloom and despondency. It was, indeed, a privilege, but a sad one, to be, with one or two others, the companion of his walks, and to try to get him even for a while to think of something else.

One privilege fell to my lot to which I shall ever look back with almost unalloyed pleasure. We had often spoken of Mozart's stringed quartets and quintets, Henselt saying that they were so beautiful as duets for the pianoforte, that to play them was, to his thinking, one of the greatest pleasures a musician can know. He had, I knew, tried one or two with a young lady (the one previously referred to), and I wondered if I might hope for the same privilege, and with this idea had a whole set of them sent to me from Leipzig. He saw them in my room, and said, 'Come in and we will play them for my wife;' and she was so charmed, that every evening at six it was arranged that I should come over to the villa and try a duet with him. When I speak of 'trying a duet,' I mean that, having in most instances carefully read over the second part, I acted as 'an accompanist' to the Meister, who from the time he sat down beside me on these occasions laid aside all his abruptness, and had such a gentle way of intimating his mode of interpretation, that he seemed—but for the sweet tones which welled up beneath his fingers—to be no more Henselt, but someone else.

This time I played with Henselt a long programme of pieces which I had been studying in Germany— his *Poême d'Amour*, Liszt's *Lucia*, second *Rhapsodie Hongroise*, Bach's *Italienisches Concert;* but it was, as I have already said, a trying summer, and as I wished to play one or two more concertos before finally returning to my native land, I went once more to St. Petersburg, and was again warmly welcomed by the friends to whom I had naturally drawn still closer during my second stay in St. Petersburg. It was then that Henselt wrote me the accompanying little note on a post-card.

Henselt was away in Moscow when I arrived, but my own special friend met me at the station, and as we were driving to the same house in which I had lived a year and a half before, she told me that, if I had arrived a few days earlier, Henselt himself would have come to meet me, and that a few evenings before he had paid her a visit, and had told her to tell me that, as I could not fix a day for arriving and keep to it (I had arranged to leave Berlin at a given date, but had been in some way or other detained), I might come now when I pleased—he did not care. But I had now served a long apprenticeship with the Meister, and only smiled with pleasure when my friend told me all this. He had one or two dear and admirable friends, who were his helpers, his daughters; but I had a place of my own, and was content with it.

One evening his Excellency's servant brought me a huge envelope, which on opening I found to contain a number of letters, addressed to his Excellency. Some were from Warmbrunn, others from Bavaria, Germany, and the various places where he had correspondents. The man who brought me this packet was a Russian, who neither spoke nor understood German; and as I neither spake nor understood Russian, it was not easy for us to understand each other. Still, he managed to convey to me somehow that his master wished me to read the letters, and that I was to return them to him when I joined him in his morning walk. I was, of course, both touched and gratified by this proof of the dear Meister's confidence, implying as it did likewise that he knew every little service I could render him would be a pleasure to me. But with rather delicate eyes, and by artificial light, to read long letters, which were often written in very crabbed German, was indeed no light task. Still, I had my reward, when I felt myself drawn so close to the Meister, and he discussed various matters, both relating to his family and to his life as a musician, with me. Among the letters which related to music, and especially to pianoforte music, I was especially interested in the very charming letters of Monsieur Conus, a Moscow professor. There were many references in them to Henselt's method and *technique;* and if Henselt's executors would entrust me with them, I would spare no labour and pains in translating them for publication.

It fell also to my lot this winter to enjoy the privilege of being associated with Mademoiselle Heinrichsen and Fräulein Calvert in correcting the proofs of the sequel to *Les Études préparatoires*—a task in which all three were wound up to generous emulation, for each of us was naturally anxious not to be outdone by the other in discovering the printer's oversights. This sequel to the *Études préparatoires* was to be followed by a long and exhaustive work, consisting of seven sections, and entitled *Les expériences d'un Pianiste.* These sections contained numerous difficult passages occurring in most of the great classical composers, both ancient and modern, and they were so fingered and grouped as to give advanced students a very fair idea of how to conquer them. These studies, being, as Henselt himself said, drawn from his own personal experience, would be of immense value and interest to all those who aim at playing with perfect finish; but, sad to relate, this storehouse of the wisdom of a life is locked up for many a year to come. Many of the examples are taken from the works of composers whose copyrights would be infringed by their publication.

It was my privilege this winter to be the companion of Henselt's daily morning walks, and at the hour he left his own door never did he fail to find me waiting to join him. Perhaps at some time or other I may relate a little of what he, as man and musician, talked to me about as we—two fur-clad figures—walked in the snowy streets, at a temperature often twenty degrees below zero.

This time I had resolved to have the best piano that money could procure, in order not to lose the chance of the rare moments when the master might be pleased to play; and the Beckers, at his request, sent me a new *boudoir grand*—for my rooms were rather small. But this was not until after Henselt's return from Moscow.

When I heard the hour he was likely to be at the station, I went to meet him there, just had a word of affectionate greeting, and left him to enjoy the quiet which he so much needed after his night's journey.

He gave me a letter to Mr. Peterson on the following day, and three or four days afterwards they sent me the pianoforte. My morning walks above alluded to had not yet begun, so I went at the time when he was always accessible, *i.e.*, after breakfast, to tell him that my piano had come; and, according to his usual fashion, he just came into the anteroom, said, 'It is you!' looked kind and pleasant, and added, 'I will be with you a little after two to-day.' I turned at once to go away, as one must always do with the Meister, who (especially in the morning hours) never tolerated a superfluous word, and was already in the hall, when, to my surprise, he called me back, and, passing into his sanctum, motioned me to follow him, saying, 'Come in here for a minute.' As I walked in after him, he had already seated himself at his dumb practising piano, and was soon arduously absorbed in wrestling with a technical tone-problem. I was so intensely interested, and so profoundly suggestive was every movement of those marvellous fingers, hands, and wrists, that I would have willingly watched him for hours. I suppose I stood there for a quarter of an hour or more; he glanced once or twice at me during this time in a scrutinizing manner, and I knew full well that if I had, by taking a seat, shown either that I expected to remain there, or was tired of standing, he would then and there have risen and sent me away. But to observe the Meister at work was a privilege of which I showed my

appreciation by my silence and my moveless attitude;
and I was indeed rewarded, for without a word, a look
towards me, he suddenly rose with a light in his eyes,
and a swing of conscious power in his whole form,
and, going over to his pet instrument, he played on it
as I had never but once heard him before during the
three years I had been privileged to know him. This
day all the glow of youth, all the maturity of manhood, was there; it was the artist at his culminating
point, and he himself knew it and felt it, for during a
brief moment's pause he observed—and it was more
to himself than to me that the words were addressed
—'I have attained what I have desired, and am content; but it is passing from me. Such moments now
are rare, and each time of late that such is given to me
I say to myself, "It may be perhaps for the last time."'

He played the *Concert Stück* of Weber, repeating
many parts several times over, and with each repetition floating up on a higher plane, evolving each time
from the keyboard tones of more intense, more
spiritual beauty; Weber's Sonata in D Minor, of
which he said when playing it, 'There is heaven and
there is hell here;' his own lovely *Gondola*; Chopin's
E Minor Concerto; and then, rising from the piano,
he said, 'I am out of breath, and much heated, and
must rest myself.' On this I moved to go away; but
he said, 'Stay with me a little, and sit down there,'
motioning to a seat near his arm-chair. How strange,
and often how trifling, are the causes which bring

disturbance into the even current of our lives! I
was deeply moved, especially by his words, 'It may
be perhaps the last time;' but I naturally did not wish
to show this feeling, so, saying to him, 'I will amuse
you, dear Meister, with some chit-chat *à propos* of
Rubinstein, and the St. Petersburg Conservatorium,'
I told him that a lady, at whose house I had been
dining on the previous evening, had said, in speaking
of Rubinstein, 'Is he not brave and strong and
resolute? for when the professors in the Conservatorium objected to the new order of things which
Rubinstein wished to introduce there, and he would
not yield a jot to them, the majority turned out in a
body, without giving him time to fill their vacant
places. But Rubinstein faced them, saying, 'You
think that you will frighten me, gentlemen; but I
feel in myself the strength of an ox, and both will and
shall be able to give all the lessons myself!"' To all
this, and much more in detail on the same subject,
Henselt listened without much comment; and then,
to my joy, went over once more to the piano, and
once more enchanted me with tones such as he, and
he alone of all then living, could draw from the
instrument. Deeply thrilled and moved, I went
home, and mused long over all I had heard that
morning. Such memories are among the most
precious possessions of an art-nature.

The reader will probably like to hear a little more
detail about 'the new order of things' which

Rubinstein had introduced into the Conservatoire, of which he had been nominated director when Monsieur Davidoff (an eminent 'cellist) resigned that post. When Rubinstein accepted the position, Madame Sophie Menter had been for two years occupying a professorship in the Conservatoire, which had been left vacant by the death of Louis Brassin. This post had been in the first instance offered to and declined by Lesschetizky of Vienna. When Madame Menter accepted it, there was a clause inserted in her agreement which gave her the privilege of remaining away fully a month longer than the other professors. She also, without being formally given such a privilege, had assumed for herself the right of frequently having the class to meet at her own house for their lesson, instead of at the Conservatorium. Rubinstein's first act of power was to signify to her that he should cancel the clause which gave her the liberty of absenting herself for a month after all the other classes had begun. He at the same time informed her that he could see no reason why the class should attend at her house, it being her duty to meet them in the Conservatoire.

Madame Menter, who has a large circle of friends and admirers, and has been for years in the habit of having much of her own way, found that it would not suit her dignity to conform to Rubinstein's rules. She accordingly at once sent in her resignation; and Rubinstein was supposed to have been very well pleased at her withdrawal.

His next step concerned a good many musicians, and placed them in a worse position than they had previously held; and it naturally excited great opposition, and made him very unpopular with the St. Petersburg professors. For perhaps twenty years most of the pianoforte professors in the Conservatorium had been accustomed to teach those pupils who commenced studying with them until the pupils had completed their course, and left the Conservatoire. This is not the order of things in Rome; for the pupils of St. Cecilia begin their studies with sub-professors, then advance to those who are more highly qualified, and finally reach the *classe di perfezionamento*, over which Sgambati himself presides. I do not suppose that Rubinstein was following the order of the St. Cecilian; but he was resolved to institute an order of things pretty analogous to that which I have just described. When he first intimated his purpose, everyone seemed to think him in the right; but when professors, who believed themselves competent to teach the most advanced classes, found that *they* were only asked to take the position of sub-professors, they at once rebelled, and as a considerable number of these were Russians by birth, and Rubinstein had wished to place them under professors whom he invited from Germany and Italy, they not only turned out in a body, but raised the cry against Rubinstein that he was favouring foreigners and depreciating native talent. And such was the bitterness of the feeling against Rubinstein at that time among the middle-class Russian professors, that friendships of long standing were (at least for the time being) dissolved by it.

I will give one instance here, but without naming the individuals concerned in them. The sister of a friend of mine was the wife of a Russian professor, who had known Rubinstein intimately for years. This lady had received me with great kindness when I first arrived in Russia, and had often asked me if I would like to accompany her to visit Madame Rubinstein, and be introduced to the great *virtuoso;* but I had declined, because I knew, from friends of Rubinstein whom I had met abroad, that he always asked people who were musical to play to him. ' Every hand I see on the keyboard presents me with a new problem,' he used to say; and I knew full well that it would not have been interesting to him, nor agreeable to myself, to hear one who was just getting into a new school of *technique;* I therefore declined her kind offer.

On my third visit to St. Petersburg, it seemed to me rather a pity not to have once seen Rubinstein in his own house, and I was no longer afraid of doing Henselt's school injustice, even in playing before Rubinstein. I therefore went to my friend, and told her that the next time she was paying a visit to the Rubinsteins I would be very glad to accompany her. But the stars had otherwise decreed. My friend, who was an Italian, clasped her hands in the true Italian fashion. 'Ah, signorina, what a pity you would not come before! For now I am no longer visiting at the Rubinsteins' house. This affair in the Conservatorium! You know, signorina, that my husband has been obliged to take part with his countrymen, and, in an article written by him in one of the daily papers, has animadverted strongly on the mode of proceeding adopted by Rubinstein. The result was that when I met Madame Rubinstein in the street the other day, she paused for one moment, just to tell me, with expressions of regret, that her family and mine could not continue to visit each other.'

On this same day when I spoke to Henselt about Rubinstein, a little before two, I heard his well-known step on the stairs, and as I opened the door to admit him, he took off his fur in silence; and instead of at once making me sit down to the piano, he said briefly, 'Please, some plain paper, a good pencil, and don't interrupt me for a quarter of an hour.' And sitting down, he wrote rapidly, every now and then saying, as he paused for a moment, 'You will be surprised, very much surprised!' When he had finished writing, he handed the paper to me, saying, 'Read that'; and I was indeed surprised, but even more concerned than surprised, for it was a draft of a letter to Rubinstein which he had just written, and in it he had, in expressing his sympathy with Rubinstein's difficulties,

placed twelve hours every week of his own time at
Rubinstein's disposal until the difficulty should have
been tided over, and the recusant professors should
have been replaced. I feared not only that the
Meister was overtaxing his physical powers, but I
saw (as I invariably do) 'rocks ahead,' and I ventured
to entreat of him to think well before giving away so
many hours of a life so valuable to art, and so dear
to us his followers (I may say disciples); and this,
too, in a direction which was wholly contrary to his
lifelong bias. He promised me that he would think
it over, and then (it was indeed a day of days) he sat
down to the piano, and played his own *Aurora Valse*,
and a considerable part of his Concerto. Taking up
Beethoven's E Flat Concerto, he allowed me to play
it all through to him, glancing *en passant* at the
printed fingering (Rheinecke's edition), and showing
me why, and wherein, he differed from it. He impressed me during this lesson as he had never before
done in the same degree with the conviction that, as
regards ideal purity of tone and faultless beauty of
expression, he stood—perhaps will ever stand—quite
alone. In his presence all false pretences vanished,
and every shred of vanity and self-conceit fell away,
leaving behind them devotion to the pursuit of an
unattainable ideal, and grateful reverence for the
man who, ever reaching and aspiring upwards and
onwards from height to height, compelling, by the
force of his strenuous will, vista after vista to open

out before him, yet condescended to take some of us by the hand. We fail to climb to a height, and can only reach a gentle slope in art; but we are at least on the way which leads to ideal perfection. We can look up with a joyful pain to the heights which we shall never reach, and say with Elizabeth Browning, 'I would not wish my art low, to suit my stature.'

It may interest the reader to read the letters which passed between Henselt and Rubinstein on this occasion. The first of these letters—the one written in my room—must have been last, for the friend at St. Petersburg, who up to the present holds all his Russian correspondence, has failed to find it. I give, however, Rubinstein's reply, written within twenty-four hours after he had received Henselt's letter. The letters are exact copies of what has been sent me from St. Petersburg:

'Dear Herr Henselt,

'My whole career has been based on the worthiness of artists. Latterly I have become confused, and have almost come to the conclusion that artists are not nobler than the public. Here comes your letter. I see, I hear, I believe!

'Permit me to look about for a couple of days, and then to answer you by word of mouth.

'Yours in art-brotherhood,

'Ant. Rubinstein.'

'St. Petersburg, 11th May, 1888.

'HIGHLY HONOURED HERR HENSELT,

'However flattering it may be for me, and an honour for the Conservatorium, that you are inclined to take an active part in this institute during the ensuing year, yet I see it to be my duty to communicate to you two points which must unluckily cause me to doubt whether you will be disposed to accept these.

'1. There is so large a deficit in the budget of the Conservatorium that reductions in every department are inevitable, and I therefore, alas! cannot offer you more than a hundred roubles for the yearly lessons of the next academy term.

'2. The personal presence of the professors at the committees, musical evenings for the students, and examinations are indispensable—a condition which you told me you could not possibly agree to; if, however, these two points do not deter you, and you would not be indisposed to agree to them, I would here express to you my cordial thanks, and would await you with open arms in the Conservatorium on the 15th of September; that is, at the time you yourself mentioned to me. You would then, as a matter of course, have to name an assistant-teacher (lady or gentleman) who would accept without demur the usual fee, and would enter on his or her duties at the same time as yourself.

'With best wishes for a pleasant journey and a safe return,
'Your
'Ant. Rubinstein.
'I await with impatience a favourable reply.'

Henselt's reply to Rubinstein.
'St. Petersburg.

'Highly honoured Herr Rubinstein,

'The first point, namely, the monetary one, plays no part in the matter, as I offered my services gratuitously; and instead of this you agreed with me for a very high fee, which I, from a very different point of view, indeed, appreciated very highly. But, alas! the second point is quite impossible for me; it would be against my nature, and this is too difficult for a man in his seventy-fifth year. I regret much that my good intentions have not led to a better result.

'Wishing you and your dear colleagues a happy summer and good health,

'I remain your thankful and obliged
'Henselt.'

I meant to spend the whole of that winter in St. Petersburg, but it was otherwise decreed. I was obliged to leave in February, to fulfil a duty which I could delegate to no one else; and though I hoped to have returned—in fact, I left all my heavy luggage in the charge of Henselt's housekeeper—I was compelled with much reluctance to give up the idea of seeing again (at least in Russia) the revered teacher, the loved and valued friend.

As all, however, that touches either more or less on the person and character of such a remarkable man must interest lovers of music, I shall not take leave of my reader without mentioning several other little facts and incidents which may serve to give a very fair idea of what he was all round. First of all, in speaking of him as a teacher, I will not disguise the fact (indeed, I have already said as much), that it was not always an easy task to study with him. I am by no means prepared to say that if I had not gone to him with so entire a conviction of his power to help me—if I had not, as Beatrice tells Dante to do, 'flung away from myself,' and let myself be freed from every shred and particle of pretension—I could not have borne with him, before I had come fully to understand what his sudden bursts of anger at what seemed trifles really meant. I wished for the utmost rigour of the school, and had told him so; but seeing me rather panic-stricken on the first occasion that he spoke very bluntly, and with a very loud voice, he said, in wishing me good-bye at the close of that lesson, 'You know it is not to have an agreeable hour with me that you come here; yet if you cannot bear my point-blank way of fault-finding, I will draw in, and not let fly as I did just now.' But I wanted

to have the old Meister just as he was, and not as he
might feel it necessary to be when he was teaching in
one or two princely families. He said one day in
Warmbrunn, when his wife had observed, 'You are
hard on her,' 'She will get accustomed to it in time.'
And I remember well that, making use of the homely
expression, 'I am neither sugar nor salt,' I begged him
when he said this not to restrain himself, but always
to speak out, and in his own fashion—that my aspira-
tion towards perfection was, as compared with my
smaller art-faculty, as intense as his own. 'You are
a sensible creature,' he replied, 'and can see that my
anger is *for* you, and not *against* you.'

When I was still in the first book of Cramer he told
me that he had played all these as a boy, and had
then no small opinion of his own powers as a *virtuoso;*
but when he heard Thalberg he was in despair, and
was convinced that he must make an entirely fresh
start—that he, in fact, knew nothing. The result of
this despair, this conviction of impotence, was that he
shut himself up to grapple with the problem alone and
unassisted. He thought out the question of how the
hand can be extended without losing either its strength
or elasticity. He re-studied the whole of Cramer,
with changes in the fingering, which were intended to
plant the fingers so as to produce perfect tone. 'Yet,'
he observed to me, 'sometimes the old Adam peeps
up here and there.' Henselt's similes were always
most characteristic, and this is one which I have

often heard him use. The sensation one had very often after a lesson with him was twofold. The art-sense was keener, the perception finer; but, as a pupil, one felt, I suppose, much like a horse who has been goaded and spurred up a steep incline, or forced to leap a high wall by the application of both lash and spur. It was not everyone who could bear such severe drill; and I was told more than once, in circles which were antagonistic to him, that there was a saying, 'Henselt kills.' The meaning of this obviously was that his was too strong and severe a training for those who either wished to accomplish much without delving deep below the surface, or who had not the physical or mental pluck to take the bitter with the sweet, and console themselves, after getting one of these moral boxes on the ear, with the reflection that the demand on the part of the teacher implied his belief in the power of the learner to do the thing demanded. But as I think over Henselt's teaching, and all I could relate about it, I feel that to enter every detail, to relate every word that fell from the Meister's lips, would in itself fill a small volume, and this I must reserve for another occasion.

And now looking back, before taking leave of Henselt, I mean to give a picture which shall present him both as a young and an old man—two pictures which, much as they differ, are one and the same. But in doing this I must ask the reader to accompany me back to the days when I was still studying with Stern-

dale Bennett, and ask them to transport themselves
in fancy to a small and quiet pension, Rue Pradier,
Geneva. It is only nine o'clock a.m., an hour when
musicians and musical students often begin their work,
but scarcely the time when lovers of music would
meet in order to enjoy a practice together, or listen
to one; and yet three persons—three musical natures
—are in yonder room, each giving the other a farewell
specimen of their individual and singularly differing
reflexes of art-feeling. A gentleman, young and pale
and dreamy-looking, has sung *Das Veilchen* by Mozart,
and *In diesen heiligen Hallen*. An older and a younger
lady play Beethoven's *Choral Fantasia*, at which they
have both worked very thoroughly; the younger lady
(myself) plays two pieces from Bach's *Suite Anglaise*,
and then the elder lady utters the words, 'We all
three are truly musical; and yet, though we have
lived for six weeks or more under the same roof, we
have been so stiff and conventional, so slow in recog-
nising the bond that existed between us, that not until
a week or ten days ago have we expanded to each
other, and interchanged what we each possess. But'
—and here the lady's voice took a more earnest tone,
and her dark eyes glanced sadly at the other two—
'what might we not have done for each other had it
been otherwise! and what have we not missed which
life may perhaps never again present to us! For it is
a rare circumstance when three so essentially musical
natures, at once so sympathetic to each other, and yet

so essentially different, have such a chance as this of mutually stimulating and supplementing each other. And we all three have let it slip. Let this parting warn us to seize the next opportunity when we find ourselves with congenial spirits, and use it to the full.' The speaker was a Russian lady, who was much attached to me. She lived in St. Petersburg, and one or two letters passed between us after my mother and I had left Geneva and gone home. Her letters then ceased; I wrote once or twice again, and, receiving no reply, thought she was no more.

I had not, however, forgotten my enthusiastic elder friend, and curiously enough, several years afterwards —the year before I saw Henselt—I had while in Italy heard from a casual acquaintance that Madame I—— was in good health, had returned to St. Petersburg after a long absence, and was as musical as ever. One of the first things I did, accordingly, on reaching St. Petersburg, was to write to her, and ask her to come and see me. She at once replied that she would come the following day; she did so, and we met after the lapse of many years, as friends drawn all the closer by the fact that in the years which had passed since we had last seen each other we had both known much sorrow and bereavement. She was much gratified when I looked at her arm after the first greetings were over, and asked, 'Where is the bracelet you used to wear? I remember "*Dieu vous garde*" was graven on it.'

Touching lightly on what neither of us wished—that day, at least—to enter on more fully, we passed on to subjects of general interest. She asked me what I had been doing in music during those years, and when I told her that I had come to Russia to study the Henselt method, she was amused and somewhat indignant—said it was absurd, ridiculous; she remembered how well I played, etc. I begged of her just to wait a month, and I was certain she would be of a very different opinion; and meanwhile she begged me to come and dine with her on a stated day every week.

We had so much to relate to each other, that for the first three times I went to her we did not seem to need music, but on the fourth occasion I brought Cramer and the *Exercices préparatoires*, and when I sat down and showed her how I had been working, the amused look which had come over her face when I had first seated myself at the piano, was soon succeeded by one of great surprise. She looked at me most earnestly from time to time the rest of the evening, and one or two days after came to me with what she called 'a great request'—namely, that I would drill her into what I had been learning with Mademoiselle Heinrichsen. And then she told me that in her early youth Henselt was a constant guest at her father's dinner-table; that as a girl of seventeen she had had ten lessons from him, that her parents had arranged a marriage for her not long after, and had persuaded the man to whom they gave her that music was her greatest bane—that it was his duty to let her pursue it as little as possible. And thus she was drifted off into a circle utterly antagonistic to Henselt—so much so, that when *she*, a childless woman, who had been a good wife to a man who crossed her only in this one thing, was left a widow some years before this, she had wished to take up music, and yet it had not occurred to her to go to Henselt. She had engaged the brother of a pianist who is a great favourite at court to come to her once every week, and he had never taught her anything—had just come in with duets which they played together, and this was supposed to be a lesson.

After she had begun working (though very little at Cramer and the *Exercices préparatoires*), she discontinued her lessons with this gentleman; and on his meeting her at a dinner shortly after at the house of a friend, and asking her whether she was laying aside music, she replied, 'Oh no; but I am very busy studying Henselt's method with Miss ——.'

The discarded professor was naturally very angry, but took an extremely clever way of trying to vent his spite on Henselt, whom he naturally looked on as the indirect cause of his having lost a pupil. Instead of seeming to disapprove of what the lady was doing, he told her that he was sure she could not do better for a while than try to improve her fingers, which had never had any proper drill. 'But your friend,' said this man, 'what can she want with such grinding? Tell her "Henselt kills."' And so persistently did this professor work on my friend's mind, that she nearly quarrelled with me, when I would not leave off studying with Henselt after the first winter.

The second winter we saw much of each other, and I had spoken of her once or twice to Henselt. The third time I visited St. Petersburg, as I saw the Meister daily, and he related much of his early life, he mentioned the name of my friend's father, and asked me to tell him more about her. Becoming much interested, he declared his intention of going to see her. I knew well that such a visit would indeed be a pleasure to her; and knowing that she was very hospitable, and would be only too charmed to have him as her guest, I suggested his dining there on the same day that I went. He seemed quite pleased with the plan, but said, 'She must write and ask me.'

She was in high delight when I went out and told her all this; and then I was to get him to fix a day, and to let her know through me exactly what he would like to have for his dinner. I was to get the receipt for his favourite soup, to find out what sort of beer he drank, and I was myself to bring with me the Polish bread which he always expected to find at the houses of those intimate friends who knew his tastes, and felt proud and happy to gratify him even in these little details. It was also settled beforehand that two friends of the above-named lady were to be asked in after dinner, to make up a whist-party for Henselt, who had a great weakness for this game.

Before the day fixed for going to dine, Henselt, however, managed to pay the lady a visit, and I, therefore, did not see their first meeting; but she related it all to me as we sat together awaiting his arrival on the occasion of his dining there.

All except the soup went well. The calves' knees, which my friend had been at much trouble to procure, were well cooked; the vegetables were to his liking. And as he sat there he told madame many little things that had happened in the days when he had frequented her father's house; he had just as good a memory for the way her father's coat was made, and how it hung on his diminutive frame, as I had for the bracelet which his daughter had worn when we first knew each other in Geneva. After dinner I was amused to see that my friend was following the lead of the Meister's disciples even more than myself; for she rose from table, brought him *eau-de-Cologne* mixed with cognac to rinse his mouth, and finally presenting to him a tiny bowl of perfumed warm water, she herself wiped his fingers with a fine damask napkin.

The whist-party that evening was not a success, and Henselt left about half-past eight (the dinner had been at half-past five), I accompanying him, as we both were going the same way. He asked me, in the interval between his after-dinner nap and the arrival

of the whist-players, whether I had brought one of
the duets which I had tried with him in Warmbrunn
(Mozart's stringed quintets and quartets, to which I
have before alluded); and on my replying that in St.
Petersburg it had never entered my head to think
even of having such a pleasure, he smiled and said,
'Well, we shall have them the next time.' And here,
returning back a little, I note the fact that one of the,
alas! too rare occasions when I heard Henselt at his
highest, was on an afternoon when he had been
playing with me for more than an hour at the house
of a friend. One of the members of this very same
household (people who had been intimate with him
for at least thirty years or longer) had been talking
about the Meister a day or two before, and saying
how people seemed to vie with each other in spoiling
him. But on this afternoon, when the duets were
over, and I left Henselt sitting alone at the piano, as
his fingers wandered among the keys, he all at once
flung himself into 'Der Freischütz'; and it was at the
same time orchestra and piano—grand, exciting, mysterious, and sweet—and this same lady, coming up to
me afterwards, said in German, which I translate,
'One forgives everything to anyone who can play
like that! No wonder so many have lain at his
feet!'

To return, however, to my St. Petersburg friend.
Henselt dined again with her, and on this occasion
took me with him in a sleigh; but it was an anxious

evening for me, for the following reason: My friend had perceived that the Meister did not care for the whist-players whom she had invited to meet him on the first occasion; and not being aware of his great peculiarities (he was choice in general as to whom he met), she arranged that the next whist-party should consist of Herr K—— and his wife, who, with herself, would make the party complete. Now, this Herr K—— was the very gentleman who had tried so many times, through her, to draw me away from Henselt. He belonged to a party whose entire aim seemed to be to cry down the Meister as a pedantic old schoolmaster—a man out of date—and Henselt knew all this, and when I told him who were to be his partners in the next whist tourney, he at once boiled up, and said, 'I won't meet them, I won't play with them; and you must write at once and tell your friend that if she cannot manage to put them off, I must beg her to excuse me from keeping my engagement to her.' I wrote, of course, at once, and received a telegram to the effect, 'All settled. I expect H. and you.' We accordingly arrived, and I was in a very happy mood, for we had had a delightful drive in a most comfortable sleigh. I had the Mozart duets with me, and all seemed to promise for a really charming evening. But all my pleasure vanished when my friend whispered to me as I was getting off my wraps, 'I could not be so rude as to put off Herr K—— and his wife, whom I have known for so many years, but I told him whist would not begin until after nine, and as Henselt always goes away early, it will be all right.' All wrong! was my internal ejaculation when I heard this, for, after all, how can one be so sure that Henselt will really be clear out of the house before nine? or that those 'good folks' will not take it into their heads to drop in half an hour earlier than the time named? Fortunately, however, my fears were only so far justified, that as we (Henselt accompanied by me) were going through the court which led out into the street I saw a gentleman and lady pass us whom I recognised as Herr K—— and his wife.

As to the duets, the Meister tried one or two with me that evening; but he was very tired, after a somewhat longer day than usual of teaching and examining in the Imperial Schools. He was not 'aufgelegt' (not in the mood), although he it was who, turning to me early in the evening, said, 'Well, where are the duets?' and as I was in a state of disquiet, picturing to myself what would happen if Professor K—— and his wife walked in. One thing I knew for certain, and that was that the whole blame would be laid on *me;* and it would be difficult for me in the first instance to persuade the Meister that I had expounded his wishes to my friend as strongly and positively as I ought to have done.

Ten days after this last sociable dinner, I found that I must go away, and to no nearer a place than Belgium. The Meister, to whom I told all my plans, etc., asked me what money I was taking for my journey, which had been rather suddenly decided on. (I mention this as an instance of his kindly and paternal feeling to those who, like myself, belonged to the small circle of his intimate friends.) On my saying, 'I shall have twenty or thirty roubles over when I reach the end of my journey,' he said, 'How can you tell, my dear, what may happen to you on the way? You must let me lend you at least a hundred.' I gratefully availed myself of the Meister's kind forethought; and, turning into his rooms to take the money, asked his leave to carry with me on the journey his copy of Bach's *Clavier tempéré*, from which I had been playing during the last few weeks, and told him, in making the request, that it was a superstition of mine, retained since the days of early childhood, that by carrying with me some article which belonged to a friend from whom I was about to part, I should secure a meeting again.

When the foregoing was penned, little did I dream that in a few short months the dear Meister would be called away from amongst us! What that loss means to his pupils and friends, no one living outside of that circle of which he was the sun and centre can possibly imagine. If I say that we feel ourselves to be like a flock which has lost its shepherd, an army that has lost its general, I am using no mere figure of speech, but am only indicating the very real relation that subsisted between the members of the school and their head. I am also quoting from his own expressions. For in the preface to a long work of his—the outcome of his lifelong thought and action—entitled *Les Expériences d'un Pianiste* (which is not yet in print), he refers to 'victories won on the battle-field of Art'; and I have been amused by hearing him say, referring to his different treatment of different pupils, 'I don't comb all my lambs with the same comb.'

It was my sorrowful, yet most dearly valued privilege, to be one of a few who stood beside his couch and caught his last conscious glances, and heard the last tones of his voice. That wonderful hand lay in mine—so soft, velvet-like, and warm, that even when death had transfigured his face, and given it a look at once sweet and solemn, I could not realize that he was indeed gone until I felt the fingers stiffen and grow chill in my clasp. It is not my present purpose to speak of these last weeks, days, hours, but just to add to the very slight sketch I have previously given of the Meister as a teacher and my relations with him as a pupil, some few traits characteristic of him as a man—traits which have come under my own personal observation, and (people will say, women-like) which have deepened and intensified my loving reverence for the Musician, Artist, Meister.

He was not only so good and generous as to give lessons for long years to those who were qualifying themselves for becoming teachers—and who could not have afforded to pay him anything—but he treated all such pupils with a delicacy of feeling, a consideration and thoughtfulness, of which I believe we should find but few examples in any profession. The following two instances came under my own personal observation, and in both I derived my knowledge of the fact that he was giving, and they receiving, through others, and in quite an incidental manner.

It was in the middle of winter, and the snow lay deep on the ground in St. Petersburg, when I went one day by appointment to take my lesson from Henselt, and was, according to the usual custom, ushered into his anteroom, after leaving my fur and other wraps in the hall. Instead, however, of being called in as usual by his man, the Meister himself appeared after a few moments, and (it was always his fashion to come at once to the point without prelude or preamble) greeted me with, ' My dear friend, I am in a sort of fix this moment, for I find that I have appointed the same hour for you and another lady. She is here, and as she is a teacher, her time is valuable—she cannot come backwards and forwards to me : what is to be done?'

I naturally at once said I would either wait, if he would have time for me when she was done, or else would go home and come back later, whichever might suit him best. It was settled then that I should have he next hour after hers.

As I lived only about ten minutes' walk from him,

however, I went home; and, after finishing a letter, came back to Henselt's house, thinking I was to play to him then. But (first and last time that such a thing occurred during all the time I knew him) there had been *another* appointment made by him for that same hour, and just as I set off for home, a pupil for examination from one of the Imperial Institutes had arrived with her governess. He had been obliged to give her the hour which he had taken from me; and there was the young teacher still waiting, and Henselt quite nervous and worried about her, and her loss of time.

'I have been so stupid to-day,' he said, 'and have treated you badly; but you will forgive me, won't you? You shall have an hour to-morrow, for I have no more time to-day.'

I was so sorry, even though I got the lesson from him the next morning, for to play to him was always 'an event,' something for which one had got one's self wound up, and even to have it deferred for a single day was a disappointment, and he knew it. But what could one do but tell him not to worry? It was not until long enough afterwards that I found out, in quite an accidental manner (and I never told him that I knew it), that the young lady to whom he had shown such consideration was one of several sisters, all of whom earned their living as teachers, and all of whom had been his free pupils for years. She was, moreover, a girl of only average ability, and he could have had no special personal interest in her.

This was but one among the many instances I gradually learned to know of poor girls owing their lifelong subsistence to him. One of them, a valued personal friend of my own, told me that during many years she found him invariably the same—kind and considerate—and never given to putting off a lesson, for which, however, he would accept no remuneration.

Another instance, also drawn from personal knowledge, will still more exemplify his utter unworldliness.

The second winter I went to St. Petersburg I had the happy sense of being one of those who belonged to the inner circle of his intimate friends. He allowed me to rummage among his music when he was absent; his housekeeper was fond of me, and loved to tell me of his ways and doings, so that when on arriving I did not at once find suitable rooms, and therefore could not hire a piano, I went to Lisette (the housekeeper), and told her I would come round and practise during the evening hours, when his Excellency was out. He sent me word through her that there were days in the week when I was quite welcome to practise there in the mornings as well; but that there was a young lady who had been coming for months to work there every evening, and that I must settle with her what time she could leave the piano free for me. This young lady was one of the younger teachers, so poor that she could not hire a piano for study; I learned this from others, not from Henselt. These were some among the many things which so endeared the Meister to all who came into near contact with him. There was a charm about the rugged, yet warm and sturdily honest personality, which so inspired many of his followers that they thought nothing of any sacrifice of time, or trouble, if only in so doing they were serving him.

Fräulein Calvert, one of his most gifted pupils and best teachers—so sought after that week after week she gave ten hour-lessons every day—had been for years the privileged one to whom he at once sent any new idea which he allowed himself to trace with a pencil (for in later years he never noted music with a pen). Here I may observe that whenever a new way of either rendering a passage, or fingering it in any given piece, occurred to Henselt, he insisted on his publisher reprinting the whole; and as he was always very eager to get this done at once, Fräulein Calvert thought nothing of copying out the entire piece, and sending it back to him ready for printing.

Fräulein Heinrichsen, called in St. Petersburg 'his right hand,' for twenty-eight years teacher in two Imperial Institutes, is the most rigid and completely methodical teacher of his *technical* side; and I here record my sense of obligation to her once more; here record, too, that having entered the school in mature years, having enjoyed a wide culture in other fields, I was for a long time at odds internally with her on the ground of her refusal to hear any artist, or to recognise any excellence beyond that of his school. Although I believed, from the first time that I saw and heard him, that I had found something which would remain with me, not only in time, but for ever, yet to recognise that, wherever you took him, Henselt stood on a tone-plane where none I have ever heard have come near him,—this was a perception which grew upon me the more I heard him. Yet I did not always hear him at his best; I often heard him when he could not soar, but just fluttered as it were above the ground. I was often angry that he would play his passages over and over again; but it grew on me, a film fell from my eyes, as I began to understand that every repetition with him meant, and was, an intense upward struggle out of the 'fleshly' into the 'spiritual.' I understood—as much as disciples may dare say they understand of something immeasurably above them—I understood that one may seem to have achieved much, and yet be on a low plane; that one may be gasping and inarticulate, and in pain, just because the plane we have struggled up to is high, and one cannot remain on it without growing giddy.

I was not there to hear it, but his last performance —the swan-song the day before his last illness—was the overture to *Oberon*. He fainted after that wonderful performance. He never again was heard in his strength.

I have read with pleasure and gratitude F. Nieck's

very interesting though brief notice of the Meister, in the *Musical Record* of November, 1889. It is a comfort to know there are those who acknowledge that he stands third with Chopin and Liszt; that to this trio we can add no fourth—at least, not of their generation.

*   *   *   *   *

La Mara.

The writer of the following interesting sketch of Henselt, a sketch which includes a long letter from the Meister when quite a young man to a young lady friend and pupil, and two letters from Robert Schumann, has been for many years past well known in Germany as a biographer of musicians, and one who holds a high rank among art-critics, having had the good fortune to be reared in an atmosphere of learning and culture, and enjoyed personal intercourse with many eminent musicians. La Mara has brought to the task, to which her entire life has been devoted, qualifications such as few possess. The choicest libraries have been accessible to her, and she has spared neither time nor labour in getting hold of every detail which relates to the great masters of whom she speaks. 'Her Musical Portrait Studies,' several volumes of which are about to appear in a seventh edition, are for this reason not only vivid and intensely interesting, but true to nature and lifelike. 'Five Centuries of Musicians' Letters' are being printed by Breitkopf and Härtel, and the present little paper will be included in a work just published by the same firm, 'The Classical and Romantic in the World of Tone.' Professor Rüst, of Leipzig, said to me in reference to La Mara, that she was more thoroughly acquainted with her subject than almost any living author who wrote about music, and as he is a musician of high standing, and, according to some, the greatest living authority on the works of Sebastian Bach, an opinion like the above would naturally carry with it much weight.

In Memory of Adolf von Henselt.*

In Adolf von Henselt, whose birthday falls on the 12th of May, we have, in the autumn of the past year, lost the last surviving representative of the older grand school of virtuosity. A contemporary of Liszt and Chopin, he was, like them, at once an incomparable master of his instrument, and a genial tone-creator for it. United with them, he carried to the tomb the Hummel-Field epoch, an epoch in which virtuosity was its own aim and end, in order to replace it with the virtuosity of the romantic school —a virtuosity rich in its subjective and idealistic tendencies, and in its supreme control over the material

---

* Translated from the German of La Mara in the Scientific Supplement to the *Leipziger Zeitung*, and published with the sanction of the author.

—the *technique* by which these are expressed. Rooted in the solid and classical soil of the Hummel school, and developing himself still further on the model of Thalberg, he became finally his own teacher. According to his own testimony, he is indebted to himself alone for his peculiar pianoforte *technique*, with its extension and fulness, its legato and song-like phrasing, and its beauty and depth of tone. As a composer he has also established his claim to be regarded as a specialist. He is the troubadour of the Clavier, and all tones of the heart are at his command. Music is for him the art of expressing the feelings which pass from one soul to another. When she leaves the domain of feeling, and passes over into that of speculative thought, she has then struck into paths which lie quite out of his beat. His artistic individuality is characterized by a gently elegiac undertone, a touch of Weber's romance of feeling and of Chopin's enthusiasm. Yet there is in him no vein of sentimentality. If he may be aptly termed the Chopin of Germany, the essential healthiness of his nature constitutes an essential difference between him and his Franco-Polish favourite. The abstruseness to which Schumann gives the name of 'crotchetyness,' the mysterious backgrounds, the ingenious pikanteries, the nervous capriccios, the impassioned bursts of sorrow which are so inherent in Chopin's tone-poetry, do not exist in Henselt. The song which had its source in the inner depths of his being wells forth in a rich, clear stream. His melody is at once simple and spontaneous, and yet full of aristocratic grace and distinction. It is a fact beyond dispute that his studies, so brimful of poetry, and each bearing a motto indicative of its inner meaning, his *Poême d'Amour*, his *Concerto*, his *Duo*, etc., will always continue to rank with the noblest, the most beautiful compositions which have been written for the instrument.

Hardly had he appeared before the public as a pianist when he took his place among the first, and was ranked with Liszt and Thalberg. Joyfully welcomed as a composer by the best of his generation, foremost amongst whom were Mendelssohn and Schumann, his MSS. passed from hand to hand, and were everywhere received with delight. Henselt saw opening out before him such a career of fame and splendour as fortune but rarely offers to any one individual of the race. Yet, with a spirit of almost unparalleled self-renunciation, hardly had he entered on a career so rich in promise when he turned his back on it for ever: he exchanged the golden laurels, which were showered on him by the hydra-headed multitudes of European cities, for the sober joys of a teacher. In the quiet hours of study, when he directed his pupils towards the path which leads to the ideal, he who had never been content with himself experienced a satisfaction which he never found in the concert-room. To stimulate the aspirations of the young, to foster in them an enthusiasm for the beautiful and true, and to strengthen and develop their individual aptitudes, was his life-task, and he pursued it with true-hearted devotion to the very last. Nor did he fail to receive a full meed of grateful thanks and honourable recognition. Many signs of distinction were conferred on him, and the seed which he took such pains to scatter abroad has borne fruit a hundredfold, which shall witness for him long after he has passed away. Yet all the while we cannot forbear to lament that so melodious a singer should, just as the world had begun to admire him, have lapsed into prolonged silence, that the virtuoso and composer should alike have retired from the scene. He ceased to shower his rich gifts around, for, from the time that he gave himself up entirely to teaching, all that he wrote, including his numerous arrangements of other composers' works, were, with but a few solitary exceptions, meant for instructive purposes. We must, furthermore, lament that one who was so essentially German in his art, should have withdrawn his genius from his Fatherland, and lived and worked among a foreign race for upwards of half a century.

He was born in Schwabach, near Nuremburg, on the 12th of May, 1814. His father, a cotton-weaver, of Saxon extraction, was in narrow circumstances. The wife of Privy-councillor Flad, who had been a pupil of Abbé Vogler, fostered his gifts in early years.

Later on, Hummel, then in Weimar, developed them pianistically. Sechter, of Vienna, was his master in harmony. It was in the last-named city that he acquired a mastery both as a virtuoso and composer, which was recognised there in the first instance, and afterwards met with warm recognition in Weimar, Berlin, Dresden, Leipzig, and Warsaw. In the April of 1838 he came to St. Petersburg, and was induced to remain there for the rest of his life. The friend and protégé of three successive emperors, he found in this city a congenial sphere of work, and never afterwards left it, except during the few months of summer-rest which he permitted himself to spend every year in his country home at Warmbrunn. Ceasing to take any part in the musical life of Germany, gradually withdrawing himself from all contact with the younger generation, and ever more and more retreating from all intercourse with his brother artists, Henselt went on isolating himself until the day arrived when he found that he was all but a stranger in Germany, and only at last returned to lie down and seek a final resting-place there.

He was still in full vigour when he entered into correspondence with the writer of these lines. It was in the spring of the year 1874. The first two volumes of the 'Musical Portrait Studies' had reached a second edition, and a third volume was in progress, in which a portrait of Henselt was to have a place. I talked the matter over with Liszt, who had been for many years past the honoured friend and adviser, without whose approbation none of my artistic plans were ever brought to completion. I was well aware that not only the utter seclusion in which Henselt lived, but a shrinking from all publicity, which was quite peculiar to himself, rendered him extremely difficult of access. Clara Bauer, a pupil of his, well known by the literary name of Carl Detleff, had already initiated me into his peculiarities, both as a man and an artist. I was, therefore, prepared for not attaining my purpose without many rounds and much trouble, though, on the other hand, I knew well that he had a bitter consciousness of being nearly forgotten in Germany. I wrote accordingly to tell him of my intention, and to ask at the same time if he would help me in the matter by replying to some questions which I would lay before him. He was, I had been told, no friend of expansive letters; and such a mode of proceeding was therefore quite in accordance with a nature which always leaned towards the tangible and practical. Eight days later I was in possession of his reply:

'Warmbrunn in Silesia, July 6th, 1874.

'MADAM,

'I regret extremely that, although I feel in my heart grateful to you for all the pains you are taking—all your goodness to me—I must seem not only unheedful, but also most thankless for the same.

But at sixty years of age I can no longer change. I am persuaded that because I performed so little of what I had promised in my youth, it would be impossible to speak about me without censure. In the goodwill with which you address yourself to me, I perceive no intention of this kind. Yet I am convinced that when you hear me speak in person (this you will have no difficulty in doing if you permit me to visit you), I shall be able to convince you that I am arguing aright. With the deepest respect,

'Yours, etc.,
'ADOLF HENSELT.'

It may well be imagined that I did not rest content with this result. A second letter was despatched to Henselt, and received the following reply:

'Frankfort-on-the-Oder, October, 1874.
'HIGHLY HONOURED MADAM,

'I know that it is an honour for anyone to be mentioned by your pen. For this reason I from my heart beg of you not to be angry with me for not having fallen in with your wish. It is, with regard to myself, my unalterable conviction that, judging from my early beginnings—I was but nineteen when I wrote Op. 14*—the world had a right to demand far more from me than I have accomplished. Any other opinion than this could not fail to encounter opposi-

* The lovely *Duo* for the pianoforte and horn.

tion in many quarters. Taking the most favourable view, it could only be said that if I had not been devoted to pianoforte-playing I might possibly have done something more remarkable in composition. Believe me, this is the correct opinion to form about me. Each individual artist is the best judge of himself when vanity does not darken his understanding. Constant indisposition has this year obliged me to defer the pleasure of at once making your acquaintance, and of thanking you for your kind intentions with regard to me. For this, however, I hope, with God's help, to indemnify myself in the season of 1884. Accept the assurance of profound respect from

'Your obedient servant,
'A. D. HENSELT.

'P.S.—Kindly excuse my writing—writing is a great difficulty to me.'*

Meanwhile, though in the first instance without my knowledge, I had in Frau von Henselt won a secret ally to my plan. She became interested as well for my work in general as for this particular design, and, without her husband's knowledge, sent me, through a friend of his, a reply to the questions I had in vain put to him. Her communications,

* Henselt's writing was all the more illegible from his habit of joining one word to another. It is very characteristic, and rather reminds one of Beethoven's.

which entered into some further particulars, placed me in a position to carry my wishes into effect. In the long-run, however, her correspondence with me could not remain a secret to Henselt, for she was, of course, obliged to put many a question to him here and there. When the catalogue of his works, which I had grouped together for adding to my sketch of them, was to be submitted to his criticism, it was impossible for me to avoid addressing myself again directly to him. The 23rd of April, 1875, brought me the following lines in his handwriting:

'HONOURED MADAM,

'You do me far too much honour! I always grow fearful and timid when people speak of me as a composer, and talk of my works. You think perhaps that I undervalue myself; by no means, but I live in no illusion about myself. I know, for instance, quite well, that some of my compositions are among the best which have been written for the instrument—that I have written better studies than many a so-called composer. Still, this is far too little; that is to say, the works that deserve mention are far too few in number; I have but given a proof that I might have been a composer: the circumstances of my life were, however, not favourable to it. Above all, the passion for virtuosity should have never taken possession of me. As you have taken so much trouble about me, as even yourself to note down with your own hand all my compositions and transcriptions, I now willingly hold out my hand to you, and in order to help you to carry out the wish of omitting nothing in this catalogue, I am asking my chief publisher here to send me a complete catalogue of all my works. As far as I can remember, there is not only no omission in your catalogue (I wonder how you came to know even the utterly worthless trifles), but it is far too full. In order to make it easier to you, I let you have it again, only adding to it my observations, etc. You seem to know nothing of my misfortune in getting the left arm broken at the wrist, and how, after five months, I still suffer from stiffness, swelling, and pains—have swollen fingers, cannot move the wrist; in short, that I (being in my sixty-first year) can never hope to be perfectly well again. Notwithstanding this, and although, as I cannot play for you, I can offer you but little that is interesting, yet for my own sake I will certainly not let pass the first opportunity of making your acquaintance. I cannot as yet quite foresee what journeys and what treatment this accident will necessitate during the summer; the present idea is that I should first try what my second native country in Warmbrunn can do for me; if this does not cure me in four or six weeks, try something else. We shall remain anyhow in correspondence, and I shall not fail to keep you *au fait* of what I am doing. Accept my thanks for the undeserved kindly interest which you bestow upon me, and accept the assurance of profound respect from

'Your very obedient servant,
'ADOLF HENSELT.

'P.S.—I believe that there are no compositions corresponding to the numbers Op. 12, 21, 26, 27, 38; but if forthcoming, they must be something quite insignificant. This confusion has been caused by various publishers creating at their own discretion, and without coming to any mutual understanding, the Opus numbers. My publisher may perhaps give us a little help in the matter. I will, however, forward his report to you, for this tardy reply burns under my fingers. I beg you will kindly excuse me, for I have become stupid through this accident' (the breaking of his arm above alluded to); 'I labour painfully through the masses of letters before I get at what I want. I am an official, and having once accepted service, must discharge my duties thoroughly. It sometimes happens that I do not come at reading the letters I like best on the day they reach me. The fact of its being just now Holy Week helps me to perform my duty towards you. I do not recognise the six themes of Paganini as my work. What sort of valse is *Petite Valse pour Piano*, Leipzig, Siegel? I do not remember any such composition. The two earlier of the same kind are, of course, those in F and C major. I beg you not to mention "Silent Love" as a song. It is taken from the *Duo* for pianoforte and horn, and gives evidence of my numerical poverty, though the melody is indeed one of my best.

'"Evening Thoughts for the Pianoforte," in the Elizabeth Fest-Album, is quite unknown to me. "A Few Observations derived from my Experiences,"* is this known to you in the Russian edition, and by what means? I thought it was only to be had here' (in St. Petersburg). 'I beg of you not to include in your list the "four vocal numbers." The overture of Llwoll has no business to be named here with the others.†

'I have received Stellowsky's list, and enclose it to you here.‡ I believe that you have omitted nothing, but, on the contrary, that you have named rather too many. Perhaps you may think it desirable to make mention of an Étude in A minor, which is just coming out in the school of Lebert and Stark. Also a morning song in G major, printed here for the benefit of those who suffered in Samarow, and in the burning of the

* 'On Pianoforte Teaching: as a Guide for Teachers and Students in the Imperial Institutes entrusted to me.' I had become acquainted with this work through a friend of Henselt's.

† By Weber and Beethoven, arranged by Henselt as a pianoforte solo for concert performance.

‡ The Russian catalogue mentions Opus 51 of Henselt, while in Germany only forty have appeared with the Opus number indicated. The Russian catalogue has accordingly named several compositions without giving the Opus number, and differs from the German edition by giving them in quite a different order of succession.

musical college in Chicago. Both the above pieces will appear separately. I must again apologize for my writing. Not being able to hold ' (the sheet) ' with my left hand, I find writing very difficult.

'Once more,
'Yours, etc.,
'A. HENSELT.'

['Do not take it amiss that on account of my questions I take it for granted that you will write to me again. I await with impatience the book so kindly promised me.']

In the middle of the following summer the third volume of 'Musical Portrait-heads appeared,' and Henselt thanked me for the gift in these words:

'Warmbrunn, September 3rd, 1875.

'HIGHLY RESPECTED MADAM,

'After all the kindness, all the honour you have shown me, the least I could do, according to my feeling on the subject, would be to convey my thanks to you in person. But the accident that happened to my hand demands so many things, that, if God will, I must look forward to the next year as being more favourable. Do not therefore disdain to receive in this manner my most heartfelt thanks. I have read your other essays with the deepest interest. . . .*

* Henselt's very warm expressions of appreciation are here omitted, as it would not have been becoming for me to publish them myself.

Allow me to hope that next year will bring with it the pleasure of your personal acquaintance. Once more receive with renewed thanks an assurance of profound esteem from

'Your very obedient servant,
'ADOLF HENSELT.

'P.S.—My wife desires to be particularly remembered to you.'

After this there was a long pause in our intercourse by letter. It was not until early in the year 1878, when there was a question of my preparing a fourth edition of my book for publication, that I again addressed a few questions to the Meister—questions which had for their end the filling up of the sketch which referred to him, and making it more complete. He answered me on the 7th of April, 1878:

'HONOURED MADAM,
'I do not deserve so much goodness and attention on your part. Pray accept my thanks for it all. The time when people will perhaps be able to take an interest in me will only begin after my decease. Even then, only when the heads of the notes either speak for or against themselves, when all other interests, acquaintanceships, and relationships have long passed away. You have, I hope, still many years before you, and may therefore recall these words of mine. I have answered your questions to the best of my

ability, though it continues to be my opinion that you ought not to take any more trouble about the article on me. I know of a certainty that more people will cavil over it than enjoy it. Yet all the while some have done me the justice to say that I seemed to stand before them in bodily presence' (in La Mara's article on Henselt above referred to). 'Yet all that has appeared with reference to me must be uninteresting. With regard to my arrangements, it is a question of time (whether they will find due appreciation). People have been so used to hear them taken up by mere *finger-heroes*' (a word of Henselt's coining). 'This has given rise to a well-founded mistrust, which will never be effaced until every other interest except that of the thing itself shall have passed for ever out of view. Ah! if you cannot make up your mind to come to Warmbrunn, I fear greatly we shall never know each other, for I am always growing shyer and shyer. Could I but come to Leipzig and just pay a visit to you yourself, and there was nothing further to come out of it, I would have done so long ago. But so many would feel themselves slighted—Liszt, for instance (not to speak of others). Get the school of Ryba with the high school of Henselt (*i.e.*, des pièces tirées de la dernière). Zschocher,* indeed, thinks I believe very little about it; he is, however, quite in the wrong. You are perhaps aware that I

---

* The director of a large music-school in Leipzig, and Henselt's friend.

have lost my only son' (the only child of the Henselts) 'in his thirty-ninth year? You will, I hope, under these circumstances, be kindly indulgent to

'Yours, etc.,
'AD. HENSELT.

'P.S.—In compliance with your wishes, I have replied to all queries. But I repeat once more that all you could say about me must be uninteresting. You would, I am sure, do better to leave the article on me just as it stands. When and how is there any hope of our becoming acquainted? Do you not know what a lovely neighbourhood we live in? Do but ask Zschocher and his wife! There we might mutually come to know each other a little better!

'Get from Hofmeister' (a music warehouse in Leipzig) 'the first movement of Hummel's Concerto in B minor for the pianoforte, arranged as a solo by Henselt.'

The work mentioned in the postscript is at the same time the first number of Henselt's *Haute école du piano*, and the last a most advanced piece in Ryba's 'Rational Pianoforte Teaching,' and connects the two. Henselt prefixed to the preface of the above a verse of Boileau, which very aptly shows his (Henselt's) intensely rooted convictions:

'Hâtez-vous lentement, et sans perdre courage,
Vingt fois sur le métier remettez votre ouvrage.
Polissez le sens et le repolissez,
Ajoutez quelquefois, et souvent repassez.'

He had a profound belief in the importance of this undertaking. He writes thus on the same sheet as the questions, which, together with his replies to them, he reinclosed to me: 'I hope that after I have been for many years gone away, you will discover that it is only when *teaching ends* are in view that I am in my own true element.' To a question put to him, on the other hand, as to whether any new composition of his was coming out, he observes thus characteristically: 'Ever since my youth I have gone backwards in productivity, and this even where I really wished to have done something. I thank God that I can see this clearly.' His morning song in G major, so full of deep feeling, and his arrangement of Weber's E flat polonaise, are, according to him 'not worthy of mention.' He disposes of his arrangement of Mendelssohn's G minor concerto for two pianos with the words, 'Will be attacked by many; do not let it appear.'

A few days later he sent me his photograph with the following lines:

'April 1/13, 1878.

'MOST ESTEEMED MADAM,

'I just now remember with consternation that I omitted to enclose you the wished-for carte. Kindly excuse me, and allow me to request that you will favour me with your own.

'Your obedient servant,

'AD. HENSELT.

'P.S.—Should you ever have an opportunity of being able to do something for "Ryba's school," I should be very grateful to you. The school deserves to be recommended, not, indeed, for the sake of the giver, but for that of the receiver. The disinterested and active share I take in it will show you the strength of my conviction; for these two years past I have taken my share of work in it, *just to help the good cause.*'

At this time Henselt's friend Zschocher made me acquainted with his *Préambules dans tous les tons majeurs et mineurs* (only published in a Russian edition). This suite of unpretending miniatures in the narrowest possible proportions (they do not overstep the limits of one to three lines) are full of poetry and of Henselt's flow of melody.

The following lines are in reply to my request for a copy of this charming work, which was quite unknown in Germany:

'St. Petersburg, April 9th, 1878.

' DEAR AND HONOURED MADAM,

'Pray never and nowhere touch on my *Préambules*. They were only written for the children in the institutes (because the directresses of these latter did not wish the pupils to play their pieces without something introductory; as if, indeed, doing so placed the children on a higher standpoint); they have, therefore, been written without very much thought, and are so likely to be brought into comparison with Chopin's genial and intellectual creations in the same genre. I perfectly well know that I cannot measure myself with Chopin, and am therefore but human in not wishing to figure beside him just at my weakest. As you, however, just out of pure friendship for me, are kind enough to take an interest in them, I have great pleasure in sending you a copy. May I beg you to make use of this letter if necessary (I hope it will be sufficient for the purpose), in order to authorize your receiving a copy of the "Ryba School" from Hofmeister. I will make it all good with Herr Ryba. I take this short way of doing things both for your sake and mine. Had no idea that your outer and inner being were in such complete harmony' (Henselt here refers to the likeness of La Mara). 'Pray accept a thousand thanks for the much-valued gift. You will, I hope, excuse the mistake that arose out of my wish to answer your valued letter at once, and according to the order in which I received it, and pardon

'Yours, etc.,

'AD. HENSELT.'

CONCLUSION.

In the summer of the following year Henselt came to Leipzig, but unfortunately did not find me there.

The following lines contain the first direct news I had of him afterwards. They were intended to be made use of by me, in bringing out the new edition of my third volume.

'Siegsdorf, near Trauenstein in Bavaria, July 17th, 1883.

'Highly respected Madam,

'Your letter has been sent after me, and as I am always, when travelling, little *à mon aise*, I must beg you courteously to excuse me if, without any preamble, I go at once right to the point. The greater number of the compositions you so kindly mention were only produced for stated occasions, in order to make amateurs take pleasure in their bad compositions. They are, therefore, really not worth mention, and would, I even believe, serve as welcome weapons for my enemies to use against me. The few numbers which I am not ashamed to own are: 2.* *Thèmes d'Auber;* 3. *Sehnsucht;* 4. *Romance de Davidoff;* 10. *Epistodischer Gedanke;* 11. *Abschiedsklage;* 12. *Maienzeit;* 14. *Frühlingslied* (1832); 15. Mendelssohn's *Wedding March*, interpreted for the piano by Henselt. I must beg you to leave the intermediate numbers unnoticed. I will send you a good cabinet photograph with the greatest possible pleasure, but, unluckily, cannot do so until I reach

---

* The numbers refer to a supplement of his catalogue which I had sent for his inspection.

St. Petersburg, for it is locked up there, and no one can get at it. If you, however, must really have it without delay, there is one of the same to be had at Haufstengel's, in Dresden.* Let me, however, hope, honoured madam, that in some way or other I shall succeed in making your acquaintance. My wife, who wishes to be especially remembered to you, is quite as impatient for this event as

'Your very obedient and obliged servant,

'HENSELT.

'Our address for the four summer months is always Warmbrunn. May I ask you to enlighten me with regard to No. 13, Würst, Op. 64, for I know nothing about it?† May I beg your kind indulgence for this letter? You can no doubt perceive with what difficulty I write.'

I answered his question about Wurst in my next letter, but, to the annoyance of the pedantic composer, wrote the name Wurst so indistinctly that he at once cut the piece out of my letter and enclosed it to me with the following words:

'Warmbrunn, September 11th, 1883.

'HIGHLY RESPECTED MADAM,

'Pray accept my best thanks for your kind

---

* The composer's portrait was to appear in the new edition of 'Musical Portrait Studies.'

† I had seen indicated in a musical journal 'Three Pianoforte Pieces by Würst,' fingered by Henselt, Erler, Berlin.

letter and *Offerte*. That there should be anything in
your letter which I could not decipher is to me so un-
endurable that I have taken the liberty of cutting out
the illegible name, and beg you to make it clear to
me. My health is by no means all I could desire. I
will not fail to send the photograph from St. Petersburg. With special greetings from both of us, and
with the most profound respect,

   'Your very faithful and devoted
          'ADOLF HENSELT.'

The next lines refer to the new edition of my book
which had been sent to him :

    'Warmbrunn in Silesia, June 13th, 1884.'

'HIGHLY RESPECTED MADAM,
  'Accept my best thanks for your interesting
book, which contains views which do me so much
honour. My wife commissions me to do the like, for
you have given her a real satisfaction, for which
she cannot omit to thank you. Neither she nor I
have forgotten that you once had the project of
visiting our beautiful neighbourhood, and that you
wished to procure us the great pleasure of making
your personal acquaintance. Don't give up this
idea; and don't forget that we are old folk, and,
according to the laws of nature, cannot live long.
May this decide you on not putting off your plan too

long! With the greatest respect, I am, and continue to be,

'Yours very faithfully,

'AD. HENSELT.'

Just a year later than this the editing of 'Five Centuries of Musicians' Letters,' a work in which I had been long engaged, was so far advanced that I made no delay in asking Henselt to sanction some letters of his being included in my collection. I sent him a long and very characteristic letter which he had written to a Fräulein Bonterwek, a friend of early youth. Among various other matters, this letter made mention of an offer made to him to undertake the tuition of certain princesses. The three following letters from Henselt are in reference to the above:*

'Warmbrunn, July 30th, 1885.

'HONOURED MADAM,

'I have received your kind letter, and gladly comply with your wishes. Yet, unless there are too many difficulties in connection with doing so, don't you think that for my own sake and that of the world in general I ought to see the original of my own letter? For—you will be surprised—I have no recollection of the offer referring to Berlin. Such an

* The letter was finally not included among 'Musicians' Letters,' but I give it in the context of Henselt's letters to me.

offer would have surely played such a part in my life at that period that I must at least have spoken of it to my wife; for it was just at that time that I became acquainted with her. The whole thing is, therefore, quite a puzzle to me, especially as the letters look quite like mine. I return, therefore, to the point that it is due to us all that I should see the actual original of the letter to Fräulein Bonterwek. It is, to be sure, quite possible that, owing to the varied impressions of that time, the incident may have slipped out of my memory. I expect your opinion, at all events, on the above, and only repeat once more that it is always my wish to oblige you. With most cordial esteem,

'Yours most faithfully,
'AD. HENSELT.

'P.S.—It is an understood thing that if Fräulein von Holstein is so kind as to send me the original of my letter, I will send it back to her directly. My wife's best regards, and our united regret about your change of plan.*

'A. H.'

'August 19th, 1885.

'HIGHLY RESPECTED MADAM,
'They have shown little delicacy in keeping back the letters all this while. It is the 19th, and

* A journey to Vienna, taking in Warmbrunn on the route.

you are at the given address only up to the 25th inst. I shall, therefore, for security's sake, have them registered. I am quite convinced that there has been no forgery, and yet, unless I were driven to it, I could not swear that the letter in question was mine. I am also convinced that you have wished to know that the letter had been seen by me. You need not be uneasy lest Fräulein von Holstein should be at the loss of the letter. My wife desires her best regards, and with the wish of some time seeing you,

'I am, your very obedient
'AD. HENSELT.

'Forgive my hurried letter; I have to write so much, and am old.'

'Warmbrunn, July 13th, 1886.

'HIGHLY RESPECTED MADAM,

'Five weeks ago my dear wife had an attack of nervous paralysis, which came on during a violent thunderstorm. Taking into account the depressing influence of this, and also my own indisposition, I hope for and crave your kind indulgence and forgiveness.* Some few people do indeed recover the power of speech, but the weakness of nature at my dear wife's advanced age leads me to fear the worst in her case. The letter to Fräulein Bonterwek dates between

---

* For the long delay in returning the letter just referred to, a delay which had called for a reminder on my part.

1833 and 1836. I have no recollection of what official post was referred to. Once more entreating your kind indulgence and pardon,

   'Your obedient and much afflicted
         'ADOLF HENSELT.

'My wife begs me to send you her best regards, in which I unite.'

A few weeks after I had received the above letter Liszt passed away, July 31st, 1886, and in editing a collection of his letters I felt that I was fulfilling a long-projected and dearly cherished plan. Applying for the sanction of the Meister's chief heir, the Princess Wittgenstein of Rome, with whom I had long been on friendly terms, she did not refuse my request, and in order from the outset to exclude every other unauthorized version of Liszt's letters from other quarters, the princess gave the copyright of these to the firm of Breitkopf and Härtel, in Leipzig. It is of my present task in collecting from out of many lands the scattered materials—materials so rich in matter—that Henselt speaks in the following letter as 'an undertaking.' He encloses me a letter of Liszt's to him, which, at the request of Fräulein Ramann, he had already communicated to her for her 'Liszt Biography.'

    'Warmbrunn in Silesia, June 13th, 1887.
'HIGHLY ESTEEMED MADAM,
  'Having heard by chance that you are starting

on such an undertaking, I have, according to my feeling on the subject, done you a wrong in complying with the wishes of that other lady' (Fräulein Ramann, who had obtained from Henselt a letter of Liszt for her biography of this musician). 'I should like, as far as lies in my power, to make good this fault, and awaiting your possible decision—perhaps your silence on the subject—remain with the most profound respect,

'Yours,

'A. H.'

'Kindly excuse the laconic brevity of my letter. I leave no one without an answer, and am accordingly almost killed with writing.

'P.S.—The kind sympathy you express for my poor wife's condition lays on me the agreeable task of telling you that her bodily state is far better than we could have dared to hope.'

The three following letters, written to me by Henselt, are also on the subject of the Liszt correspondence. The first of these mentions the *Epistodischer Gedanke* of Weber, arranged for the pianoforte, and completed by Ad. Henselt. It was dedicated to his friend Fr. Liszt.

'Warmbrunn, May 5th, 1887.

'HONOURED MADAM,

'I anticipate your projected journey by my

rapid reply. Liszt's writing in reference to the *Epistodischer Gedanke* is not in the form of a letter. I will gladly let you have it. But, then, you must have patience until September, for it is under lock and key in St. Petersburg. It seems to me, however, that you can make use of the letter which you have copied out. I chance to have one with me belonging to the Baroness Wrangel, and willingly let you see it. I expect, however, that you will let me have it back at once, as the baroness has asked for it. It breathes all the *Liszt large-heartedness*. I can give you one other letter (but not until September) which refers to my offer of hospitality to him in St. Petersburg (we unfortunately did not have this experience). Fräulein Ramann is in possession of the letter I sent to you. Fräulein Ramann did not ask for this letter, but for the one referring to the *Epistodischer Gedanke*. This, however, as I have above said, does not exist in the form of a letter. Still, just as it is, you may willingly have it. I think I have now settled all your questions. With the most profound respect,

'Your obedient
'AD. HENSELT.

'P.S.—After I had just now read the enclosed letter referring to Liszt, I find that you ought to have the lines and musical quotations which refer to it. I am, as I have said, ready to do all I can, but you must have patience until September, *i.e.*, until, with God's help, I arrive in St. Petersburg. (It refers to my official jubilee of the year 1888.)'*

'St. Petersburg, April 16th, 1888.

'Highly honoured Madam,

'I beg ten thousand pardons; thought all had been despatched. I send you all that I still have of Liszt's. Forgive my unbecoming brevity and hurry; I am under the influence of the many engagements arising out of the jubilee. With the greatest esteem,
'Your obedient
'Ad. Henselt.'

Letters of Liszt which I shall make known elsewhere were enclosed in the letter. A few days later he also sent me letters of Hans von Bülow, Llooff, Hummel, Schumann. I let Henselt's last letter follow here. It runs thus:

'July 30th, 1888.

'Highly honoured Madam,

'I cannot with certainty recall the year that I was at Liszt's for two days; I had not the honour of

* Liszt's letter to the Baroness Wrangel, as likewise his album-leaf to Henselt, with the letter of thanks which the latter wrote to him, were published by me in the third volume of the 'Musical Portrait Studies,' fifth and sixth edition (Henselt-sketch); also in the second volume of 'Five Centuries of Musicians' Letters.'

playing whist with the grand-duke. The two bars referred to the *Epistodischer Gedanke*. With distinguished esteem,

'Your obedient
'AD. HENSELT.

'My poor wife is not better in health, nor am I, either. It becomes always more unlikely that I shall have the pleasure of coming to know you.'

The letters in Henselt's handwriting end here. One more leaf lies before me; it is in print, with a wide mourning border on which the following is written:

'This morning, at forty minutes after nine, my dearly-loved husband, Adolph von Henselt, state councillor (a title of honour) in the Russian Empire, and director over all the music schools throughout the empire, passed away calmly. His long and severe sufferings were borne by him in patient submission to the will of God.

'From his deeply-afflicted widow,
ROSALIE *née* MANGER.

'Warmbrunn, October 10th, 1889.'

I here add as a supplement, the earlier mentioned Viennese letters of Henselt to Fräulein Bonterwek which fall between the years 1833 and 1836. She died a few years ago, having been a protectress of art and artists at an advanced age, in Ilmanau. To these I also add two of Schumann's letters to Henselt.

[*Author's Note.*—In the summer of the year 1887, being in Warmbrunn and much with Henselt, I have heard him speak more than once about this identical letter. He seemed to believe that it was his own, for it was, he said, written quite in his style. Before giving it, a word or two may, however, be necessary, both for the sake of the writer and the lady to whom he wrote, and the abrupt and almost uncouth form in which the translator seems to have placed it before the public.

A conventional reader might be disposed to imagine that Henselt was either a lover of Fräulein Bonterwek, or perhaps on the way to become such. But from his youth up the Meister used this simple and hearty language to all those whom he liked. There never was a question of anything more than a cordial and entirely open friendship between him and the young lady in question. The translation is as literal as I well could make it, for I wished to preserve as far as possible the roughness and directness of the original. Henselt disliked writing, and took such short-cuts in coming to the point that his letters were full of elliptical sentences, not always quite intelligible, even to the persons whom he addressed, and full of enigmas to any outsider into whose hands the letter might happen to fall.]

'To Mdlle. M. Bonterwek, in the house of the President Conta.

'Most valued Friend,

'Is not this my usual way of addressing you? But I am in earnest; believe me, my love, that I really value you. Will you be able to forgive me for having delayed so long in writing to you? It seems not. But if I had known of this I would not have had the confidence to ask for news.

'Your letter, which rejoiced me greatly, and for which I thank you greatly (although it was indeed through one which was not addressed to me that I really perceived what you are to me), is lying before me. It gives rise to much which I ought to make you observe, and much to which I ought to reply. The first being too tedious to write in full, and as I, besides, shall soon have the pleasure of seeing you, I shall wait until then. You ask for my other songs. Once I am with you, you may have what you wish. Can you have so little knowledge of your own capacities that you cannot even compare yourself with N.? I certainly like her much; but I confess that I do not believe she will ever be a good performer. She has been too much spoilt from the first. For this reason I have not recommended to her the "Five-Finger Exercises." For even if she were to follow me blindly, and to play them, it would be a year at least before the *old man* would be able to see the good of it. I shall talk much over this—not write. You must have written a very flattering letter to Frau von Flad, for she asks most graciously after you. Has she already replied to you?

'Since then she speaks better of me. As to Hummel, I am really touched, and believe now that he, on the whole, means well with me. Thank him, meanwhile, in my name, and speak of a letter which will soon come to him. But I want you to tell me something more definite about this appointment. I am very happy about it—is it for life? Frau von Flad is also much pleased about it. She says I must not go to Vienna till I have something in writing. One of my kind acquaintances, who would rather have me in Vienna than Berlin, has written the enclosed questions. Select out of them what you think well, and speak with Hummel about it.

'Here I have been interrupted. I am with Frau von Schallhammer. She gives me leave to write my letter here. I do not, however, know what I said to you before, and am not taking time to read it again through. You asked me in your last letter if I were still working hard at the octaves. Oh yes! But I have set myself another task, at which you will be very much surprised. It is the "*extension* of the hand." I have brought this to such a point that I am able to stretch the following extension, but not to play it:

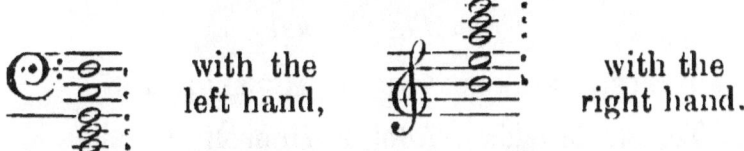

with the left hand,   with the right hand.

'While I hold this extension with one hand, I practise with the other; I can, besides this, also read or learn by heart. It is now eight o'clock in the evening. Perhaps I shall to-day yet write to Hummel when I get home. If not, however, I beg you to give him my best respects, and to thank him in my name. But now write me soon something in full—if you are but able to read and understand this letter, for, though there are but three women in the room, they speak twice as much as about double the number of men! I hope to find you in Weimar now when I come there. You write so much about your independence—then, why can't you stay on in Weimar? You must not let yourself be led astray by the above lines, and perhaps think that I make great demands; if the terms are in the least acceptable, I shall with pleasure leave my present position. Have I now forgotten to tell you anything? I can't think of anything more. Now a cordial good-bye; I am as glad as a child at the thought of seeing you.

'Your true friend,
'ADOLF HENSELT.

'I have already announced my intended departure to all my pupils.'

From the German.

LETTER OF SCHUMANN TO HENSELT, 1837.

'To the Musician Adolph Henselt, Breslau.

'Leipzig, August 31st, 1837.

'MY DEAR SIR,

'Your letter has been a great pleasure to me; I trust mine will be the same to you. To begin with, best thanks for so speedily complying with my request. It will not, however, quite answer to take the Study in B Major,* as the Schlesingers might not be pleased. I thought of the Study in E Minor,† which Clara played lately at her concert; but it is not a composition for the many. I will, however, see. What would please me best of all would be, if you could send me as soon as possible a study, or some smaller piece that would not be published anywhere else before the New Year. Accordingly, nothing that Hofmeister is bringing out, but anyhow something fine.‡ I cannot fall in with your idea of making the B Major Study begin with the simpler form; they both lose when so placed, and make the study look like a variation. Let it remain as an andante, and give it the title of "Andante and Etude," or, if you wish an antique title, call it "Preludium and Study," or whatever else you like. I am not for

---

* The celebrated *Poème d'Amour*, Op. 3.

† Op. 2, No. 8.

‡ Schumann evidently wished to have one of Henselt's compositions as a supplement to his new musical periodical.

the title of "Romanza." Do look at Bennett's compositions' (Sterndale Bennett). 'You will find much in them both for your nature and your heart. I am writing to you just as if you were an old friend; for have not both Becker and Wieck brought me so near to you of late that I can almost believe that I am touching your hand? But you must come—you must come: and you shall have a good time of it. Here there is life and go; here there are friends and artists who know how to honour you. You mean to go to St. Petersburg? Is this really true? Before you do so, write, however, again to your

'R. Schumann.'

Letter from Schumann to Henselt, 1837.

'To the composer, Adolph Henselt, at present staying in Salzbrunn.

'Leipzig, September 21st, 1837.

'Forgive me, my dear friend, for having remained so long silent after receiving so many tokens of friendship from you. These last days—they have been difficult. But more about this at some future time.* Besides, I have been able to do but little for you, as Hofmeister has been visiting the Naturalists in Prague. The Studies† are in hand, and in four days I am to have a proof of them. But

---

* Refers to difficulties which he had to fight his way through before winning his future wife, Clara Wieck.

† Henselt's Op. 2, published by Hofmeister.

with regard to metronomic indication you risk a great deal, for just on this point I frequently differ from the composer; and, after all, of what great importance is it? I shall, however, place the metronomic indications in the pieces as you wish. I quite agree with what you say to me about the pedal, for I also mark nothing more than " Pedal " at the beginning of my compositions. A whole number of quite new effects could be brought into play, where the pressure has to fall on the second (the unaccented) note of the bar. A question regarding the indications of performance, if we could possibly introduce them in German? I mean to send you soon my *Phantasiestücke*, and you can see that it looks very well. Thus, instead of Allegro, Rasch or Feurig, and so on, etc.* As to R. R., make yourself easy; at the bottom he is an ass, who thinks that with words he is able to say everything; in other ways, a good sort of fellow in whom one can feel no further interest. Clara plays the Study in the way in which it is most effective, *i.e.*, beginning with a Wave figure; and it is well that you only mean to publish it so. The variations in F are not yet out;† I believe Clara plays them incomparably. I don't enter the house, as you may perhaps know.

'The F Minor‡ is my especial favourite, as you

---

* Henselt retained the usual Italian indications.

† Henselt's Op. 1.

‡ Most probably the rhapsody, Op. 4.

may well imagine. Becker plays it with an Introduction in G Major in 2/4 time; and this might pass well enough if it only suited the close in F Minor. "Allegro Appassionato" is quite correct. My indication in German would be "äusserst bewegt," or else "schnell," and with "äusserst starker Emmpfindung" (extremely agitated, or else rapidly, and with extremely deep feeling)—*à propos* before I knew anything of you I gave mottoes to some of the smaller pieces in several of my cahiers—*i.e.*, in the *Carneval*, for instance, in *Phantasiestücke* and others. You find there "Traumeswirren," "in der Nacht," "warum"—a considerable number. The last-named compositions will please you, but the *Carneval* not quite so well. In the midst of my hard-working and active life I have just written eighteen *David's-bundler-tänzë*, and for this reason you must forgive me my bad writing.

'I can hardly get beyond one thought,* being full of thoughts; and yet all the more I am full of the pianoforte, and especially of you, whom I so love and value. If I only don't forget the title for the Studies, which will be ready in eight days! What are you going to do about the dedication? If the sanction from Munich were once in your hands,† a new one

---

* The last two words are nearly illegible.

† The studies, Op. 2, were dedicated to Louis I., King of Bavaria, whose assistance had enabled him to study under Hummel.

would have to be made at a pinch. They say here that you are married. May it go right well with you, as you indeed deserve! Farewell! I am weary with too much happiness and too much sorrow.

'R. SCHUMANN.'

The report of Henselt's marriage had not been correctly reported, for it was not until four weeks after the receipt of this letter that, on the 24th of October, 1837, in Salzbruun, Silesia, Henselt was united to his Rosalie. He had known her as the wife of Dr. Vogel, who was a friend of Goethe, and physician to Carl August in Weimar. His wonderful *Poème d'Amour* is dedicated to her.

At length, on the 29th of December, he accepted Schumann's invitation, and on being heard at Leipzig for the first and the last time in public was received with endless *salve*, and fêted with the highest honours. A few days later, without any presentiment that he was doing so, he in Dresden bid farewell for ever to an art career in Germany. It was but in death that Adolf Henselt was given back to us.

The accompanying letters from Liszt and Von Bülow, and the letter read to Henselt on the occasion of his jubilee, were given to me by Frau Mila, of Berlin, Henselt's niece by marriage.

Letter from von Bülow to Hensfelt.

'October 27th, 1864.

' Highly honoured Meister,

'You may have probably taken it somewhat amiss that when you were staying in Gersdorf I did not return you the manuscript which you had lent me, *i.e.*, your truly enchanting arrangement of Weber's Sonata in D Minor. Yet, though accountable for this delay, I am not altogether so much to blame as you may imagine. I have just passed through a very trying time, and it is only within the last fortnight that I have so far recovered from a very distressing form of indisposition as to be able to resume my pianoforte studies. The copyist had, moreover, left me in the lurch, and there was nothing else for it but to imprint your arrangement firmly on my memory. If I had not done this, it would have been impossible for me to enrich my Concert Répértoire with this pearl (as you have kindly sanctioned my doing). My performance of it will, I hope, leave you no occasion to regret that you have granted me this favour. It may perhaps even prove me worthy of your bestowing on me another of the same kind, *i.e.*, your letting me see your interpretation of Weber's second sonata, that in A flat? I earnestly hope, highly-esteemed and much-honoured Meister, that these lines, which the Schlesinger firm have kindly undertaken to forward with the manuscript, will find you in good health and spirits. It is with a sense of the deepest gratitude that I now recall the enviable hours which I had the good fortune to spend with you in St. Petersburg; above all, the never-to-be-forgotten enjoyment which fell to my lot when one day you were so good as to let me listen to your incomparable playing. This has, if I may so express myself, left a deep imprint on my memory; so much so that, in now resuming my pianoforte studies after a long interruption, the memory of what I then heard is a source from which I draw most fruitful instruction and helpful stimulus. May I at the same time be permitted to lay at your feet a work in which I believe I have not only given a useful guide to pianoforte literature as regards the general public, but likewise a useful help for instructive purposes. If it meets with your approbation it will be a great pleasure to me, but I in no way count upon your expressing any open opinion with regard to it. I may say, great Meister, that my life has taught me how to estimate the great value of time.

'It will interest you to hear that I found my father-in-law, Dr. Franz Liszt, in the best of health and in the full swing of productivity. During his short visit to Germany last autumn my illness unfortunately prevented me from bearing him company in any of his various tours to Carlsbad, Weimar, and Paris; and the happiness of being with him for any length of time—at all times seldom possible—was accordingly much diminished. My wife accompanied her father as far as Paris, and from there he, after a few days, returned to Rome, which, I am sorry to say, he for the future looks on as his settled home. I make free to take this opportunity of acquainting you that I am just about moving to Munich, where I have been summoned by his Majesty the King of Bavaria' (Louis II.). 'This change in the sphere of my activity is, I must say, in every respect an advantage. The over-exertions necessitated by Berlin life and the various strains on the nerves which were an inseparable part of it, were, I may say, the main cause of my indisposition during the past summer.

'I think of beginning the second half of the winter with my concert cycles in Berlin, Dresden, Hambourg, etc., and mean to open each of these with *Weber's D Minor Sonata.* According to your wish, I do not give the arranger's name; you will not, I hope, on the other hand, think me indiscreet for having spoken about it to Mr. Robert Lenan, the very musical and intelligent successor of Schlesinger : he is longing to make some agreement with you about these "arrangements." I have, however, most highly honoured Meister, taken up already much of your time; you have something better to do than reading this present letter. May I just add that I hope you will preserve a friendly recollection of me? On my side, you may be assured that I shall always occupy myself with your beautiful works, in so far as they may be accessible to my narrower range of activity. Pray accept, highly honoured Meister, the expression of my unalterable admiration and grateful devotion. I have the honour to sign myself

'Your very obedient servant,
'Hans von Bülow.'

Franz Liszt to Adolph Henselt.

'Weimar, June 5th, 1878.

'Highly honoured Friend,

'The original works of Adolph Henselt are most exquisite gems of art. One can but long to have a greater number of them. When Henselt, moreover, sets himself to revise—to interpret—to effectuate the compositions of others, he succeeds so admirably that both pianists and the general public are thereby greatly enriched and benefited. Even my insignificant *Lucia* transcription has, honoured friend, gained much through your interpretation. Cordial thanks for this reminiscence of our St. Petersburg intimacy. I simply return you the proof copy without a single touch or alteration, for all the " Varianten " suit most admirably. I leave entirely to you, moreover, all arrangements with regard to the publication of the same. The German copyright of Hofmeister does not, I suppose, hold good in Russia ? I am going to Paris to-morrow, and when there shall follow up your recommendation of the Russian pianofortes. Many of your admirers here, especially

Zschocher and Topfer, often talk with me about you.
When you visit Leipzig and Dresden, why not also
come on to Weimar? ' Please answer this modest
question by coming yourself to see.

    ' Yours, etc.,

          ' FRANZ LISZT.'

  Translated from the German.

Address read and presented to Henselt on the occasion
 of his Jubilee, April 21, 1888, by Rubinstein, at
 St. Petersburg.

 ' HIGHLY HONOURED HERR VON HENSELT,

  'This day fifty years since, you who then
already were a famous and honoured member of the
European world of music, devoted your great powers
and faculties to our Fatherland. Faithful and highly
gifted, you have, without interruption, throughout
these years served our noble art as a brilliant virtuoso
—the composer of a series of pianoforte works which
have ranked, and shall never cease to rank, with the
choicest masterpieces of contemporaneous musical
literature. You have, finally, been the representative
of a pedagogic system which, in your hands, has
received a genuinely earnest productive and formative
stamp. In all the above departments your energy
has been untiring. Active throughout a whole half-
century, you were on all sides met with the most profound respect, the most unfeigned admiration, the
most cordial affection.

'The Conservatoire of St. Petersburg, which is proud to rank you amongst its members, greets you to-day with such feelings as the above. But to feelings, which our community hold in common with the entire world of musical art, there is added a deep and unalloyed feeling of gratitude, awakened in us by the fact that when the Conservatoire recently passed through a difficult crisis, you generously came to us of your own accord, and, wholly in the interests of art, gave us the help of your pedagogic experience, continuing, with rare self-abnegation, all undaunted by the pressure of work, to labour in our midst for the benefit of the young.

'Accept, then, highly honoured Herr von Henselt, the most heartfelt brother-greeting of your associates and sincere admirers, who see in you the last surviving representative of the brilliant art pleiad of the last quarter of our century.

'Accept with this our greeting our not less earnest wish that it may be granted you to occupy for many, many years to come your fame-crowned position, a bright example to all conscientious disciples, all laborious servants of art in our Fatherland.'

THE END.

www.ingramcontent.com/pod-product-compliance
Lightning Source LLC
Chambersburg PA
CBHW021156230426
43667CB00006B/426